MAKEUP MAN

MAKEUP MAN

FROM *ROCKY* TO *STAR TREK*: THE AMAZING CREATIONS OF HOLLYWOOD'S MICHAEL WESTMORE

MICHAEL WESTMORE

with JAKE PAGE

Guilford, Connecticut

An imprint of Globe Pequot

Distributed by NATIONAL BOOK NETWORK

British Library Cataloguing-in-Publication Information Available

Library of Congress Cataloging-in-Publication Data Available

ISBN 978-1-6307-6190-5 (hardcover)
ISBN 978-1-6307-6191-2 (e-book)

♾™ The paper used in this publication meets the minimum requirements of American National Standard for Information Sciences—Permanence of Paper for Printed Library Materials, ANSI/ NISO Z39.48-1992.

To my most beautiful and precious wife, Marion, my partner for life. I thank you for the past fifty-plus years together. Through your strength, encouragement, dedication, love, and our family, we are all better people. Like The Man of La Mancha *with his many adventures and battles, Don Quixote was my hero and knight errant to my Lady Marion. I thank you for all of your support, and for never leaving my side. I thank you, Mrs. Westmore, for just being you. I will love you forever and always.*

A TRIBUTE TO JAKE PAGE

In memory of my cowriter, friend, and adviser, Jake Page, and to his talented wife, Susanne Page. Thank you for the hours of guidance and hard work you contributed to organize my thoughts. When we met, Jake was already a prolific author and editor. In the year 2000 he was asked by Smithsonian *magazine to write an article about my Hollywood career. Our collaboration quickly developed into a friendship. Jake Page was too modest to reveal that in his career he had written forty-nine books and hundreds of articles. He was a kind, witty, and generous man. This book is a tribute to his life and our friendship.*

Jake, I miss you.

Contents

Foreword

When I scanned the first cast and crew list before shooting began on the pilot episode of *Star Trek: The Next Generation*, there were only two names I recognized—LeVar Burton and Michael Westmore. I am sure LeVar will understand and forgive if I say that it was the name Westmore that set my pulse beating. I had been a crazy movie fan since the late 1940s. I was one of those who sat through to the end of film credits until the screen went black. I had seen the Westmore name many times on many wonderful movies. But sometimes I wondered if there were lots of Westmores, or just one who couldn't decide what first name he liked best. There was Monte, Perc, Ern, Wally, Bud, and Frank. What a thrill for a nerd like me to hear the real story from the horse's mouth. There was George, Mike's grandfather, who created the Westmore Hollywood dynasty in 1917. He was the father of the six named above, which included Michael's father, Monte. They were all makeup artists, and had at different times run most of the major Hollywood studios' makeup departments.

I knew Michael had won an Academy Award for his work on *Mask*, and as I had only worked with a couple of Oscar winners, and never before in Hollywood, Michael's presence on the show added a glamour that was already buzzing around me each time I drove onto the historic Paramount lot. But if I might have been expecting superstar behavior from Michael, I was to be disappointed. Dedicated, modest, and friendly, he was happy to tolerate the impressionable fan who was playing Captain Picard.

Michael's work was outstanding. He inspired his coworkers, and his passionate professionalism set a standard for all of us actors. We respected and adored Michael.

He was a natural leader, and his wit and perpetual good humor got us through many a long day, often into the early hours of the next day. Through our association with Michael, we were all touched with the magic of moviemaking at the highest level. He is, quite appropriately, an important part of the history of Hollywood, and I am proud to have shared a tiny part of it with him.

—Patrick Stewart

Preface

I ask you, why would anyone want to document all the trivia that has occurred in one's career? First you must understand my heritage if you want to know why I have spent so many years contemplating and recording my busy life. I was born into filmdom's Royal Family of Makeup Artists. My grandfather, George, started the whole thing when he became a wig maker in England before the turn of the last century—that's 1900, not 2000. His specialty was to construct and style wigs for the crowned heads, barristers, and hookers. For the hookers he traded wigs for favors. Upon leaving the Isle of Wight in England with my grandmother, Ida, and the oldest children, they first landed in Canada, then went on to New York, where he opened a wig shop. There is a photo of him proudly standing beside his new sign. The family didn't stop for long, as they traveled down through New Orleans and then on to sunny Southern California. From England to California, Grandmother always seemed to be pregnant, giving birth to a total of eighteen children, of which six males survived. George opened a new wig shop and added to his credits some very impressive silent films, like *The Three Musketeers* and *King of Kings*, and stars, including Clara Bow.

Each of his six surviving sons, including my father, Monte Sr., became world-renowned makeup artists, setting the standards and styles for makeup around the world. Each one became the makeup department head of a major studio at a young age. To make everyone's life more exciting, grandfather George got pissed off with his new wife, and committed a nasty suicide. Not to allow my grandparents to outdo them in numbers, all six sons were betrothed more than eighteen times, and some of the beauties were well-known actresses of the silver screen. Even my dad was married to my mom twice, and I became the twinkle in round two. Well! After being born into all this, why shouldn't I keep score?

I think every makeup project in my personal and work-related life has become a passionate adventure. In the middle of a conversation, a single word, name, place, or action will conjure up in my mind an entire past encounter which I am compelled to share. I'm compelled to the point that I will have to interrupt the flow of the present conversation to interject my thoughts.

My studio career as a day laborer and trivia expounder started in 1958, when I was working during the summer between college semesters. My entry into showbiz started at the bottom, if that includes pulling nails out of reusable lumber, sweeping empty studio stages at eleven p.m., removing empty bottles from the Rat Pack's dressing rooms, and picking up elephant poop. From there it was all uphill.

My career time also includes the eighteen years I spent at Paramount Studios, immersed in Gene Roddenberry's world of *Star Trek*. It was exciting, as each one of the more than six hundred television episodes and features I designed and supervised was a special moment in time.

Beginning in 1987, I was the makeup creator and supervisor of everything *Star Trek*. I held this position at Paramount for eighteen years. At that time I occupied a spacious corner office upstairs in the Dreier Building. Directly across the bustling street, known as Avenue "P," was Stage 18 with its high, gray cement walls and huge, ancient doors. This exterior location was the setting for a scene in the 1950s movie *Sunset Boulevard*. This was the exact spot where Gloria Swanson, playing the fading silent star, is driven up in a 1929 classic Italian limo. Later inside the stage she performs her grand entrance and exclaims, "All right, Mr. DeMille, I'm ready for my close-up."

Back across the street in my upstairs office is the movie location where a young William Holden, Swanson's costar, plays a hack screenwriter. Another scene called for the writer, typing away, to be next to his window that looked out at the stage across the street. I had the same view in which to ponder. Nothing had changed in fifty-three years. In the afternoons around four p.m., after all my special makeups had been applied, I would take this time to design the alien creations which were needed for the upcoming *Star Trek* episodes. One afternoon during my creative hour my mind wandered from fantasy aliens to reflections about my present career and continued to regress in time. I thought about John Chambers, my mentor, who devoted much of his talent and time to the CIA. Did he recruit me? I will get killed if I tell!

Staring out the magic window I thought about my roots, my famous family and their accomplishments, my wife Marion, my children, my father, my mother, and my childhood. I asked my assistant Valerie Canamar for a legal pad and started to compile everything I could remember about growing up in a show-business family. I included all the movie stars that I had met—during my youth, on the lot at Warner Bros. studio, and in our home during the holidays. Within a year or so I had filled three legal pads that only took my life's timeline up through college and my makeup apprenticeship in 1961 under Uncle Bud at Universal Studios. I couldn't stop there. I was possessed to continue documenting my adventurous career, my family, and just simple moments that went *bump* in my mind.

For the next thirteen years, "My Hollywood behind the Camera" memories came flooding back like a giant tidal wave. The year 1965 represents what Robert Wagner calls the dividing point in Hollywood history. It marks the end of the classic studio system and the ushering in of independent productions. I experienced this moment firsthand, as it was the year a Westmore (me) was honestly married (just once, for life), and I could quit wearing a tie to work.

Like many of my peers, for years I stood quiet and motionless behind the lights and camera, ready to rush onto the set to attend to my performer's visage. A blot with a tissue or a puff of powder and I would return to the shadows as the director called "Action!" For some strange reason I filed all that happened away in my mind.

I found my creative involvement always meant more to me than money or the accolades from the Academy Awards. This is my account of Hollywood and my life as I saw it. This was my time to dream the impossible dream, and to make it come true. Like my favorite character, Don Quixote from *The Man of La Mancha*, I've completed my quest.

Tributes

At one time there were as many Westmores as there were major studios in Hollywood. The historic achievements of the Westmores started with George, a makeup genius and pioneer, who founded the Westmore dynasty.

—A. C. Lyles, producer

The contributions of the Westmore family to Hollywood are enormous! They were consummate professionals who set the standards for makeup artists, not only in Hollywood, but on an international level. There is no other family who so greatly influenced beauty in the movie industry.

—Robert Wagner

The Westmores were pioneers in the makeup industry, and their influence continues today. I think it's time Hollywood recognizes the Westmores with a star for their tremendous talent and contribution to the world of film.

—Paul Newman

I feel the Westmores were vital in our motion picture history, and should definitely be included in the Walk of Fame.

—Debbie Reynolds

Acknowledgments

To Rick Rinehart, my editor, and Jacques de Spoelberch, my literary agent—you are very much appreciated for making my Hollywood journey a reality.

A special thank-you to Helen Cohen, my manager, and Barbara Hein, for caring as much as you do, and for being true friends.

To my namesake, Michael Jr.—in you, I see so much of myself. Thank you for your support, and for your abundant talents that allowed us to complete this journey. I am proud to have you by my side.

To Michele Westmore Meeks and McKenzie Westmore Tatopoulos, who with hard work and determination have become such talented and beautiful women. And to their husbands, Martin Meeks and Patrick Tatopoulos, thank you for taking such good care of my little girls. And to Maddox, our grandson, who is on his way to conquering the world with his genius and talents. Mema and Deda love you.

In memory of John Chambers (Mr. Argo), my mentor and friend—without his teachings and generosity, my life's path would not have been possible.

To Robert Barron, a real master of disguise, and the greatest prosthetic specialist in the world—if I tell you everything that Robert has done, he will have to kill me.

To Christiana Benson, the keeper of the Westmore family history—thank you for your knowledge and support.

Finally, to all of my relatives, friends, and acquaintances—there are not enough pages to mention everyone, but you are in my thoughts, and I am blessed just knowing all of you.

Walk of Fame

At eleven a.m. on a sunny October 3, 2008, the Westmore clan and friends gathered near the crossroads of Hollywood and Vine—1645 Vine, to be exact—not far from the original House of Westmore beauty salon. Tourists walking past the assembled group stopped to listen in on the event, whatever it might be. The first speaker was Leron Gubler, president of the Hollywood Chamber of Commerce, followed by A. C. Lyles, a living legend who seemed to know everyone in Hollywood, and is said to have introduced an actor named Ronald Reagan to his future wife, Nancy.

A first-ever event occurred on the sidewalk that October day. The podium had been erected next to the building, and many floors up a resident stood on an overhanging balcony and decided at that moment to water his plants. He overwatered them. A small torrent cascaded down the front of the building. I stepped back and watched Mr. Gubler get drenched. I was next to speak, and hoped that my notes, written in washable ink, had survived. (They did.) I spoke of our family heritage, and my brother Marvin followed, giving tribute to our parents and our recently deceased brother, Monty Jr. After the speeches I was given a plaque with a miniature version of our star, which reads:

Hollywood Walk of Fame
Presented to
The Westmores
On the occasion of the placement of your star in
The Hollywood Walk of Fame
October 3, 2008
Hollywood Chamber of Commerce

The sidewalk beside the podium was covered with a red carpet, in the center of which was a cut-out area covered by a wooden replica of the permanent star. As the family gathered around, the wooden star was lifted, revealing our new family tribute, Number 2,370. Like the others, it is a pink stone star engraved with our name, a bronze symbol embedded into it. The symbol denotes which part of the entertainment business the honoree is associated with. Our symbol is an old-fashioned camera.

After many photographs and congratulations, relatives and friends gathered around to toast the family. That day, I couldn't help but feel that every Westmore, past and present, was with us as we celebrated the heritage the Westmore family had brought to the land called Hollywood.

Star ceremony on Hollywood Boulevard.
My family left to right: Michael Jr.,
McKenzie, Marion, me, Michele.
Bob Freeman, Hollywood Chamber of Commerce

The Family

The Westmores are the longest-lasting family dynasty in Hollywood, especially in the creation, innovation, and application of makeup and hairstyling. No family has been more prominently associated with this field over the last ten decades than the Westmores, famously known as Hollywood's Royal Family of Makeup. The first three generations include George, the visionary father, his six sons, and his three grandsons, along with four highly successful women, and a fourth generation. All family members combined have accumulated an enormous amount of film and television credits—well over 2,500. The family's impact on the motion picture and television industry is monumental.

Each of my makeup and hairstyling relatives touched me directly or indirectly with their spirit and genius. In Hollywood's heyday, almost every major studio had a Westmore heading up its makeup department. Since 1917, when George arrived in Hollywood, there has never been a time when Westmores weren't shaping the visages of stardom.

GEORGE WESTMORE (1879–1931)

George Westmore, a wig maker on England's Isle of Wight, was given a boost of confidence as a barber by a young war correspondent, Winston Churchill, and set off to become the makeup and hairdressing genius he believed himself to be. By that time

My grandfather George in front of his one-chair beauty parlor in Hollywood. *Courtesy of the author*

George had produced four sons, and after a brief sojourn, he noticed that prostitutes in Hollywood were better turned out than the famous actresses who appeared on the silver screen. The constant traveler would wind up in Los Angeles working in the famous salon, Maison Caesar. Off he went just as the city was becoming a major center of the American film industry, arriving in 1917 determined to be famous.

He established the first movie makeup department in cinema history with an outfit that made jungle movies. Over his career he accumulated more than eighteen film credits. He created Mary Pickford's signature curls; arched and shaped boxer Jack Dempsey's eyebrows; fashioned a new wig for actress Billie Burke, and then did the unthinkable—he applied her makeup.

This was during a time when all the performers applied their own makeup. Soon any actor or actress worth their salt had their makeup applied professionally. George had created a ready market for his skills. He completed Billie's new look by creating one of the very first pair of false eyelashes. He tied real hair around a straight piece of clear catgut, then curled the hair with a hot curling iron. To put his young daughter-in-law to work, he taught her this new technique; that person was my mother, Edith. It was not long before George soon became the indispensable intimate of the young stars.

He also created a new technique for cutting hair into layers, and one of his first subjects was movie legend Douglas Fairbanks. Grandfather's silent film credits included the original *Ben-Hur*, *Robin Hood*, and the 1921 version of *The Three Musketeers*.

All was not rosy in the Westmore household, however. The patriarch was a strict disciplinarian. With his sons he was a stern taskmaster with an appetite for cruelty. He seemed to take pleasure in playing one off against the other. Following the completion of *King of Kings*, George opened a new salon on Hollywood Boulevard and thought of himself as the makeup, wig-making, and hairstyling czar of Hollywood. He was now in competition with some of his sons, and he was losing. As each major studio decided to establish a makeup department, George was passed over for one or the other of his sons. Those studios included Warner Bros., RKO, Paramount, and Selznick.

Westmore family in profile, 1935: Perc, Ern, Bud, Wally, Monte, and Frank, who is twelve years old.
Courtesy of the author, photo by Christiana Benson

In 1931, his son Ernest won an industry award (at this time there was no Academy Award category for makeup) for his work on the film classic, *Cimarron*. In a fit of jealousy and despair the combative Westmore patriarch, now completely playing second fiddle to all of his sons, attempted suicide by drinking mercury bichloride, a very toxic chemical. He evidently changed his mind, but doctors could do nothing for him. After four days of excruciating pain and an awful stink, his insides were eaten away and he passed away. The brothers mourned their father, but went on climbing the makeup ladder of success.

MONTAGUE WESTMORE, "MONTE" (1902–1940)

Montague Westmore, known as Monte, was the oldest of the six brothers, and my father. He originally had no intention of going into the makeup profession, but one day in 1921, he saw a dark-haired young man known to be something of a gigolo. Monte couldn't resist. He befriended this not altogether savory gent and created the "Valentino look." He pulled back Rudolph's hair and dressed it with a thin coat of Vaseline, shadowed his jawline with makeup, plucked and reshaped his eyebrows, defined his lip line, and trimmed the ends of his sideburns at an angle. Valentino became the first global matinee idol. Monte followed Valentino for the duration of his acting career as his personal makeup artist and friend.

The flapper sensation was created in 1927 when Dad taped down Clara Bow's breasts for the movie *It*. Clara became forever known as the "It" girl. In 1932 he was hired to design the makeup for Paul Muni in the film *Scarface*. The cosmetic material used to create the scar running down Muni's cheek was a liquid called collodion, painted on with a small brush. When this material dried it would shrink and create an indent in his cheek, a very realistic-looking scar. After having it applied day after day during the filming, it left an actual red scar that Muni had for the rest of his life. In the early days of film many people were not listed in the credits, and makeup artists were rarely credited. Dad was not credited for *Scarface* or *Mutiny on the Bounty*, with Clark Gable playing the mutinous Mr. Christian. Monte is credited with over seventeen films, his most memorable being *Gone with the Wind*. He spent a year preparing for it and another year working during the filming. At the same time he was working on Alfred Hitchcock's best picture Oscar–winner *Rebecca*, 1940, and *Intermezzo: A Love Story*, 1939, with Ingrid Bergman.

My dad lived up to what would become the family reputation of being married several times, but twice to my mother Edith. I was two when he passed away. I am sure that the pressure from the mega-films he was supervising created a great deal of tension, stress, and frustration. In any event, in 1940 he entered the hospital for a routine tonsillectomy but had a massive heart attack that killed him. My only recollection of him was passing by a couch in our living room where he lay sleeping. Even the angle of this image in my mind is very low, at about the eye level of a two-year-old. Did this really happen, and was it really my dad?

In 1940 my mother was pregnant for the fifth time when Dad passed on. The previous five had all been boys, and they had always wanted a girl. The only name they had picked was Patricia. With Dad gone, Mom lost the baby (it was a girl). In the throes of despondency she searched out a medium, not telling her about the recent circumstances. The medium told my mother she could see a man on the other side of the veil, holding a baby girl, and that he would care for her until they were all together again.

PERCIVAL WESTMORE, "PERC" (1904–1970)

It has been said that volumes could be written about Uncle Perc's (pronounced *purse*) illustrious career. He and his twin brother Ern were born in England in 1904. When they came to America, still in their youth, they were learning the hair trade at a salon known as Maison Caesar and Wm. Hepner Wig Company in Los Angeles. One morning an actor burst through the Hepner door, panicking because he had accidentally shaved off half his mustache. Perc put down his broom and in a short time had hand-tied a perfect match. The actor, Adolphe Menjou, was able to return to the set of *The Three Musketeers* and continue filming.

This simple act brought much attention to the newly arrived Westmore family, so in 1921 the twins started the first film studio makeup department at National Pictures. By the 1930s nearly every studio was headed by a Westmore. National Pictures had become Warner Bros., and Perc was signed to a lifelong contract. He was always inventing something new to enhance the art of beauty and hairstyling. My earliest recollections of him were in the early 1940s, as we would make an annual Christmas-morning visit to his large mansion, located just north of Sunset Boulevard in West Hollywood. He loved to show me his latest woodworking projects located in one of his two workshops. Uncle Perc collected two of everything. Behind the big house on

The first known Westmore makeup guide, 1939. Perc Westmore is on the cover. *Courtesy of the author*

separate levels were two swimming pools, and his prized workshops each contained the same hammers, electric saws, drill presses, and so forth.

Perc was the most powerful and competitive of the Westmore brothers. He transformed Bette Davis into a pale, imperious Queen Elizabeth. Davis was a difficult-to-handle hellcat who insisted that Perc do her makeup while she was totally naked. After Perc passed away I took on her makeup duties, and thankfully, she remained clothed. "You're no Perc," she told me. In 1936 when Paul Muni accepted the Academy Award for his lead role in *The Story of Louis Pasteur*, he thanked only one man: Perc Westmore.

In the early 1930s, led by the driving personality of Perc, the Westmore brothers opened the most exclusive beauty salon in the world, the House of Westmore, located on the Sunset Strip. Women from far and wide made pilgrimages to sit among the Hollywood elite, where they would receive the same styling as the stars. At Warner Bros., Perc was a giant, totally trustworthy. Bette Davis even let him shave half her head when she played Queen Elizabeth in 1939. After letting her hair grow out, he restyled it and produced her famous bangs. Also in 1939 he became the "makeup master," loaned out for $10,000 to RKO Radio Pictures to create the makeup and body suit for Charles Laughton when he played the deformed character in *The Hunchback of Notre Dame*.

The House of Westmore Hollywood stood on Sunset Boulevard from 1935 to 1965. This photo was taken in 1940.
Courtesy of the author

At this time Perc and Ern designed what is now used by any enterprising makeup artist, the Seven Basic Face Shapes, published in a 1939 booklet. By using the measuring steps to calculate her face shape, any woman can dial in the perfect way to apply her cosmetics and design the most flattering hairstyle. (My philosophy: Steal an idea from one makeup artist, and it's plagiarism, but take it from more than two—Perc and Ern—and it's called research.) Perc was also instrumental in designing the Westmore eyebrow, which is applied in three steps. It is the classic style that became so popular in the 1940s. A good example is Elizabeth Taylor's eyebrows, which didn't change throughout her life. Perc even calculated the angle, sharpness, and cutting technique to properly shape the pencil. During the time I spent with Elizabeth Taylor, I always had pencils sharpened and ready to go.

Not only did new techniques flow from their minds, especially Perc's, but they also developed the first natural makeup foundation, where oil and pigments were suspended together. Other makeup artists were known to pour this liquid gold into another bottle and sell it to Hollywood stars at 1,000 percent markup. Translucent powder, a staple today with most any woman who uses powder to blot, is more than seventy years old, a product of Perc's ingenuity.

When I was a kid I went to work with my mom on Saturdays to Warner Bros. Studio, Uncle Perc's domain for decades. I had the run of the entire makeup department, but didn't see much of Perc, because he was a workaholic with a lot of responsibility. The day the place was bulldozed to make way for modernization, Perc stood across from his beloved cement structure and cried with every crashing blow. His contract with Warner's had ended, but instead of retiring he went to work for Uncle Bud at Universal. I was already there on staff, so we did become close, talking every day as he applied his great artistic skill and knowledge once more.

By now Perc had downsized his home and was on his fifth wife, Ola. She turned out to be the love of his life and a wonderful aunt to me. She had managed the House of Westmore for many years, and I believe she knew where all the bodies were buried. In their living room hung an almost life-size portrait of Bette Davis, painted to hang as a prop in the 1944 film, *Mr. Skeffington*. Somehow Perc had spirited it away from the studio, and from then on, everywhere that Perc went, Bette went with him. Their living room was decorated to enhance its elegance. Bette tried for many years to have Perc give it up, but he never did, not even after his death. I am not positive of its exact location, but I know that it survives today.

Uncle Perc tried for years to have the Academy of Motion Picture Arts and Sciences establish a makeup category, but his request fell on deaf ears. He told me

Brothers Westmore on the phone, from a publicity photo in 1935: Wally, Bud, Perc, Monte, Ern. *Courtesy of the author*

that a very influential producer once said that as long as he was president, there would never be recognition for makeup artistry. One of his reasons was that a Westmore would win it every year.

Upon Perc's death I felt a sense of total loss. He was my go-to man for any makeup problem. Whenever I would ask, "How do I do this?," he would reply with ten solutions. After the funeral the first thought that crossed my mind was, *My answer man was gone.* My second thought: *I am going to have to step up to the plate and become my uncle Perc.* To this day I still get "How do I do this?" calls from associate artists needing help.

ERNEST WESTMORE, "ERN" (1904–1968)

Ern and Perc were identical twins with highly successful careers before I was born. In 1931, at a ceremony at the Ambassador Hotel, the trade magazine *Hollywood Filmograph* presented Ern with a silver cup for best makeup, for the film *Cimarron*. He was only twenty-seven years old. This was the first known recognition for makeup for a motion picture, and many years would pass before it happened again.

Ern headed makeup at RKO and was intuitively brilliant. Before Perc got to Bette Davis, Ern created a whole new look for the film star when he refused to make her up with the typical cupid's-bow mouth, instead painting her upper lip straight across. The brothers developed a way to disguise irregularities in a nose's profile and to make it appear thinner for the camera, using it on Claudette Colbert, Ginger Rogers, Hedy Lamarr, Barbara Stanwyck, and a host of others.

Ern's talents launched him into other related fields of makeup. He coauthored several cosmetics books with his brothers, and was a partner with them when the doors first opened at the House of Westmore at 6638 Sunset Boulevard. Ern and his brothers also created a line of cosmetics that could be found in most dime stores from coast to coast. Ern acted in several movies and hosted several television shows, including a series titled *The Ern Westmore Show* that dwelled on glamour and beauty.

Uncle Ern Westmore's makeup trophy for the film *Cimarron* in 1935. *Courtesy of the author*

I know he loved me like the son he never had because I always had his full attention when I needed it. And indeed, he was the father I lost when I was about two years old. The last of his four wives was Betty, who had a daughter, Colleen. In the beginning they lived directly behind us. I would crawl over the back fence to visit. Aunt Betty always reminded me that when a stranger came to their door I should hide in the fireplace so she always knew where to find me. Later, they moved several miles down the way, so I would visit by bicycle. Unannounced, I would appear at their back door, and Aunt Betty would welcome me with a "Hi buckaroo," or her cheerful greeting, "God love ya." Another nickname for me was "Goober Feathers" (I have yet to figure that one out). If I arrived early enough in the morning, I would be served a normal meal, and I would watch with amazement as Uncle Ern was served everything on a breakfast buffet. I remember wondering where he could put all that food. I was often tempted to look under the table.

Ern was my hero. He took me to the circus every year. Those were the years when the circus had a large menagerie tent and a mesmerizing freak show. One year I brought home a chameleon that could change its body color. It was pinned to a chain on my shirt for several days before meeting its inevitable doom. Another time I came home with a stuffed purple monkey that slept with me for many years. Where we lived in the San Fernando Valley, summers were always extremely hot. As a surprise, Ern installed an aboveground swimming pool on his outside patio. It was actually an army surplus water storage tank about five feet deep. It sure felt great to slip beneath the cool water, even though it smelled like rubberized canvas.

Not long ago, my five-year-old grandson, Maddox, asked me if I had ever participated in an egg hunt. Did I ever! For many years Uncle Ern sponsored a community egg hunt on the several acres that were next to his house. Every year zillions of kids would show up to run the obstacle course for eggs and prizes. Even though I didn't find many, I always seemed to wind up with a prize-winning egg.

In 1948, as a youth of about ten, I got a birthday gift that every child should experience. Uncle Ern and Uncle Perc took me to a toy store and gave me a hundred dollars to spend. I searched every shelf, purchased everything I wanted, and had money left over. It was better than getting lost in Michael Jackson's candy store, which I did in later years. One of Ern's ways to relax was to take a boat out deep-sea fishing, and I accompanied him several times. That was when the Pacific Ocean waters were teeming with fish, especially halibut, just waiting to be caught.

During his studio career Uncle Ern moved around to several studios, accumulating more than sixty-two credits. In 1949, he was supervising a studio called Eagle Lion, and my mother was a hairstylist there, working on a film called *Port of New York*. Like so many other Saturdays, Mom took me to work with her. I met all the actors and actresses and became very comfortable with my surroundings. The next scene to be filmed that day was a comedian in a bar telling an off-color joke, and the tag went something like this: "The Duke is feeling much better, and the Duchess is feeling herself." Ern started to wonder where little Mickey was (another of my nicknames). Little Mickey had been sitting at a table in the front row of the nightclub, laughing along with all the other patrons (even though he didn't know what he was laughing at).

Ern's film credits were fewer than his brother's because in the early 1950s, he left Hollywood to become designer and spokesperson for a door-to-door cosmetic company called Holiday Magic. He kept an exhausting lecturing and traveling schedule, hard work for a man of sixty-two. One day he was going to speak to a sold-out audience in New York's Carnegie Hall. I was twenty-nine years old, working at Universal Studios. The day before Ern's performance at Carnegie Hall, my phone rang very early in the morning, and Ern said, "Mickeroo, I'm very tired, but I'm going to speak in Carnegie Hall tomorrow, and then I want to come home and take you fishing."

Both my wife Marion and I sensed that something was wrong about his voice. Several days later we got the message that Uncle Ern had had a heart attack, falling dead on the floor of the hotel lobby before his lecture. Time healed my sorrow, but I will never forget the kindly man who spent his life pleasing people, developing ideas for products and tools that are still in popular use today, and being a surrogate father for me.

WALTER WESTMORE, "WALLY" (1906–1973)

Uncle Wally was the one uncle whom I saw the least. When I was growing up, the only contact we had was an occasional Christmas morning visit or a passing hello when my mother was working at Paramount Studios on Saturdays. Over his forty-one-year tenure at Paramount he is credited with over 376 films. He and his wife, Edwina, were very social, and lived in a Tudor-style house in Beverly Hills, across the street from Elizabeth Taylor.

Wally's success as a creative makeup artist probably began with the gruesome facial transformation that he created on Fredric March for the 1931 film *Dr. Jekyll and Mr. Hyde*. By applying red hair to March's face and red filters on the camera, facial contouring and hair growth were made to subtly appear or disappear. You could almost say this was a forerunner of today's computer-generated imagery (CGI). In 1935 he designed and patented the inner working movements of several oversized latex fantasy masks, for several characters in the film *Alice in Wonderland*. In the hollow spaces between the actors' skin and the inner surface of the balloon-like mask, rubber contact points were adhered in specific movement spots. For example, if the actor smiled, the contact point at the mouth made the mask smile. You might say the mask acted like a puppet, transferring the actor's facial movements to the surface of the latex.

At one point in his career Wally is credited with inventing one of the first flesh-textured prosthetic hands. His prototype had a series of wires embedded in it, allowing the hand to move realistically. Like all the Westmores, Wally's reputation didn't stop with special-effects makeup. He was also a creator of beauty and glamour, designing Audrey Hepburn's heavy black eyeliner and eyelashes in *Breakfast at Tiffany's* and the signature eyebrows of his Beverly Hills neighbor, Elizabeth Taylor. The third-floor makeup department at Paramount was always a bustling place. Even at lunchtime the likes of Bing Crosby and others would arrive to play cards with Wally. Many a business tip was passed along at the games, such as the day the inner circle heard that Crosby was going to purchase an orange juice company.

Wally was not very happy that once I finished college I accepted an apprenticeship at Universal, where my uncle Bud ran the show. Wally had thought of me training with him at Paramount, but Bud had offered first. Nonetheless, Wally welcomed me into the family tradition by having me come over to his studio and giving me one of the most generous gifts I ever received. He took me into the makeup storeroom where he unlocked a big cabinet that was filled with the most expensive cosmetic brushes in the world. As my eyes bulged out, he proceeded to fill my makeup case with all the necessary (and unnecessary) brushes that I would ever need. Now all I had to do was work as an apprentice for the next three years.

One thing that Wally and I had in common aside from makeup was that we were the only two in the first generations of the Westmore family to be married only once, and in this business, that is quite an achievement. In all, the six Westmore brothers had eighteen wives, which still stands as a record in Hollywood.

GEORGE HAMILTON WESTMORE, "BUD" (1918–1973)

The uncle I was closest too as a young adult was Bud. In my late teens I decided to build a wooden cabinet to hold my portable record player and speakers. Who best to seek out for assistance but Uncle Bud, a woodworking master. His shop at home held all the perfect tools and the sharpest saws to build my money-saving dream. After many months of weekends it was finally done. As I had spent so much time there, I grew very close to Bud, his wife Jeanne, and my cousins. I was part of the family.

After a long day Bud would fall asleep on the red shag carpet and Jeanne and I would talk for hours. Bud deserved the rest, because over his film and television career as a makeup artist supervisor, he is credited with over 479 projects that spanned the years from 1938 to 1973. In 1961, as I was graduating from the University of California at Santa Barbara, Bud asked me if I was interested in accepting a makeup apprenticeship under his wing, at Universal Studios. With my bachelor of arts degree in hand, I left Santa Barbara on a Monday and arrived at the studio two days later, on January 31, 1961.

Bud had apprenticed under his family, too, his brothers Perc, Ern, and Wally all taking him under their wings. He quickly rose to makeup department head at Universal Studios. Prior to my arrival, the most notable of Bud's creations were *Creature from the Black Lagoon* (1954) and an earlier film called *Mr. Peabody and the Mermaid* (1948), starring a young Ann Blyth. Both of these special costumes had something in common: They were constructed with foam latex and caused a problem when first submerged in water. Due to her costume's buoyancy, Ann flipped upside down, tail in the air, and the creature did the same. The costumes suspended the wearers upside down in the water with no way of righting themselves without assistance. Back to the drawing board. Lead weights were inserted into the mermaid's tail and the creature's feet, to allow for proper stability.

When I started at Universal, the last existing mermaid tail and creature suit were hanging in the special-effects lab, but they were slowly disintegrating due to the increase in ozone (smog) that was being generated in Los Angeles. Other items sitting on dusty shelves were the alien latex heads and hands from the sci-fi film *The Mole People*, and a headpiece from *Spartacus* that could be worn on top of an actor's head. It was made to spring open and spray blood when hit with an ax—brains, anyone? It had been used in the first eight minutes of the film's battle sequence, along with cut-off arms and other mutilated body parts that also sprayed blood. It seems there was too much gore for the premiere's audience, so all the early blood and guts were eliminated.

Another prop left over from Bud's *Spartacus* was a full-length latex body of Woody Strode, with his arms extended over his head. It stood over eight feet tall. Ron Walters was another apprentice at that time. We would wait for the tourist bus to pass by the upstairs lab, then wrestle the naked latex body out onto the stairway balcony and throw it over onto the street in front of the passing tourist bus. We were the first unplanned attraction for what is now called Universal City Tours.

In another dark corner were several small dolls. Bud was friends with a toy-making couple who had designed a new doll and wanted his advice in 1957 on how the doll should appear cosmetically. That new teen fashion doll became known as Barbie. Other memorable moments with Bud occurred in the special-effects lab, where I spent most of my time.

Another film called for a full-figured mannequin of Claudia Cardinale, an Italian beauty. What better way to do this than to lay a nearly naked Claudia on the marble lab table and take a plaster cast of her whole body? It took several hours to complete, and we all became very familiar with each other during the process. When it was completed, Claudia announced that we all had become her honorary brothers. The body cast created a life-size mannequin of her that appeared as a prop in the 1965 film with Rock Hudson, *Blindfold*. Bud had kept a scantily clad copy of her mannequin, with wig, eyebrows, and glass eyes, standing in the back corner of his makeup room. Anyone who entered the room not knowing of her presence always jumped a mile. It was always good for a laugh.

Under Bud's guidance, I had the opportunity to work on such films as *Rosemary's Baby*, *To Kill a Mockingbird*, and *The List of Adrian Messenger*, which was the largest makeup-budgeted film until the original *Planet of the Apes*. I owe my career and livelihood mostly to Uncle Bud, and when he died in 1973, I couldn't stop crying.

FRANK WESTMORE (1923–1985)

Uncle Frank was the youngest of the brothers. In fact, he was born only two months (April 13, 1923) before my brother Monty (June 12, 1923). Frank's father George, my grandfather, died when Frank was very young, so he had no real Westmore roots until he came to live with us. Monty Jr. and he both attended Hollywood High School but ran in totally different social and athletic circles. Our housekeeper Kate used to put two fresh hot pies in the kitchen window just so the boys could steal one. Kate was like a second mother to all of us. She came to live with our family after my father passed away and Mom had to go to work.

After a stint in World War II, both Frank and Monty Jr. started makeup apprenticeships at Warner Bros. Frank's greatest film achievement was Cecil B. DeMille's *The Ten Commandments*, in 1956. Under the burning Egyptian sun he was in charge of makeup for the huge cast. DeMille loved Frank for all his devotion, and rewarded him with a small percentage of the film's royalties until his death in 1985. His personal film and television credits are listed at over fifty, but a single series name can include many episodes. Two films that really displayed Frank's talent were *My Geisha* and *Gambit*. In both, he transformed star Shirley MacLaine into an Asian beauty.

Robert Mitchum was another good friend, and Frank's second wife Gloria was Mitchum's assistant. Much to my surprise, I discovered when researching material for this book that Frank had worked with Jimmy Stewart on the film *Shenandoah* at Universal (a film that holds a special meaning for my wife and me).

In the early 1970s the Academy of Television Arts and Sciences added a new award for Best Makeup. Frank couldn't be bothered with "whatever it was." I had been a judge on the first go-round year, and the makeup contestants' work had been pretty boring. For example, how do you judge Tom Jones's straight makeup on a variety show? Uncle Frank had been working on a television movie, *Kung Fu*, with family friend and actor David Carradine. Frank had perfected the art of making a performer appear bald with the use of a plastic cap. I told him he could win if he would only submit the paperwork. He wasn't interested. Not wanting to let this opportunity slip by, I picked up the paperwork, filled out the application, took it to the studio for Frank to sign, and delivered it to the Academy. He not only made it onto the first ballot, but Frank was the first Westmore to win an Emmy, for his work on *Grasshopper*, in 1972. I don't remember, but he must have said thanks.

We only worked side by side a few times. I asked him to help me on *Rocky*, *Raging Bull*, and *The Lou Gehrig Story*, the last of which we both were nominated for Emmys. With all Frank's prizewinning work, his single most amazing contribution was to write *The Westmores of Hollywood*, a family biography. It chronicled our history from its beginnings to 1976. Frank didn't pull many punches, and the tales of happy days are more than matched by the accounts of the Westmore brothers. They cut a swathe though the Hollywood of their days. What I have written about them is largely based on my own experiences.

The competitiveness was long over when Frank mentioned Monte Sr.'s three sons, who followed in their father's footsteps. What Frank wrote about me toward the end of the book suggested a whole new style among the inheritors of the royal lineage of Westmores:

> Then there's Michael, the youngest of Monte's three sons. He's as handsome as Bud was, strikingly similar to him in appearance, though Michael has inherited his mother's beautiful blue eyes, and he has now surpassed Bud's skill in fabricating the rubber-plastic prosthetic types of makeups in the lab. Ranked second only to John Chambers in this specialized field, it was Michael who was called in by ABC to change actress Jane Alexander into Eleanor Roosevelt for the network's classic four-hour drama, *Eleanor and Franklin*.

There would be no competition among the Westmores as a third generation began to flower. Today, there is an active fourth generation still engaged in makeup, film production, and acting that continues to represent the genius that an old Brit, George Westmore, brought to Hollywood in 1917.

EDITH WESTMORE, "MOM" (1902–1994)

My mother and protector was born in 1902, high in the mountains of Colorado, as Edith Adeline McCarrier. She lived an exciting life for ninety-two years. She married my dad for the first time in the early 1920s. My master craftsman grandfather took her under his wing, and she became one of Hollywood's finest hairstylists. Mom and Dad divorced, but remarried several years later, in 1934. That's when Marvin and I were born. In 1940 after Dad died, she had to leave her few precious years of retirement and return to the business. With my mom off to work, a little Irish lady by the name of Catherine Cunningham stepped in to wipe my nose until I was eighteen.

Those were the times when the motion picture business worked long hours, six days a week. The only way I could see my mother more often was to spend my Saturdays at the studio. The makeup department and grounds at Warner's became my playground. I knew the location of every ice-cream machine and bathroom. I also knew where every stage was located. I have a faint recollection of being dazzled one Saturday by a giant swinging gate lined with singing chorus girls from the 1944 film *Shine On, Harvest Moon.* Ann Sheridan and Dennis Morgan were the stars of this musical. They shot the gate scene over and over, at different angles, and each time a recording would play the orchestral music theme, "Shine On, Harvest Moon." I sat there watching and listening all day. I heard it so many times, there was no way I would ever forget the melody and the words.

At that time Mom also worked with Humphrey Bogart, Lauren Bacall, and Gary Cooper. She continually went from one film to another. In 1950 I was visiting the set of *The Flame and the Arrow*, which starred Burt Lancaster and Virginia Mayo. It was a Robin Hood–like story, and Lancaster was the swashbuckling hero. He had been a trapeze artist in his earlier years, so it wasn't any problem for him to jump off a three-story balcony hanging onto a chandelier or curtain and swing across the entire length of a large banquet hall and fall to the floor. The director was never happy doing it just once; there was always room for improvement, so Lancaster did it several more times. My mom's advice to me was, "Don't even think about trying it."

Mom was very adventurous and she loved to go on location. These were the days when cowboy films were popular, and there were a lot of places to film, from the mountains to the desert. She was especially adept at putting long black wigs on actors to become on-screen Indians. We have a picture of her on one of her Western locations, standing in a Nogales, Mexico, bar surrounded by a number of smiling whores. She was smiling and looking as if she was a member of the sorority. Mom did get her name in lights, or at least, a theater program. The director and family friend George Schaefer was directing a play called *The Linden Tree* in 1948, and Mary Kimber the actress was playing, onstage, the role of Edith Westmore. A coincidence, George?

Mom could fit in anywhere; she was only five-foot-two, with bright red hair. She was respected by everyone; in fact, crew members would apologize if they swore in front of her, although she had a few sayings of her own, like "Balls on a brass monkey" when she didn't agree. She claimed she knew who murdered George Reeves of

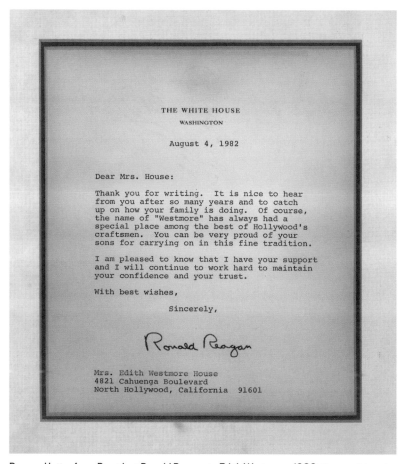

THE WHITE HOUSE
WASHINGTON

August 4, 1982

Dear Mrs. House:

Thank you for writing. It is nice to hear
from you after so many years and to catch
up on how your family is doing. Of course,
the name of "Westmore" has always had a
special place among the best of Hollywood's
craftsmen. You can be very proud of your
sons for carrying on in this fine tradition.

I am pleased to know that I have your support
and I will continue to work hard to maintain
your confidence and your trust.

With best wishes,

Sincerely,

Ronald Reagan

Mrs. Edith Westmore House
4821 Cahuenga Boulevard
North Hollywood, California 91601

Personal letter from President Ronald Reagan to Edith Westmore, 1982. *Courtesy of the author*

Superman fame, but would never reveal her secret. She said it was too dangerous to know. She was also on the set of *Genghis Kahn* when Jack Palance got carried away with his character in a passionate love scene and bit clear through a leading lady's lower lip. Mom said there was blood everywhere.

She finished out her career attaching herself to several television series. From 1957 to 1963 she worked at Universal Studios on the all-American show *Leave It to Beaver*; I can't say there was a lot of excitement there. That was followed by nine years of creating period hairstyles for the cowboy series *The Virginian*. In 1961 I had become a makeup apprentice at Universal Studios. Although it was never spoken about, I know that Mom was the power behind the throne to move that mountain for my appointment. After three years of training, and ready to go it alone, I was assigned to the television show *McHale's Navy*. Who was the hairstylist for the moment? My mother! Actually, it was good; with her finger buried in my back and a little push, she taught me timing, and through her example, set etiquette.

During her early days of punching out cowboy movies, Mom was hairstylist to a young star named Ronald Reagan. After Mom had retired and Ronny became president, Mom sent him a personal letter addressed to the White House, exclaiming about how proud she was of all his accomplishments. Not long after, she received a personal reply on White House stationery, asking about my mother and the family. This was one of her treasures.

PATRICIA WESTMORE (1926–)

Patricia is a half-sister to the brothers, the offspring from George's second marriage (1925–1931) to Anita Salazar, after Grandmother Ada passed away. As Pat grew up, she shared her mother's beauty and style, which made her very popular in a business predominantly populated by men. I am sure she has more film and television credits than can be found, as much of her professional hairstyling career went unaccredited. Pat started in the motion picture industry as an independent hairstylist in 1955, about the time I was playing football at North Hollywood High School. By 1957 she was styling hair for the likes of Joan Crawford. Designing modern hairstyles wasn't a job to Pat; it was a hobby. Over the years, she would switch back and forth from blockbuster movies to popular television shows. Her clients included Ann Baxter, Sandra Dee, and Lana Turner. Her most epic film credit was the 1956 movie *Giant*, with Elizabeth Taylor, Rock Hudson, and James Dean. Dean was killed in monstrous automobile crash the same year the picture was released.

In the early 1960s Pat worked with my brother Monty Jr. on the ever-popular Middle America television show *Ozzie & Harriet*, which also included their sons, David and Ricky Nelson. The show was so widely viewed that strangers would stop Harriet on the street. Not being able to instantly place her face they would ask this sweet-looking everyday mom, "Don't I know you from somewhere?" Patricia is also known for a little space adventure that went where no man (or woman) had gone before. It came too soon and only lasted on-screen for several years. These first shows are known as the Original Series, the beginnings of the *Star Trek* franchise.

MONTY WESTMORE JR. (1923–2007)

Monty, or, as I always referred to him, Junior, was my big brother. When it came time for Mont to practice making false beards at eight years old, I became the guinea pig. Night after night I would sit in a barber chair that was in our garage and he would paint my face with sticky spirit gum and lay into it loose hair, several strands at a time. After it was all laid and the hair covered my face, he would curl and shape it with a very hot curling iron. More than once I left the chair with a burned badge of courage. It was so uncomfortable, I swore then that I would never do it again unless one of my own decided to become a makeup artist. For his talent and exceptional personality, Mont's services were specifically requested by many stars. For seven years he remained with the Nelson family on their comedy series *Ozzie & Harriet.*

Working in the Westmore lab, late 1940s: Uncle Bud, Monty Jr., and Uncle Perc. *Courtesy of the author*

His favorites to work with were Morgan Freeman, Patrick Stewart, and Gene Wilder; he was written into the contracts of Joan Crawford and Paul Newman. He attended to Newman on more than seventeen films. He is credited with over eighty-four films over his fifty-seven years as a makeup artist, including *The Shawshank Redemption*, *Jurassic Park*, *Hook*, *Alien Nation*, *Stand by Me*, *The Towering Inferno*, *What Ever Happened to Baby Jane?*, and many more.

Over the years Mont and I collaborated on several films. We tramped through the jungles of Hawaii, causing trouble on *Uncommon Valor*. We made bodies fall apart and guts splatter on the ground in *Endangered Species*. On *Doc Savage*, he had me applying body makeup to some pretty smelly background people, and made me miss a plane that crashed. Away from the hustle and bustle of filming he loved to grow roses, do origami, and write poetry. Here is a poem he wrote in 1975 while working with Paul Newman:

Old Tree

Old tree, old tree, standing there
I've seen you leafed and seen you bare.
What stories you must hold,
within each branch, each twig.
If you could but speak, life's history unfold
of lovers in the spring,
who etched their names and had their fling.
In summer your great shadows
cast a place of rest.
And in winter you gave haven to
some wayward birds to nest.
But now, old tree, many seasons,
they have passed, and I leave you
to linger last.

—Monty Westmore, 12/2/75

Mont (ever Junior to me) was so loved and respected in the motion picture industry that all of Hollywood mourned his passing. He was the best of the best.

MARVIN WESTMORE (1934–)

Marvin was born on December 24, 1934, which meant he was screwed, receiving just one set of gifts for both birthday and holiday, like everyone else who was born the day before or the day after Christmas.

His career started with *The Red Skelton Show* on television. In 1964 he worked on *My Fair Lady*, and then in 1967 he met up again with Rex Harrison for the popular film *Dr. Doolittle*.

At Universal in 1969, Shirley MacLaine starred in *Sweet Charity*, and it became a family affair. My uncle Bud was the department head, Uncle Frank was Shirley's personal makeup artist, my mom was doing hairstyling, and my brothers Mont and Marvin and I were on the makeup staff.

In 1976 Marvin worked with Yul Brynner on *Futureworld*, a movie where you can't tell the robots from humans. In later years, as Yul toured the world doing *The King*

All the Westmores worked on the movie *Sweet Charity* in 1969: Uncle Frank, me, brothers Monty Jr. and Marvin, and my mom, Edith. Uncle Bud is not shown. *Courtesy of the author*

and I onstage, Marvin would send him his daily dose of dark brown makeup so he could play the King of Siam. Marvin also hit it off with Kurt Russell when he made him up for a TV special called *Elvis*, and then teamed up with him again for the 1996 film *Escape from LA*. His most noteworthy film was *Blade Runner*.

Marvin has over fifty credits to his name and numerous awards. He was involved with the original series *V, The Autobiography of Miss Jane Pittman, The Rat Pack, Space Rangers*, and *Frankenstein*. The latter was a televi-

sion special that I was involved with, so I called brother Marv to help me sew up the creature's face. It took several hours for the two of us to glue individual stitches into all the scars that covered Bo Svenson's face.

Monty, Marvin, and I all belonged to the Motion Picture Academy and the Television Academy, but I think Marvin's proudest years were when he was president of the Makeup Artists and Hair Stylists Guild, and the founder and CEO of the Westmore Academy of Cosmetic Arts and the George Westmore Research Library and Museum.

The family crest of Hollywood's royal family of makeup. *Courtesy of the author*

Marvin's children didn't stray far away. They have also been involved with many aspects of film and television production.

All of these ambitious and talented men and women have touched me, some more deeply than others, but all of them have included me and helped lift me into my place in the unprecedented Westmore dynasty.

The Sixties

In 1961, two days after I graduated from the University of California at Santa Barbara, I started my three-year apprenticeship program at Universal Studios under the tutelage of my uncle Bud. I reported on a Wednesday morning in January, and, like Alice, I was "Michael in Wonderland." Little by little I had responsibilities heaped upon me; everyone expected more out of me because I was a Westmore. I was watched like a hawk, even by my mother, Edith, who was a hairstylist there at the time. I became the stocker, runner, and delivery boy, the clerk, the receptionist, and the secretary to my uncle, even down to forging his signature on most documents. I was the number-one gopher. Every morning before completing my aforementioned duties, I would slip into a makeup room and watch one of the professional makeup artists prepare some famous face to go on camera. Uncle Bud usually had Sandra Dee in his chair, so in between watching him apply her rouge, lipstick, and eyelashes, I would bring Sandy her coffee. After everyone had left the makeup department I noted in a black book every technique I thought I could use when I became what is known as a "journeyman."

Not only the makeup and hair department, but the entire studio in 1961 was like a big family, from the top executive to the bottom laborer. Many times I would trade cosmetics or eyelashes to a person in another department for a gallon of paint, a roll of wallpaper, or even a bucket of nails. It was a very happy and congenial environment in which to learn my craft, work long hours, and, on top of it all, be paid. I started out at $75.00 per week. In the afternoons I would trudge up the outside stairway to the Makeup Lab. It was a large room, whose walls were filled with famous plaster faces, the shelves full of masks and molds. In the corner, slowly disintegrating, hung a full latex suit from the *Creature from the Black Lagoon* and an upside-down, full-length body with arms stretched downward from *Spartacus*. In 1962 I started to receive my most extensive, special makeup effects training under the tutelage of John Chambers, who had just joined our staff. Every day I would practice hour after hour the many makeup techniques that I would need to know, and then take my artistic endeavors to be critiqued. Most of the time I was sent "back to the drawing board" to improve myself; I had a heritage to uphold.

This was the happiest kingdom in the world for me until late in the decade, when Uncle Bud was terminated due to a serious medical condition and fast-approaching tenure. He was less than a year away from becoming fully invested for retirement, meaning that the studio would have had to pay his full pension. With Bud gone from the picture, it left his two assistants, me and Nick Marcellino. Nick had been a friend, but he had a better seat with the production end of the studio. Nick was appointed the new makeup department head, and I was promoted from assistant number two to being a regular day-to-day makeup artist.

When my cowboy series *Alias Smith and Jones* finally closed its swinging saloon doors in 1973—the same year Uncle Bud died, and after Pete Duel's suicide—I became what is commonly known as laid off, or temporarily out of work. Temporary started to stretch out, and Universal Studios didn't come calling for my services, so I started in 1974 to work for Sid and Marty Krofft, building the lizards and monkey people for *Land of the Lost*. I had now become an independent makeup artist, no longer tied to any one studio.

KIRK DOUGLAS, 1960

Over a four-year period I had two encounters with the man of steel. During the summer of 1960, between college semesters at the University of California at Santa Barbara, I would work as a day laborer at Universal City Studios, which was before they added the word "City" to their incorporated township. The first day on the job I walked into the assignment office on the backlot. An old grizzled man behind a much-cluttered desk looked up, paused, and said, "I bet you're a Westmore." *How did he know?* I thought in amazement. I wasn't wearing any name tag, and my name wasn't tattooed across my forehead. That was the defining moment when I learned that the Westmore blood carried a very prominent gene: our nose.

I particularly discovered this when I took my family to visit the English Westmore clan on the Isle of Wight. At the turn of the twentieth century my grandfather had set up his wig shop on this island, located off the southern coast of England. My cousin John insisted we stay with him and his family, and he arranged for a number of the cousins to attend a little meet and greet. It was there I discovered that all the Westmores looked alike as I gazed around the room full of men and women with similar noses.

I spent my early days sweeping stages, pulling nails, and following an elephant around with a shovel. One warm summer morning at Universal the office assigned me to a crew of older men. We were to report to the exterior gates of the Appian Way, which had been constructed for the historical film *Spartacus*, starring Kirk Douglas, the rebel who defied Rome. From the top of a mountain a cobblestone road wound down the hill to the entrance of the Roman city, which was located next to the Hollywood freeway. Spaced along the stone roadway were towering crosses where the rebels were crucified. The ragtag extras who had to hang there in the hot summer sun all day for little money might have preferred crucifixion, or at least an early lunch.

The morning that the road was scheduled to be filmed, Kirk appeared at the top of the hill, gazed down, and said, "I don't like the cobblestones; I think it should be covered in dirt." That is why I was standing on the Appian Way the next morning. It was my first job of the day to help cover the cobblestones with tons of dirt that had been trucked in and dumped at my feet. As the day wore on, the temperature reached into the 90s. At sundown we threw the final shovels full of dirt and then we all collapsed in exhaustion.

The next morning Kirk returned to the top of the mountain and offered a new revelation: "The dirt roadway doesn't work; I like the cobblestones." I hoped it wasn't something I had done. This was my first multi-dirt experience. Following our new instructions, the crew and I went to work shoveling and sweeping clean the tons of earth that covered the Appian Way. For the rest of the movie my job was to sweep and clean the mosaic floors of the villas and sets. Being an art history major, this was more like an honor than a chore. In the end I returned to college with my pockets stuffed full of money.

My second encounter with Kirk in 1963 was after I had become a full-fledged makeup apprentice.

FLOWER DRUM SONG, 1961

Universal was known for its "B" class movies, horror and comedy. Then the genre changed with the blockbusters *Spartacus* and *To Kill a Mockingbird*, but never a musical. MGM was the home of the extravagant music and dance numbers. And then it happened: Universal was going to produce a film version of the Broadway musical *Flower Drum Song*, by Rodgers and Hammerstein. Everyone was excited, as this production was filled with song and dance numbers showcasing the contrast between traditional Chinese life within American culture.

What made this film so unique was that the entire main cast, which was supposed to be Asian, were Asian. It was a known fact in Hollywood, and I heard it many times, that there weren't many talented Asians available to fill all the speaking roles. To compensate for this casting theory, Caucasians were transformed over the years, through the art of makeup, to play the Asian roles.

Much of the movie takes place in Chinatown. The old Hollywood theory was proven wrong, as the principal cast who were supposed to be Asian were Asian, and the background extras were Chinese, Japanese, and Polynesian. There were no make-believe Asians.

As an apprentice I was assigned to make up the dancers. I was to work in a room called "the bullpen," a long narrow room with many makeup chairs, all in a line. In front of each chair ran a counter on which we could lay out all our supplies. At the back of each counter, mounted on the wall, ran end-to-end mirrors that extended the length of the room. The dancers arrived and a very happy-go-lucky gentleman jumped into my chair. Following all my instructions, I tucked Kleenex into the collar of his shirt and draped a barber's cape over his clothes. I applied a foundation makeup to his face and ears, plus a touch of manly rouge. To set his makeup I dipped my powder brush into my powder box and started to dust it into his right ear. He didn't forewarn me of his sensitivity, but as soon as I touched his ear, he laughingly slid down out of my chair, onto the floor and under the counter. Being new at this occupation, I didn't know if this happened regularly. (No, it never occurred again in my career.) From then on, during the show, my dancer would grip the handles of my chair and hold on as if he was riding a rodeo bull.

In authentic Chinese theater, the dancers and actors make up their faces to symbolically resemble deities and animals. The patterns are very stylistic and intricate. In one of our big dance numbers the brilliant choreographer Hermes Pan and director Henry

Koster wanted the principal actors and dancers to wear stylistic faces, but not as a permanent makeup. The designs were painted on form-fitting plastic masks that could be easily applied and removed.

From Chinese research my uncle Bud would paint one side of the mask and then say to me, "Mick, you were an art major in college; finish it!" Part of finishing meant meeting the challenge to perfectly match the intricate painting of Bud's first half using a steady hand and precise measuring tools as a guide.

What can go wrong with a painted sign? Universal had a huge double stage, which meant it was two stages back to back with a removable middle wall. From one end of Stage 1 to the far end of Stage 2 was constructed an exterior replica of Chinatown. Many of the dances and scenes were to be played within the town, and it was awesome to behold. The individual shop windows that lined the street were dressed with food and merchandise. The advertising signs that were to be hung across the shop fronts or over the doorways were painted using Chinese symbols. When the Asian cast and extras entered the stage for the first time there was a large stir in the atmosphere. The sign painters had used the proper calligraphy, but the sign hangers, not knowing Chinese, had hung them as they pleased. For example, a symbolic sign advertising a fish market was incorrectly placed over a shoe store. The director insisted on correctness, so we shut down for half a day while the sign hangers shuffled them around to their proper placement.

It was amazing to watch all of this come together: the creative costumes of Irene Sharaff, the choreography of Hermes Pan, and the music. Remember, this was my first musical. One style of hat Irene designed for a dance number was a pink ball held on a horizontal wire several inches directly above the dancers' heads. I remember someone in Wardrobe telling me what each one cost to make; although the dollar amount is lost to my memory, I do remember my reply: "*What*?!"

Even with the tight schedule and all of the things that had to be corrected, Mr. Koster was so organized, he was able to bring the film in under budget and a week early. This was unheard of at the time. As a reward, Koster was given a shiny new car—I think it was a Mercedes—and the film crew was out of work a week early.

THE LIST OF ADRIAN MESSENGER, 1963

During the last year of my makeup apprenticeship at Universal Studios, I was deeply involved with a film that supported the largest special makeup budget to date. Because of his outstanding reputation as a makeup technician, John Chambers, my mentor to be, was brought in to the project by my uncle Bud. John's job was to assist Bud in supervising all the steps needed to create a large group of assorted disguise masks. The plot is one you have to pay attention to: A man by the name of Messenger gives a list of names to a friend before he leaves on a trip. Things become more serious when Messenger's plane is blown out of the sky. The friend finds that some names on the list have already mysteriously died, and races to find out if there are any survivors. Why were each of their names on the list? Did some die by accident, or were they murdered? The film challenges the audience to identify all five of the great disguised stars.

Bud wanted to assemble the best makeup lab team in history, so he hired the sculptor, Chris Mueller, who sculpted in clay *The Creature from the Black Lagoon*. There is a real art to casting perfect plaster molds, so Elmer Lund was brought up from the staff shop, a studio term for the building where all the architectural plaster items are manufactured. Don Cash Sr. rounded out our lab team. Don was a pro at manufacturing foam latex appliances, as it had to be done on a daily basis to keep up with our filming demand. I became a full-time student to each one of them, and I must say, my career roots run deep to each one of their teachings. In the words of *Kung Fu*'s Master Po, I was "Grasshopper."

Universal studios makeup lab for the 1963 film *The List of Adrian Messenger*. The lab rats, left to right, are Don Cash Sr. (latex technician), me (the apprentice), Chris Muller (sculptor), and Elmer Lund (plaster mold technician). *Universal Studios*

After the script was completed, fine watercolor renderings and overlays of each disguised character were painted in the art department. Each of these pictures had to be approved by director John Huston before our work could begin. Each character was to have its own individual latex disguise mask, with extra pieces like ears and eye bags if needed. There were so many plaster molds that the tables, benches, and shelves were filled. All of the liquid latex that was poured into the molds had to be vulcanized with heat, just like a rubber tire. The oven where this process took place was large enough for a full-grown man to walk into. It was originally purchased to cook the *Creature from the Black Lagoon* latex suits.

After the sculpting, molding, and pouring of foam latex was completed, each character needed custom-made dentures, which was Chambers's specialty, colored contact lenses from Dr. Greenspoon, wigs, eyebrows, and facial hair.

Kirk Douglas was cast as the main character and wore four totally different disguises. Tony Curtis, Robert Mitchum, Burt Lancaster, and Frank Sinatra all played cameo roles in their own CIA type of makeup. The makeup for Curtis, Mitchum, and Lancaster worked without a hitch. Sinatra was a little more difficult, as he didn't want to sit for a facial cast or have the mask glued onto his face the day we filmed his reveal. Everything was done to accommodate him, including having his $25,000.00 check ready to hand him as he was leaving. He wasn't there long enough to even sing one song.

Elizabeth Taylor, a dear friend of John Huston, was to be our surprise female cameo. Both John and Uncle Bud flew to London to cast her face. I seem to remember them telling me that they plugged up the plumbing at the Dorchester Hotel as they tried to get rid of the plaster remnants down the toilet. She was to play the part of an old, bearded seaman, but her friends had warned her that glue and latex would ruin her skin. Without a word she disappeared into the European countryside, never to be seen again until the movie was completed. Elizabeth's friends were probably right, as the glue that was being used to stick on the masks was old-fashioned spirit gum, and it didn't remove easily.

The actor Jan Merlin was hired to replace Douglas, on film, when needed—not to stand in, but to actually act. This meant that Jan had to have a complete duplicate set of everything that Kirk wore, including faces, teeth, and contact lenses. The cameo actors were in and out of their makeup in a few days. With Kirk playing so many roles, it became quite a chore. It was common to hear "Let Jan do it," which meant that the duplicate actor had to be made up at the same time. In his duplicate makeup Jan looked very similar to Kirk's disguise, except for the shape of his eyes. I could always tell who was on-screen, and so could a few film aficionados. In later years Jan complained about

Universal makeup lab in 1963. I'm surrounded by tons of plaster molds that were used to make all the latex disguise faces. *Universal Studios*

how the entire process was handled, noting that he didn't receive much credit even though he was prominent throughout the film.

The List of Adrian Messenger was fairly successful, especially for the makeup department, and would have won an Oscar it there had been a makeup category at that time. John went on to supervise *The Planet of the Apes* at Fox Studios. For his extraordinary work he was awarded a special Academy Award, and I was promoted to lab supervisor at Universal.

A TALE FROM THE OLD WEST, 1963

During the typically hot California summer of the last year of my apprenticeship at Universal Studios (1963), a lady called our makeup department and requested a professional makeup artist to apply her makeup for her forthcoming wedding. No established makeup artist would accept the amount of money she was willing to pay. Uncle Bud thought it would be good training for me, along with a chance for me to practice all the cosmetic tricks he'd taught me while I observed him making up Sandra Dee. By that time I had also practiced on just about every secretary at the studio who would sit still during their lunch hour.

The client thought it would be wonderful if we could meet prior to her wedding day so we could discuss her style and color requests, and I could check out her face. This was to be a very businesslike consultation. She lived in a modest home in the San Fernando Valley. Wearing a sport coat and tie, I drove up in my VW Bug in the early evening and proceeded to knock on the front door. The wooden door swung open and there, behind the screen door, stood an attractive woman wearing only her underpants. A gruff voice in the background said, "For God's sake, put on some clothes!" The owner of the grumpy voice was a large man who I could tell had been, and still was, drinking straight whiskey. He rose from his old worn-out chair wearing dirty shorts with a matching undershirt.

The woman had disappeared, so Gruff Man opened the screen door and let me in to their modest living room. He introduced himself as the disappearing lady's uncle. He then plopped back into his chair to watch television. The lady reappeared wearing a thin silk robe. She and I sat down at her dining room table for our professional consultation. She kept scooting very close to me so I could see her face (I thought). Her breath was overpowering, so I realized very quickly that my client had been imbibing with Uncle Gruff. I also learned that I was privileged to be in the presence of the lead female singer of a very famous country-and-western band.

She then exclaimed that I could more fully understand her cosmetic needs if she sat on my lap, and down she plopped. This might have been the first makeup lap dance in history, and I started to get nervous. I could feel beads of perspiration popping out on my forehead. For a moment we talked seriously about the makeup, and what time I should be at the church on Saturday to apply all of my Sandra Dee knowledge.

As I was about to make a mad dash across the front room to freedom, Miss Cowgirl wanted to show me another of her many talents. Aside from singing, she said she was also a professional rope twirler. She had the ability to sing while jumping in and out of a twirling lariat. With that she moved the coffee table from in front of the couch and pulled it out into a double bed. The quietly drinking uncle in the corner said, "If you are going to f**k, I'm going to leave." In my head I was screaming out for Uncle Gruff not to leave. He exited with a full glass in hand and my champion roper jumped onto the bed with her rope in hand. She proceeded to display all—and I mean *all*—of her talents as the mattress acted like a trampoline, and between jumps her robe went flying.

This was my opening to ride into the sunset. I made a mad dash for the front door. At that moment I would have used a window to escape. As I ran to my car I politely shouted back, "Call me!"

At the time I was still living with my all-knowing mother. I once related to her another one of my Hollywood close calls. Her advice was "Let me cook you a steak." Aside from recommending Valium, a steak was her next best cure-all.

I never heard back from the cowgirl, so I don't know whether she ever tied the knot.

BRANDO, 1963/1966

I first met Marlon Brando when I was an apprentice makeup artist at Universal Studios in 1963. He had been contracted to play the role of an American ambassador assigned to an Asian country in *The Ugly American*. The film was filled with all the intrigue that was found in the best-selling novel.

Aside from being an apprentice, I was also the number-one gopher. One of Marlon's requests was to wear a mustache. Because fake mustaches itch, most actors try to avoid them. He further asked for the studio to supply him with a generous number of the little furry creatures. Because of their theater background, he and his personal makeup artist, Phil Rhodes, said they would trim, style, and care for them. (As a side note, four struggling actors living in New York made a pact that if anyone made it big, they would take care of each other. Brando made it big; Phil, the philosopher, became his makeup artist; the only female member became Marlon's stand-in and Phil's wife; and number four disappeared. They remained buddies until the end.)

It was understandable why Marlon needed so many mustaches; they weren't really cared for, so he would just dump one when it was tired and out of shape. At the time they probably cost a whopping $25.00 each. Regarding the trimming and dressing, no two were exactly alike; some were wider, some were longer. Most of the viewing audience never really noticed, but the expanding and shrinking mustache can be seen throughout the film. The magical mustache is most obvious in one particular scene, when Marlon walks through a doorway from the outside into a house. The exterior was filmed overseas in Bangkok, and the interior, at Universal Studios many weeks later. It is understandable that the traveling muff was not available, so Marlon had a different look on each side of the door. Films are full of these bloopers if you keep your eyes peeled.

The Ugly American did very well at the box office, so Marlon was hired again in 1966 to star in a Western titled *Appaloosa*. By now I had passed my exams and had become a full-fledged makeup artist. As the plot unfolds, a Mexican-American buffalo hunter has his favorite horse (an Appaloosa) stolen by a Mexican bandit. Brando's character single-handedly sets out to recover his beloved horse. In his search, much like any hero, he takes on the entire bandit gang. Brando had a love for wearing makeup, and wanted to be true to the original novel on which the movie was based. It seems it is easier to rewrite someone else's thoughts than to have an original idea yourself. According to Phil, his makeup artist, as they were growing up, Marlon always liked ethnic personalities, especially women.

As part of this new screen character with Native American blood, Marlon wanted to dye his hair black or wear a black wig and mustache. He also wanted to widen his nostrils, have a bump on the bridge of his nose, and top off the swarthy tan makeup with a very visible gold tooth. All of this was prepared and tested on camera. When Lew Wasserman, the head of the studio, saw the makeup tests, he exclaimed, "No, no, no! I pay a million dollars to see Brando, and I can't visibly see him when he is wearing all that makeup." When the movie started filming, Marlon played Marlon. That is the power of the man who pays the salaries.

Many years ago a producer told me that most actors and actresses are just overpaid employees. But never underestimate the power of an A-lister. As the story goes, Marlon was having some kind of battle with director Sidney Furie. He would enter the set disrespectfully reading a book, keeping the book up by his face until he heard the word "Action." He would then lower the book, pass it to Phil, and recite his lines. Upon the director saying "Cut," Phil would pass Marlon back the book and he would continue reading.

McHALE'S NAVY, 1963

The very first TV series that I was assigned to upon completing my three-year apprenticeship in 1963 was *McHale's Navy*, which had already started filming in 1962. It was budgeted to film each half-hour episode in three days. We would usually complete an episode in two and a half days, sometimes two. On the third day we would have to look busy until after lunch. I am uncredited on the show, as the department heads were the only ones listed at that time. I worked on the show for several seasons, until the plot left the jungle for Europe.

The cast had a camaraderie that I didn't see again until working on *Star Trek: The Next Generation*. Academy Award–winner Ernest Borgnine was the star I took care of every day. Others included Tim Conway (*The Carol Burnett Show*); unlike some comedians, who were unfunny outside of the limelight, Tim was actually funny and entertaining most of the time. Carl Ballantine was always performing some feat of magic, which I thought was a hobby. One day in 2011 I walked into an exhibit of famous Jewish magicians at the Skirball Cultural Center in Los Angeles, and there was an entire area devoted to Carl and his memorabilia. It was jaw-dropping for me—or was it Carl, pulling my jaw down? Robert Hastings always had a laugh or two to contribute.

In the beginning, *McHale's Navy* was about the daily adventures of a misfit PT boat crew in the Pacific during World War II. Every year on December 7, Pearl Harbor Day, our Japanese wardrobe man would mysteriously appear out of one of our sets wearing a torn and burned flyer's cap and jacket. He was also wrapped in a battered Japanese flag. As he stumbled into everyone's view he would moan that he had just crash-landed and needed directions. Over the five years this became a ritual that was always greeted by a cheering cast and crew.

Ernest Borgnine was the lead actor, known as "Skipper." I was applying his makeup one morning when he looked up at me and said something like "I shouldn't be doing this." I felt the hair pull tight on my head, for I knew what he was talking about. This was two days before he was to marry Ethel Merman. He was right; it didn't last long.

The most memorable dark moment occurred when Joe Flynn, wearing a long sword as part of his costume, swung around and hit Ernie in the crotch. Ernie claimed that Joe did it on purpose, and to my knowledge, it was never the same between the two cast members. Joe's apologies at the time were not accepted. I was standing right there when it happened, and it sure appeared to be an accident.

I went from the television series to work on my first feature movie, *McHale's Navy*, in 1964. Due to some studio discrepancy (and that usually means money), Ernie didn't appear in the film, but the rest of the cast members were present. An opening line in the film went something like, "Skip had to go to Bora Bora," and at the end of the movie, "Skip is coming back from Bora Bora." Skipper spent the entire movie there.

With no Ernie, I took care of our guest star, George Kennedy. George had to wear a fake mustache, and I had to keep it glued on his upper lip. One afternoon I was going to check the mustache and my more-experienced makeup artist partner said not to worry about it, it was fine—even though George was about to have his big close-up, thirty feet away. My better judgment told me to go and check. As I quietly approached George, the cameras were rolling. The first thing I noticed was that half of his mustache had come completely loose and was hanging over his mouth. In all my new wisdom I decided not to say anything or fix it.

The next day I asked my uncle Bud if I could go view the previous day's filming, and he approved. Very nervously I entered the dark screening room; the film started to roll, and there, bigger than life, filling the screen, was a close-up of George with the hanging mustache that fluttered every time he spoke. I quietly snuck out. I couldn't believe that no one had made a comment. To this day, that infamous scene features George's fake mustache, waving in the wind. That was the first and last time I wasn't behind the camera when I was supposed to be.

MAN'S FAVORITE SPORT?, 1964

Man's Favorite Sport? started preparations in 1963, while I was an apprentice, and didn't commence filming until 1964. It was another happy-go-lucky, feel-good story, and I was behind the scenes, helping to prepare some special wardrobe gimmicks. Rock Hudson was the male star, and one couldn't meet a more charming person. Along with his makeup artist, Mark, he was always laughing, smiling, and playing tricks on people. Famous costume designer Edith Head came to Uncle Bud for assistance. In the film Rock had to wear a pair of fisherman's waders that had to blow up like a balloon. They were not going to be used on camera for several weeks, but Uncle Bud, known for his impatience, had to finish them ASAP.

It was New Year's Eve, 1963, and I spent it gluing small rubberized circles onto the waders to aid with the inflation. Later I remember that when Rock put on the pants and they were inflated, he had as much trouble staying upright and afloat as did the actor in *The Creature from the Black Lagoon* on his first dunking. Rock looked like Tweedledee or Tweedledum from *Alice in Wonderland*.

Our second request from Miss Head was to construct a seamless, skintight, one-piece, pink latex suit for Maria Perschy. This condom-like suit was requested by director Howard Hawks; actually, it was more like a demand. In theory it may sound easy, but in practicability it was a nightmare. We purchased and assembled a full-size mannequin that was slightly smaller than Maria. All of the mannequin joints had to be filled in so it would be seamless when the latex was applied. To try and brush on the latex would leave brush marks on the surface. So, with a quart-size airbrush, I applied several coats of pink balloon latex to the surface of the mannequin, being careful not to create any latex drips.

After the latex had dried slightly, I placed it into our lab oven that was big enough to accommodate the mannequin. This heating process vulcanized the latex, making it easy to stretch and pull. This type of latex has an extreme amount of stretchability. To remove the latex suit, all the mannequin parts had to be individually separated and taken out through the wrists or neck openings. This took a lot of grunting and groaning, and a lot of baby powder to make the latex slide. Totally removed, the floppy latex skin looked like something from a horror movie. It was as much trouble for the wardrobe department to squeeze, pull, and tug Maria into the suit as it was for us to originally remove it from the mannequin.

Because it was so totally form-fitting, Maria couldn't wear anything underneath. During the first day of her wearing the suit on camera, everyone realized that no allowances had been made for her to go to the bathroom. It would have taken valuable hours to remove the suit and redress her each time. A light went on in someone's head. Outside the stage door was a storm drain covered with a metal grate. The drain outlet itself had a straight shot to the Los Angeles River, which flowed next to the studio. Small holes were cut open in the bottom of the latex feet. When the moment arose, Maria would go outside, stand on the drain, and relieve herself. Where there's a will, there's a way, and in show business, there is always a way. (Also, special thanks to the wardrobe department folks who had to remove it every night.)

SHELLEY WINTERS, 1964

On a late afternoon at Universal Studios in the mid-sixties, Uncle Bud informed me that I would be working with Shelley Winters and Jack Hawkins on the last episode of a long-running NBC drama series called *Bob Hope Presents the Chrysler Theatre*. That was the good news. The bad news was that we began filming the next morning. This was to be my rite of passage, I thought, the ordeal that would test my chops.

Shelley Winters was one of the most popular Hollywood stars, her story already part of the folklore of the town. She was well on her way to a life's work that would include ninety-nine films, and a host of awards, including an Oscar nomination for her work in the movie *A Place in the Sun* that starred Montgomery Clift and Elizabeth Taylor. She was a great storyteller, whether it was about herself, her friends, her husbands, or her lovers. She personified the phrase, "If you've got it, flaunt it." I was pretty darn nervous about meeting this ball of fire. (Years later, I learned that she had tried out for the 1938 epic film *Gone With the Wind*, which was the last film that my father's makeup department worked on before his death.)

That day Nick Marcellino, my uncle's assistant, escorted me down the long hallway to personally meet Ms. Winters. She was sitting in a chair facing a large mirror, and a hairstylist was trying out different styles for the film. Nick, who had known Shelley previously, introduced us. After a little small talk she asked me, "Do you know how to apply facial lifts?" As my mouth started to form the word "No," Nick interjected. "Does he know how to apply them? He invented them!" As I stood there in horror, Shelley said, "See you in the morning."

A facial lift was made from a piece of flesh-tinted silk about a half-inch wide and two inches long. One end was trimmed with pinking shears to make the edge irregular and the other end was attached to a two-inch piece of stiff wire. Tied to the middle of the wire was a light-colored string that was twelve inches long. The use of this simple device was very popular among female actresses from the 1930s through the 1960s, before plastic surgery became the procedure of choice. Up to eight such lifts could be glued around the face and pulled back to remove wrinkles and sags. How much one pulled depended on how tight the face was to appear. The silk was glued down to the skin with spirit gum. The strings were pulled up to the crown of the head and anchored with bobby pins. Then the actress's natural hair or a wig was styled to conceal all the magic. This may sound complicated in theory, but it was simple in application.

That night I took home all the materials and my mother taught me how to make them. I practiced into the wee hours, applying and removing them from my mother, the guinea pig. I was an expert. The next morning I met Shelley at about six a.m. in the makeup room, armed with my makeup case and a handful of facial lifts. I quickly glued down the four lifts and pulled them into place in record time. One pair opened her eyes and lifted her eyebrows. Another pair pulled back her cheeks (technically called nasal labial folds). Because of my speed in applying them, Shelley said she was now wary of previous makeup artists who had made this a lengthy, mystical trick, trying to convince her they were the only ones capable of pulling off (or up) this nearly secret procedure. When we finally arrived on the Universal filming stage, out of the blue she announced to everyone within earshot that I had pulled her face up so tight she didn't need to wear a bra.

Watching Shelley and the great English actor Jack Hawkins perform on camera was like sitting in the audience at an unforgettably great play. She was so thoroughly trained an actress that she could be in the middle of telling a dirty joke off-camera, something she did often, when an assistant would call her to work. Shelley would go onto the set, perform a demanding emotional crying scene, and then return to us, wipe away a tear, and finish her joke, followed by infectious laughter. A ball of fire indeed.

Shelley was known to take a little nip now and then, whether she was working or not. In the top of my small traveling makeup case I carried small two-ounce bottles of glue, makeup remover, stage blood, and, for milady's convenience, one little bottle of vodka. Whenever she would get nervous, I would get a particular nod that meant Bring it forth. The little bottle was disguised in a tissue; I would approach her and pretend to be blotting her shiny nose as she casually lifted the small bottle to her lips and took a satisfying swig. This was teamwork.

Soon after completing *Chrysler Theatre*, Shelley wanted me to accompany her to San Diego, where she was going to be filming a thriller called *Tentacles*. As the title implied, we had a giant octopus on a rampage. The time was not convenient for me to leave Los Angeles, but Shelley asked me to make a dummy of a specific actor who was drowned in the movie and then spit up by our underwater monster. During the scene the dummy of the actor was supposed to pop up out of the water with his mouth gaping wide, as if his last moment had been a watery scream. Shelley then told me that the actor was not available for the shooting of that scene—he was working elsewhere—but she thought I looked enough like the actor to model the dummy on myself. Besides, who knows what the head would look like after the giant octopus got through with him? At least the shark in *Jaws* ate his whole victim.

So I got on with it. As assistants proceeded to mold my head, I placed a block of wood between my teeth to support my wide-open mouth. The jelly-like casting material was poured over my entire head, followed with a backup support of plaster. Each layer had to dry, which took an hour each time. When sufficiently dry, the entire cast was removed, along with the block of wood between my teeth. Much to my horror, my jaw had become locked in the open position. I couldn't close my mouth. I had no idea what to do. After about a half-hour I decided I had better go to the emergency room instead of becoming a human fly trap. Before heading for the hospital, however, my jaw slowly started to relax and return to normal.

So, with proper drama along the way, the head got made and mounted onto the body. The octopus didn't do too much damage. You can see me pop out of the ocean if you ever run across the movie *Tentacles*, one of my few appearances in front of the camera.

THE MUNSTERS, 1964–1966

When we started filming *The Munsters*, we were unpleasantly surprised to find out that we had competition with a similar show being filmed across town, *The Addams Family*. *The Munsters* was based on a spoof of Universal Studios popular horror creatures from the 1930s and '40s. It was unique in that there was no sex, no violence, and no bad language, just weird-looking characters that belonged to a very loyal and funny family.

Because it took time to apply the makeup to each of the actors, they were assigned to one of five makeup artists for the run of the show. Herman Munster (Fred Gwynne) was based on Frankenstein. Lilly (Evonne De Carlo) played his vampirish wife. Eddie (Butch Patrick), their son, was a young vampire who carried around a werewolf doll called "Woof-Woof." Grandpa (Al Lewis) played the elderly vampire. Their human niece Marilyn was played by Pat Priest, whose mother was actually the Treasurer of the United States.

Out of the original five makeup artists, I am the sole survivor, so I would like to share a few of my remembrances. I completed my apprenticeship in 1963, so this was one of my first assignments as a (nearly) full-fledged makeup artist. If I remember correctly, Uncle Bud hid me in his private makeup room for several months and had me illegally applying Butch's makeup before I passed my exams. Then legally into the first season I continued to make up Eddie. Every morning I would glue on his pointed ears, lay a vampire's widow peak, and apply a coat of "Munster" colored makeup all over his face. The second season my duties doubled, as I also made up Marilyn.

Every morning after completing my application rituals, I would climb the outside stairs of the makeup department up to the special-effects laboratory. This was the hallowed room where special items were created for classic Universal productions like *The Creature from the Black Lagoon*, *The List of Adrian Messenger*, *The Mole People*, *This Island Earth*, *Spartacus*, *Frankenstein*, and *The Werewolf*. I was surrounded by film history, including the plaster face casts of famous actors hanging in rows on the walls, as if they were watching me from on high as I performed my daily duties. The counters and cupboards were filled with chemicals and the mixers used to prepare large bowls of foam latex. In the corner stood a large oven big enough to walk into, used to dry the molded latex and our plastic bald caps. Throughout the day shafts of light filled the room from an old, cracked skylight. There was a thick coating of dust on everything in the room. This was a secret place where only the anointed were allowed to enter, and that didn't include anyone with a mop or dust rag. My daily responsibility in this mysterious chamber was to make a new latex head for Herman Munster, along with a set of neck bolts, and Eddie always needed a new pair of pointed ears.

Butch always jumped into my makeup chair with a smile, but Fred and Al were not thrilled with the discomfort they had to endure on a daily basis. Their makeup application took several hours. The two shared a large room, one actor at each end. It seemed that each day they would conspire as to what mental damage they could inflict on the studio. There was always something to complain about, including Fred's IBM stock that he'd sold too soon. Al smoked the stinkiest cigars and had a

Measuring Eddie Munster's pointed ears. *Universal Studios*

habit of losing his fake sideburns. Between the two of them, they always requested fresh strawberries, especially when they were out of season; according to their contracts, the studio had to find them somewhere.

No one knew at the time that we were creating a cult classic. I helped make the original Woof-Woof dolls; only a few were produced in this lab, and I wasn't smart enough to make one for myself. Butch and I and Woof-Woof are still friends.

In show business the established bonds of friendship never seem to break. This is true for Butch Patrick and me, from the days when he would climb into my makeup chair right up to the present, when we meet at the Sci-Fi and Horror Convention, now known as Monster Palooza. It all seems like yesterday. Butch revealed to me in later years that he really looked up to me. I respected him as an intelligent and well-mannered child; he was fun to be around. From his point of view, I was tanned from weekly sailing, drove a Jaguar, and was a bachelor—until I met the most beautiful woman in the world, in 1965.

This message from Butch captures our friendship:

To: Michael Westmore
From: Butch Patrick

Being Eddie was a kid's dream come true! Hanging around with the BEST actors, special-effects guys, makeup legends, AND future legends! But by far the best part was exploring the soundstages for upcoming shoots. ALWAYS something to check out. And being in makeup, I could go anywhere and not get turned away!! I always talk about the infamous Munster Koach joyride. We were supposed to leave the house on Colonial Street and return promptly, but Fred Gwynne had other ideas. He drove out the studio gate onto Lankershim Blvd. After a quick spin we returned to a VERY upset Zimmy, our AD, and not to mention the director of the week! Tragic, not really, BUT I did miss the Beatles one day! No one even had the sensitivity to get me an autograph. DARN, DARN, DARN!! In closing, one of my first real COOL moments was when I was allowed to order breakfast to the makeup room AND have my favorite guy in the world, Mike Westmore, take care of my look. You see, Mike was a hip, single guy who drove a Jag, and I idolized him. When he told me he was getting married, it was, WHAT?? Great memories from *The Munsters*, starting every Wednesday, Thursday, and Friday, cuz those were our shoot days! And, many more from the lab, where his magic brought so many more creations to life.

Thanks for everything!
Butch

HOW I MET MY WIFE, 1963–1965

I have been asked this question and have repeated my story many times, and it is always met with a chorus of *ahhhs*. My uncle Perc and I were the first live attraction on the Universal Studio Tour when it opened in 1963. The entire experience consisted of two trams, two tram drivers, four tour guides (one of which was John Badam, the famous director), a salesgirl (whose job it was to sell overpriced souvenirs), Mrs. Ross (who oversaw everything), my uncle Perc, and me. The starting and finishing point of a quick tram ride around the Universal lot was located in the commissary, near the studio's front gate. The tourists would file down the stairs into a fairly large circular storage room where the walls were plastered with movie posters, or anything else that would convey "Hurray" for Universal Studios. In the corner was Miss Donna and her glass case of souvenirs. In the middle of the room the studio carpenters built a circular gazebo that held a real Hollywood makeup chair surrounded by mirrors.

The studio makeup department where I worked every day was directly across the street. Several scheduled times a day I would run over to the basement, hang a microphone around my neck, select a lady from the group of tourists, and apply a twenty-minute beauty makeup and try to explain it. That's like patting your head and rubbing your stomach at the same time. At that time we were servicing over a thousand tourists a week and thought we were doing pretty well. Rumor had it that the studio didn't invest any more money into the operation, and that expansion and operations were all covered by profits.

The lecture I was doing was above and beyond my call of duty as a studio makeup artist; I didn't receive any extra money, but the studio said that if I worked with them, they would take care of me later. I'm still waiting for that "later." From the basement we moved to an area called Prop Plaza in the middle of the lot; at least it was above-ground and outside, but in the summer, the temperature could reach triple digits, and in the rainy winter, we would freeze.

By this time I was teaching other artists the routine. As the Tour grew, we moved again to the top of the mountain, where the Tour exists today. For the makeup demonstration they constructed a two-hundred-seat Beauty Pavilion with a stage located next to Spartacus Square. In the center hung a monstrously expensive crystal chandelier that Mrs. Stein had installed. Mrs. Stein was the wife of Jules Stein, co-owner of the studio. One of my side jobs was to keep her dozens of eyebrow pencils sharpened. From its size the chandelier probably cost more than the building. Lining the inside walls of the auditorium were glass exhibit cases that displayed costumes created by the legendary costume designer and multiple Oscar winner, Edith Head. I continued to train more demonstration artists, as we were now performing up to ten shows a day, seven days a week.

The studio decided to expand the stage show. Edith's gowns were removed from the glass encased mannequins so they could be displayed on living models. From a casting call three young female models auditioned and were carefully selected to display onstage Edith's most admired movie fashions. The studio also had plans for these gorgeous gals to be seen in various TV shows and movies that were filming on the lot; they were creating their own celebrities for the tour. Now the live shows on the tour would alternate between the makeup demonstration and a fashion show.

Between shows the models and the artists would socialize with each other, except for one, named Marion Bergeson, who always avoided me. My take of the situation: This gorgeous, tall, blue-eyed blonde is really stuck-up! Her take on me: This tanned, brown-haired, blue-eyed, ascot-wearing, sports-car-driving, "I've dated them before" guy is really stuck-up! Besides, my uncle Bud had told me not to have anything to do with the models. I was there to work, not play, and he didn't want to hear any stories of me fooling around. I took Bud's advice and became a recluse. For three months I worked with and around the girls, including one who never spoke.

Outside, actor Robert Hastings of *McHale's Navy* would stroll through the grounds, greeting the tourists. They actually got to meet a real live actor with a familiar face. Out of boredom, or just wanting to create some hell, Robert would casually enter the Pavilion and hide in the shadows. He would lay in wait for just the perfect moment—when model Marion was parading across the stage in some very sexy lingerie that Miss Head had designed for the legendary Mae West. Robert would quickly run down the aisle while stripping off his tan US Navy coat and scream, "Mother, you don't have to do this!" He would jump onto the stage and wrap his coat around her; the audience would roar with laughter, and Marion would melt with embarrassment. None of us ever knew when the next Hastings attack would occur.

And then one day, following the fashion show finale, I was backstage sitting in the makeup chair, reading the *Wall Street Journal*, waiting to go on with my show. The fashion show ended, the yellow curtains parted, and there stood Marion. Our blue eyes locked in place. Her final outfit was a beautiful lace wedding dress that Rosemary Forsyth had worn in a Jimmy Stewart film called *Shenandoah*. The only words I could get out of my mouth were "Do you want to get married?" Instead of the usual snub, she said, "Wait until I change, and we can talk about it!"

What?! She actually spoke to me, and we were going to converse again if she didn't slip out the back door. At that moment I didn't feel cool like Cary Grant or George Clooney. How long did it take for her to change? It seemed like a decade. My heart was pounding so loud I thought she might hear it. For lack of words when she returned, I asked her if she would like to ride with me to the boat shop because I had to pick up a part for my sailboat.

On our second date we dined at a restaurant across the river from the studio. It now sits on the same site as a 1930s whorehouse frequented during the days of silent films, a fact that's not found in the present-day menu.

She accepted, so I tried for a second date, a nice dinner at a restaurant in Marina del Rey. I showed up at her door wearing black slacks, a white shirt, and a black-and-white-checked coat. Marion was wearing a black skirt, white blouse, and a black-and-white-checked coat. We looked like our mothers had dressed us as twins. We laughed about the coincidence, and went on to date every night for the next week. We are still on the same wavelength after five decades. Just to be within breathing distance of Marion was exhilarating, as she was infused with the scent of a thousand roses (what I later learned was Joy perfume).

We were engaged three months later and married soon after that. The girl of my dreams, Marion Christine Bergeson, became my wife on December 4, 1965. We all lived happily ever after with our children, Michael, Michele, and McKenzie, and our grandson Maddox.

Our wedding day in 1965. Isn't she beautiful? *Courtesy of the author*

POMP AND CIRCUMSTANCE

On a sunny summer afternoon in 1965 the Universal Tour grounds were abuzz with the rumor that Princess Margaret from England's royal family was about to make an appearance. Inside the Beauty Pavilion I was in the middle of a makeup demonstration to a fully seated house of hundreds of tourists. Suddenly an unknown person burst through the Pavilion's wide doors and shouted, "The princess is here, the princess is here!" (They forgot to add the "Hear ye, hear ye!")

My entire audience rose up and rushed for the exits. It seemed to clear out faster than if someone had yelled *Fire!* They were all stampeding just to get a glimpse of her princess ship. When the dust had settled there was a very large single male tourist sitting in the middle of the auditorium, and he exclaimed, "Go on with the show." So Leonard and I proceeded to demonstrate and lecture on the art of beauty makeup to my audience of one.

That's not the end of my story. Outside and next to the Pavilion was the only ladies' restroom in the park. After a guided and bumpy tram ride around the studio tour, the princess's bladder could wait no longer. After she entered the throne room my former audience lined the walkway from the restroom door into the park. Upon her departure, in total control, she greeted the admiring and curious crowd. Not many people can say they saw a real princess on the Universal Studios Tour. For all of us working there, it was just another story and just another day.

NEVILLE BRAND: SOLDIER OF FORTUNE

Things always seemed to happen on the backlot of Universal Studios. It had its own little hospital because stuntmen and actors would get hurt, and for emergencies, the studio had its own fire department.

Daily, many tour trams would wind their way through the empty historical streets, occasionally coming across some movie or TV show in the process of filming. The *Laredo* series was based around a band of Texas Rangers always seeking justice, and Neville Brand was one of the stars. He was also a regular at the hospital. Most days weren't any different from the others, but for Neville Brand, a highly decorated World War II veteran turned actor, trouble seemed to follow. A tourist-filled tram stopped so the tour guide could explain what was going on and who they might see. Neville approached the tram full of smiling tourists, unbuttoned his pants, and christened it right then and there, to the horror of the guests. I'm sure he also bellowed something memorable in his deep voice. This was the last time any tour tram was routed anywhere close to Neville's voice or stream pattern He was also known for other head-shaking escapades, but I will let them be lost to history.

SHIRLEY MACLAINE, 1965/1992

My uncle Frank was Shirley MacLaine's personal makeup artist and confidant for many years. Their tales alone of shared laughter and tears would fill a book. Frank was the organizer of the team and Shirley was the flower child. I first met Shirley in 1962 after she had been cast to play an Asian woman in the film *My Geisha*. Frank brought Shirley in one morning so I could meet her and take a life cast of her face. On the cast I sculpted in clay small ethnic corners that covered her inner eye. The clay was molded and transformed into latex pieces that Frank would apply to her every time she assumed her Asian character. Every morning at the studio I would make a new set, until I had accumulated a dozen pair. I then packed them into a small box and off they went to my uncle in Japan, where they were filming the movie.

Frank Westmore makes up Shirley MacLaine for *My Geisha*, 1963. *Paramount Pictures*

Shirley returned to Universal in 1966 to star in another film with Michael Caine, entitled *Gambit*. Shirley was cast to play another Asian role, and Uncle Frank was still with her. Her eyes had to appear Asian again, but not by the application of the inner latex eye tabs. Frank came up with a unique technique: He attached to the bottom edge of her eye a small triangular piece of medical tape with a flesh-colored string, and at the end was tied a Christmas decoration hook. Shirley's character called for her to wear a very stylized wig, but before applying it, a cloth covering known as a wig cap was tightly pulled over her own hair. Before her makeup was applied, the tape point was pressed onto her skin at the outside corner of her eyes. The string was pulled backward and up over her ears, putting tension on the tape. The hook was then snagged into the wig cap, thus giving her the illusion of slanted eyes. This process was much easier and faster than the latex eye tabs used in *My Geisha*. The trick was to ensure the exact same tension and angle on each side, or her eyes would appear lopsided.

Partway through filming Uncle Frank had a heart attack, and I was appointed to take over. You can't imagine my fear, as I had only been a full-fledged makeup artist for

Shirley MacLaine made up for *Gambit*, 1966.
Universal Studios

three years, and I was newly married. Uncle Frank knew how to control his hyperactive movie star, but I was new to this game where the rules were always changing. On my first day Shirley told me that I would have twenty minutes to totally apply her makeup (a session that would usually take one hour). She further told me that the reason for the time limit was that she couldn't sit still any longer. The interrupting phone calls and people passing through meant nothing. I only had twenty minutes.

One day because of a phone call she bounced out of the makeup chair at the twenty-minute mark before I could apply her eyebrows. Her passing words as she walked out the door were "Catch me on the set." That day we were on location, and I kept following Shirley through rehearsals and social engagements. When I finally reminded her about the missing eyebrows, there was a ten-foot-high chain-link fence that separated us. She exclaimed, "Oh shit," a favorite response, approached the fence, and placed her eyes next to an opening. Using a long wooden eyebrow pencil, I poked it through the fence and drew on her famous Westmore eyebrows.

Shirley had a filming contract that allowed her to quit at 6:00 p.m. every night, and she liked to stick to it. One night at about 5:59 p.m., we had one last shot to complete. I powdered her nose and grabbed my makeup case to make a hasty retreat behind the camera. I had forgotten to lock the top of my case, so I dropped makeup and brushes from one side of the set to the other. Shirley stood there and broke into hilarious laughter as I scooped everything up and threw it out of camera range. Since I was so entertaining, Shirley generously went beyond her 6:00 p.m. deadline.

As a thank-you she gave me a small engraved silver tray that is packed away with other fond memories. We didn't cross paths again until February 27, 1992, when we met at Elizabeth Taylor's sixtieth birthday party at Disneyland, in front of the "It's a Small World" ride.

Hollywood truly is a small world.

"THE PINK LADY" OF MALIBU, 1966

Not all of the Westmore clan is recognized for its makeup talent. In 1966 on the graffiti-covered rock face which stands over the Malibu Canyon Road tunnel in Southern California, a work of art appeared with the rising sun. During the blackness of night a person had been lowered down the face of the rocks on a nylon rope and removed all of the painted initials, slogans, and gang signs that had been accumulating over the years. Here was a blank canvas of stone, and on it appeared a creation known as the "Pink Lady." She was an imposing sixty-foot-tall woman with flowing dark hair and robust breasts, skipping fully naked and carrying a bouquet of flowers.

The *Los Angeles Times* writer Jack Smith described her as "exuberant and free," as if it was a gallery opening. When it was discovered the artist was a woman and her identity was established, she received marriage proposals, death threats, and invitations to join a nudist colony. At the time, our Pink Lady made more newspaper headlines in Los Angeles than President Johnson and the Beatles. Eventually the county of Los Angeles declared "The Pink Lady" a traffic hazard to all the gawking motorists that couldn't keep their eyes on the road. The city was not tickled pink. She had to go.

As the passing motorists watched, several methods were attempted to chemically remove our Lady on the mountain, but all miserably failed, so county workers were again sent up with spray guns and approximately fourteen gallons of brown paint. They were lowered in harnesses down her naked pink body, crawling over her skin

The short-lived "Pink Lady" of Malibu, painted by Lynne Westmore. *Photo by Dan L. Chambers, reprinted with permission*

like little ants. Slowly she disappeared with each pass of the paint-filled spray guns. Though the naked lady with the dark flowing hair and flowers is gone, a few patches of original pink paint are visible above the western tunnel entrance, half a century later. Much to the family's surprise, the Pink Lady painting was designed and executed by none other than my cousin, professional artist Lynne Seemayer Westmore.

BOBBY DARIN EARNED THE RIGHT TO SAY "SCREW 'EM!"

It was an interesting experience for me, in more than just the usual ways, to watch the movie *Beyond the Sea*, the story of Bobby Darin's life, family, career, ups and downs, and particularly, his relationship with Sandra Dee. It gives you a unique perspective to watch a re-creation of a piece of show-business history that you were actually a part of—even if only in a small way. In the film Kevin Spacey did a terrific job of picking up Bobby's mannerisms and characteristics, and it started me thinking about the real Bobby Darin, who I knew and worked with during his heyday in the 1960s.

When it comes to dynamic, talented, and charismatic show-business personalities— wow! It's hard to top Bobby Darin, in my experience. He wasn't the mere creation of press agents, managers, and publicity. Bobby was the real thing. Tough, smart, kind, gifted, charming—Bobby was all of those things. In this day of carefully produced and manipulated studio recordings and slickly edited music videos, it's difficult to imagine a performer who could get up on a stage, grab a microphone, and dazzle an audience with little more than the sheer magic of his presence. Like Sinatra, Bobby was a great all-around entertainer. Not only was he an extraordinary singer, but he also composed music and was an actor to be reckoned with.

Let me start with Sandra Dee. She was the great love of Bobby's life, and the first actress who was important in my development in the world of Hollywood makeup. I got my first glimpses of Bobby while I was still apprenticing with Uncle Bud, who was Sandy's makeup artist over at Universal. Sandy was one of the top-ten moneymaking stars at the time, bouncing from one movie to the next. In 1960, she and Bobby acted together in the romantic comedy *Come September,* and the on-screen chemistry between the two of them was actually real, as their working relationship turned into a full-fledged romance. They married after a monthlong courtship. Bobby would come to the studio to visit Sandy (she was eighteen and he was twenty-four). I would often see them together, and, believe me, sparks were flying.

By that time, I had known Sandy for quite a while. During my apprentice days at Universal, I would watch Uncle Bud make her up every day for films like *Gidget, A Summer Place,* and *Tammy Tell Me True.* Sandy was exceptionally pretty, with delicate features and an all-American, girl-next-door allure. Watching Uncle Bud apply and blend colors to her sweet face became my example of the perfect beauty makeup. In those days giving an actress that flawless look so common to the era was more complicated than movie makeup is today. The makeup was a lot heavier, including pancake, powder, and false eyelashes. They re-created this look perfectly on the actress Kate Bosworth, who played Sandy in *Beyond the Sea,* but Kate doesn't have the slight space in her teeth that Sandy had. A makeup man notices these little things.

While Sandy was being made up, I was happy to do little errands for her, getting coffee or anything else she requested. After her makeup was complete and she was off to the set, it was my job to clean up and reset Bud's makeup table, including the sponges, brushes, pots of rouge, tubes of lipstick, and everything else that went into the meticulous process of making an actress ready for the camera.

Once, during my tenure, Uncle Bud asked me if I would like to apply Sandy's false eyelashes. Hey, I was game, and she happily agreed. Holding the lash with my thumb and forefinger, I squirted a generous amount of liquid adhesive glue across the strip. With Sandy's eyes closed, I placed the fake lashes down on her eyelid next to her real lashes and squished them into place. Well, "squishing" them wasn't exactly the right thing to do. I had applied too much adhesive, and it ran all the way down through her lower lashes. Note to potential false-eyelash wearers: It is important *not* to open the eyes until the glue has dried. When I asked Sandy to "open" so I could marvel at my work, one of her eyes wouldn't open! I had glued Sandra Dee's eye shut! Let me tell you, the first time this happens, it's sheer panic. All I could think of was that Sandy was going to spend the rest of her career as the one-eyed "Tammy." Luckily it wasn't as bad as all that. After a hearty belly laugh, Uncle Bud came to my rescue and easily opened the eye and corrected beauty makeup lesson number one. Sandy took it in her stride. But, then, she was always very kind and easy to work with; she treated everyone on the set the same.

Years after her career was over and she was no longer in the public eye, Sandy would shock the world with the revelations that she was an alcoholic, had been sexually abused as a child by her stepfather, and had been anorexic and bulimic for most of her life. Yet even before any of these dark secrets were made public, there was an air of melancholy around her. As I said, she was always sweet to me, but I would say to myself, "Oh boy, there's something sad in her." Maybe it was just the loneliness and isolation that comes with the territory of being a huge star. Although Sandy was the envy of every teenage girl in America, it was apparent that because of her incredibly busy daily schedule, she couldn't live the normal life of a young girl. Sometimes we'd talk about things like dating or dancing, but it was clear to me that these weren't activities that were part of her everyday life—unless they were scenes in a movie script she happened to be working on at the time. Even after Sandy and Bobby Darin began their great love affair, she couldn't have the usual "honeymoon" period, with romantic dinners and quiet walks. The press was all over their relationship.

Beyond the Sea portrays Sandy's mother as being extremely controlling. Personally, I remember her mother being exactly like that—pushy and demanding. That film hinted at a flirtation between Bobby and Sandy's mother—and I must confess, a big rumor during the making of *Come September* was that Bobby was having an affair with her mother in order to get to Sandy. Whether that's true or not, I have no idea, but it was definitely scuttlebutt that was going around the studio.

After she made her last film for Universal I didn't see Sandy anymore. I read about her divorce from Bobby in the papers. They loved each other, but they couldn't live together. Yet even after their divorce they saw each other because of their son Dodd. I would read things about her from time to time, and through the years I often thought of trying to look her up just to see how she was doing—but one thing leads to another with the distractions of one's own life, and before I knew it, many years had passed. I heard about her death on the television news. She was sixty-two.

I worked on my first Bobby Darin film, *Pressure Point*, in 1962. This was a high point in Bobby's professional life. His career was going great, he was happily married to Sandy, and *Pressure Point* was a taut and dramatic film set in a 1940s prison. Bobby played a disturbed American Nazi inmate opposite Sidney Poitier as the prison psychiatrist. It was a demanding part, and Bobby was up to the challenge. Most people, myself included, thought of Bobby as an extroverted, pop-singing, finger-snapping guy. But he surprised the industry by giving a deeply felt, realistic portrayal that would earn him a Golden Globe nomination.

I wasn't actually working on Bobby's makeup for this film, but I did become familiar with his face. A young actor, Barry Gordon—who later became the president of the Screen Actors Guild—was chosen to play Bobby's character as a child in a series of intense flashback sequences. As is often the case in these casting situations, the two actors had faces that weren't a perfect match. I was working with my mentor, John Chambers, and we were brought in to make the younger actor resemble the grown-up Bobby as much as possible. The main problem was that young Barry's nose was too small. Bobby had a hook on the bridge of his nose. To remedy this we designed, sculpted, and molded a small plastic bridge to attach to Barry's nose. I used the same process and materials in my makeup creations for many years to come.

I worked on another Bobby Darin movie the following year, *Captain Newman, M.D.*, but once again I wasn't doing Bobby's makeup. The movie was set in a military hospital during World War II, with Gregory Peck playing the head doctor. Bobby had a small but important part as a shell-shocked soldier. I didn't have the opportunity to hang out on the set all day because my assignment on the picture was to make all the false plaster casts that the actors playing patients would be wearing in the hospital scenes. I was busy creating casts for arms, legs, chests, elbows, and heads. It literally took weeks to make these wardrobe props that would lend realism to the movie. When I was told what body part the actor would have in a cast, I would wrap that part in a plaster bandage, dry it carefully, and cut the cast in two pieces with a special saw. On the morning of filming, the two shells of plaster were fit back into place and secured with white adhesive tape.

If you look at the cast of that movie today, there are many actors in bit parts who went on to have successful careers. Later when I saw the movie, I was as much impressed with my miles of wrapped plaster bandages as I was with Bobby's performance, but there were no Academy Award nominations for plaster props. Bobby, however, was nominated for a Best Supporting Actor.

Now in that plaster story, everything went smoothly and everyone was happy. But I have others: Once I cut a bloody line all the way down Henry Fonda's leg while working on his cast for *The Cheyenne Social Club*, and another time the saw malfunctioned when I had Rutger Hauer in a full body cast for *Blade Runner*. But those mishaps have their own special place in my memories.

I really got to know Bobby four years later, in 1967, when my uncle Bud assigned me to be his personal makeup artist on a film called *Gunfight in Abilene*. By the time I started working with him on this movie, Bobby's marriage to Sandra Dee was crumbling.

Gunfight in Abilene was to be Bobby's last film for the studio in his three-picture deal, and I already knew that he was not thrilled with the script. It was a remake of a film called *Showdown at Abilene*, which had originally been made about a decade before. Bobby felt the storyline was predictable and lackluster. After giving top-notch performances in first-rate movies like *Pressure Point* and *Captain Newman, M.D.*, Bobby viewed this film as a step down. "Lucky me," I thought before the filming

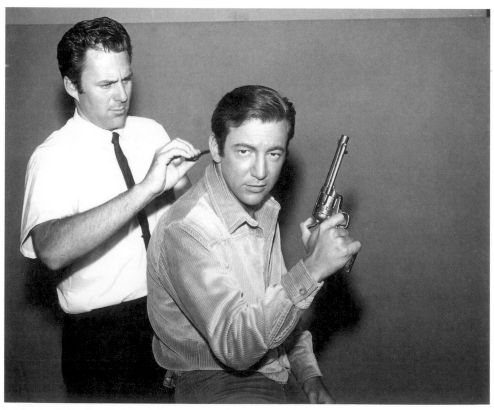

Working on Bobby Darin for *Gun Fight in Abilene*, 1967. *Universal Studios*

began. "I'll be the first one in the morning to deal with a disgruntled Bobby Darin." I was surprised, then, to find each day during his hour in the makeup chair that he was warm, friendly, and intellectual.

I applied his makeup and glued on Bobby's hairpiece—yes, even famous people go bald and have to cover it up. They make a big thing about the hairpiece in *Beyond the Sea*. Toward the end of the film Bobby comes to view it as part of a "fake" persona, but ultimately he embraces it as being part one of his many "selves." In the long shots of the movie, Kevin Spacey really did look like Bobby. In the close-ups I sometimes could spot where they went wrong, particularly with the hairpiece. Sometimes it looked good and sometimes it looked off. I guess that's the way it was in real life, depending on whether Bobby was at home and put the piece on himself, or had a pro doing it. "Your toupee is crooked" the Sandra Dee character reminds Bobby throughout the movie. On the set, I used to dress Bobby's hairpiece daily, and it's a very exact and particular procedure to make it look natural. I used a curling iron on the roots to give the illusion that it was growing from his scalp.

During the makeup process we managed to talk—and we talked about everything. He would tell me all about his life and I would tell him about mine. Over the years, I always wondered what type of lives these actors led because they were amazed at what they considered the normalcy of my world. Well, it was normal to me, but my family didn't always see it that way. The hours were long, and I would often travel on location for many months at a time. I particularly remember that Bobby was really interested when I talked about things like spending a Saturday afternoon by the pool with my family. He seemed fascinated, and maybe even a little envious, that it was possible for someone to take a day away from work and just sit around with your feet up. Bobby was always working, planning the next maneuver in his career. Even on the weekends he'd be on the phone, strategizing about club dates, movies, or recording sessions. While I talked about my family, Bobby introduced me to his world of sound. He really enjoyed talking about all the mechanics of making music.

Gunfight in Abilene was about the return of a Civil War soldier, and the studio had wanted some realism to his 1865 appearance, but Bobby Darin was Bobby Darin, and by the time I finished with him this was the cleanest, most tailored, and well-groomed soldier to ever return from battle. Realism was not Bobby's priority on this Hollywood epic. "Screw 'em!" was his exact message to the studio heads. It was a mediocre script and I guess he figured, "At least I'm going to look like a star."

After eight a.m., when the makeup process was over, Bobby was an entirely different person. I had physically transformed Walden Robert Cassotto from the Bronx into—drum roll . . . spotlight—Bobby Darin! Now he was aloof, brash, demanding, and the ultimate superstar in every sense of the word. We would hardly say a word to each other for the rest of the day.

Bobby's transformation was complete. He'd be sitting in the chair, the nicest guy you could ever meet, swapping stories and making jokes, and then when he was camera-ready he'd become the swaggering, cocksure, magnetic star—shooting out lightning-bolt looks and making demands. This was the performer who once declared, "I want to be a legend before I'm twenty-five." He was also someone I didn't want to be anywhere within twenty yards of if I could help it.

During the workday as I silently powdered his nose and kept his hairpiece in place, I observed Bobby wheel and deal and eat up inefficient agents and incompetent studio execs for breakfast, lunch, and dinner. From a distance, I would watch his trailer rocking and rolling, and the screams that were coming out weren't Bobby singing "Mack the Knife." I didn't care or want to know who the recipient of his wrath was, as long as it wasn't me! When the picture was finished he was out of there, and I never saw him again.

It's part of his legend now that Bobby had been very ill as a child due to a bout with rheumatic fever. The illness had left him with a severely damaged heart. He always had a premonition that he was going to die young; in fact, he had been told as a child that he wouldn't live past the age of fifteen, and that's why he could be so difficult—he was driven to leave his mark, trying to release all the talent and ideas he had in him, always running against time with the knowledge that he could drop dead at any given moment. When Bobby was "on," the reason his confidence wasn't as off-putting as it is with many arrogant entertainers is because he actually had tremendous talent to back it up. Bobby was so filled with genius, so ambitious, that he wanted everything to be done right—and right now. Like many great entertainers he had the ability to reinvent himself every few years. I was shocked when I heard of his death in 1973. He died on the operating table during open-heart surgery. He was only thirty-seven. I often wondered what other wonderful things he would have accomplished if he had been given a few more years. Bobby once said, "My goal is to be remembered as a human being and a great performer." So, in the end, he got his wish.

ROSEMARY'S BABY, 1968

One day in 1967 I sat down to read one of the scariest novels ever written, entitled *Rosemary's Baby*. When I had completed it I thought to myself, "Someday this is going to make a great movie." When I heard that William Castle, a master of the macabre, and his production company were bringing this project to Universal, where I was employed, I was excited beyond belief. At that time I was in charge of the makeup lab, so if any special makeup effects were needed, I would be involved.

The script called for a man with missing fingers; the visual effects process that can be used today to make them disappear optically wasn't even an option. I taped his real fingers tightly down to the palm of his hand and then adhered with spirit gum latex finger nubs to the ends of his knuckles. I vividly remember releasing them at the end of each day and the actor stretching them out with a sigh of relief after twelve hours of filming. Mia Farrow (Rosemary) had to play part of the film as a pregnant mother. A special pregnant belly had to be custom-made to comfortably fit Mia under her clothes. I went with Uncle Bud for our first meeting and body cast in Edith Head's wardrobe department. Throughout the entire process Mia continued to munch on a banana and stare at the ceiling. Hello! Excited she wasn't. Didn't she understand, she was Rosemary?

In another unexpected moment in the film a woman falls to her death from a window. In the long hours of filming she was going to have to lie there on the ground, perfectly still, in an uncomfortable position. It was decided upon to create a perfect look-alike dummy that would lay there after the stunt girl took the fall. World-famous director Roman Polanski tried to explain to us in broken English and hand gestures exactly what he desired, but the communication wasn't working, so he got down on the not-so-clean lab floor and contorted his body into the mangled pose he desired. The moment was recorded on Polaroid film. Ahh! Now we understood.

What made this supernatural movie so special was that it remained very close to the original novel's storyline, which is rare; often creative people in positions of authority think they can make improvements on the original concept, but most fail.

The Seventies

I first met Liberace in the early 1950s while trick-or-treating at his house in Studio City. This is the home where he had his signature piano-shaped pool. He always liked to come to the door personally to fill our outstretched bags with candy. The most memorable thing about him was his kindness and infectious smile.

In 1970, Uncle Bud and I were asked if we would take plaster casts of Liberace's hands and face for Madame Tussauds Wax Museum in London. At the time, he was living in Palm Springs, California. I was excited to go because my uncle Bud had been friends with him in the 1940s, when Liberace was making some forgettable films. I was told to arrive at the house early so I could set up. What I wasn't told was that he didn't arise until one p.m. Then he would have breakfast with his mother, and I probably wouldn't see him until three p.m. And to think I was hoping to return back to LA in the early afternoon.

I spent the morning with his managers, who gave me a great tour of the house. Liberace was an excellent cook, liked to entertain, and wrote several cookbooks. The downstairs contained multiple dining rooms, each one decorated in a theme that would go with a special menu. The main dining room, where he would have breakfast, was a long, French-style room with cases of silver plates, utensils, and bowls lining the walls.

In the center of the room was a table that looked to be a mile long! One end was set for his mother and himself. In front of his place setting sat a small television. With all the splendor and opulence in this room, this was his link to the world. The housekeeper told me that polishing the silver was a steady routine; it would take about a week for her to make the rounds of the room, and upon completion, she would start all over again.

After Liberace awoke and ate, we went to work. I had to make a plaster cast of his face and of each hand. These were the largest hands I had ever seen. With his fingers spread out, from the tip of the little finger to the tip of his thumb, they must have covered half of a piano keyboard. All the while I was doing this, he imparted his love for the Westmore family, and we both struck an accord when it came to fondness for food. As we exchanged tricks of the culinary world, I told him about a recipe my wife Marion had developed for cooking artichokes. We had shared this same cooking technique with a restaurant in Santa Cruz, California, and they'd put it on their menu. I traded Liberace our special artichoke delight for a signed copy of his latest cookbook. I then packed up my plaster casts and headed back into the setting sun for Los Angeles. In case you're interested in the recipe, here it is:

Artichokes in Wine

For each serving, add:

1 artichoke per person
½ teaspoon olive oil
¼ teaspoon salt
1 clove garlic (minced)
Enough white wine (Chardonnay, Chenin Blanc, or my favorite, Sauvignon Blanc) to
    cover the heart of the artichoke

Cut off the artichoke stems so they can sit on the bottom of the pot without falling over. Rinse the artichokes thoroughly in cold tap water.

Slice off half an inch from the top to remove the sharp ends and open the bud. Discard the small leaves around the base.

In a mixing bowl, combine the olive oil, salt, garlic, and wine.

Place the artichokes in the bottom of a large deep saucepan, making sure each one fits comfortably.

Pour the wine mixture over the artichokes, making sure the heart is covered.

Cover and bring to a boil.

Reduce heat and cook for 45 to 60 minutes, or until a leaf from the center of the artichoke pulls out easily. This is your test for doneness. Water may be added to keep the hearts covered with liquid during cooking.

Serve the artichokes in their own bowl. Pour the cooking liquid into a separate bowl. This is for dipping the leaves. Add another large bowl for discarding the uneaten portions.

GREER GARSON

I was lucky to be able to work with some great and legendary performers over the years. One in particular was Greer Garson. She was a popular actress during the 1940s, considered one of MGM's most valuable properties. Greer was nominated six times for an Oscar and won once. In later years she donated much to the Greer Garson Theatre in Santa Fe, New Mexico. Personally she was filled with class, beauty, and talent, and was one of my favorite people. On-screen she was a giant in her day, and off-screen, she was just as wonderful. I had the privilege of being her makeup artist near the end of her career. At that time in the early 1970s she was married to self-made oil million-aire "Buddy" Fogelson. They resided in Los Angeles on the entire floor of a high-rise on Wilshire Boulevard. This was one of several places they owned around the world. As I was beamed up to their personal floor, the elevator doors would open onto her apartment chateau; it was like you just walked into a world-class museum. The paint-ing and sculptures of the Masters adorned her home. I always liked to arrive early so I could browse. Having been an art history major at the University of California, Santa Barbara, this was like being let loose in a candy store (except there is no candy called Picasso). Usually I would make her up at home, as she desired privacy for our little tricks; then we would jump in the car and travel to the filming.

Once, upon my usual early arrival, Greer inquired if I had eaten lunch. Before I could respond she said, "Fine, I will make you a melted cheese sandwich." It's nice to have a personal chef like Greer Garson. While she was in the kitchen I was sitting at the dining room table that looked out over the rooftops of Hollywood, and in the background, the famous Hollywood sign. The house was as quiet as a museum when suddenly there were loud noises emanating from the next room. Buddy came running out, glanced around, then looked directly at me and said, "I have to tell someone! Mike, my company has just discovered the largest national gas deposit in North America!" Okay; one of the wealthiest men in North America just got wealthier, but I got a melted cheese sandwich made by Greer Garson.

In the late 1960s, early 1970s, I was the makeup artist for a Universal Studios tele-vision series titled *Alias Smith and Jones*. Greer was cast as our guest star for one particular episode, and I was to take care of her, too. Greer had an aura about her; everyone wanted to be in her presence, and that included the entire cast, crew, and studio executives. In her eyes we all played equal parts in this world, and everyone was just as important as the next.

One thing she didn't do was drive herself to work every day. On the last day of filming she sent her chauffeur out in the classic Rolls-Royce that Buddy had given her as a wedding present many years ago, to pick up a dozen five-gallon containers of ice cream from Baskin-Robbins 31 Flavors. Very properly and civilly the chauffeur tried to serve each crew member individually. His assistance didn't last long, as one hundred people were waiting in line. This was Greer's thank-you gift to all of us for the wonderful time she had spent working and socializing on the show. Not anticipating her ice-cream generosity, the crew had so loved being in her presence that we had all chipped in to purchase her a thank-you gift: one hundred long-stemmed red roses. This is the only time I have ever seen a crew respond with such love to a parting guest star. We filled her Rolls with roses, and she departed with a wave out the car window as she drove through the studio gates. A classy lady.

SKULLDUGGERY, 1970

This is a film about a safari to New Guinea. The expedition discovers a group of furry creatures, which raises the question: Are they human or animal, or possibly a living descendant of the missing link to modern humans?

As the head makeup lab technician I was told by the studio that very soon I would have to fly and work in Jakarta, Indonesia, for several weeks. This was my first distant location and longest length of time away from home. It was exciting to think of traveling to Indonesia, but not so thrilling to leave my wife, Marion, and our two babies, Michael and Michele. Uncle Bud said there was no time to take family along; we were going to travel light and fast. We were going to meet up with a group of Indonesian students who would play our missing links in the movie. It was my job to prepare and cast twenty-four plaster face impressions and twenty-four plaster molds of their upper teeth. I would also take body measurements for the production of the hair suits which would be manufactured in Hong Kong. We were supposed to swing through Hong Kong for a couple of days before our return flight home. To complete the missing links' creative makeup, we would have to construct Neanderthal-type latex foreheads and nasty-looking snap-on teeth back at the studio.

The journey to Jakarta was the longest plane ride in my life. I was in constant motion for twenty-four hours. We only touched the ground long enough to refuel. I boarded Japan Air Lines in Los Angeles with our luggage and pounds of casting materials. The first stop was Honolulu, and then on to Tokyo. On the first two legs of the flight the stewardesses wore traditional Japanese kimonos.

Sushi and sake were abundant, and the female stewardesses bowed frequently and spoke very softly. We landed in Tokyo for just an hour, then started our journey south through Hong Kong, Bangkok, Singapore, and into Indonesia. For the rest of the flight from Tokyo the flight attendants' clothes had changed from traditional Japanese costumes to dark blue skirts and jackets that resembled the United Airlines uniforms. In perfectly spoken English, our food of choice was chicken or steak, and the offered beverages were beer or wine.

Once in the hotel, Bud and I set up a room as a lab so we could quickly accomplish our assignment. The students were scheduled to arrive a few hours apart. We completed all our plaster impressions in five days. Then the plaster faces and teeth had to be dried and carefully packed for their journey back to Universal Studios.

Jakarta wasn't the island paradise one might imagine. It had just broken relations with its Communist friends, and the Indonesian military was in control. There was higher than 90 percent unemployment and the streets were lined with beggars, including those that had been purposely deformed at birth so begging would be their occupation for life. Needless to say, we were told not to venture too far from our hotel once it became dark. During the day the humidity in the air was so heavy, it felt like you were inhaling hot water. The humidity level was just a tad below rain.

The most stressful thing I had to cope with was communication back to the United States. Indonesia was connected to the pacific cable that ran under the Pacific; there were no satellites. Phone calls both in and out to the United States were only possible from seven to eight p.m. on a "maybe basis," several nights during the week. There was no guarantee of a hookup, so communication was sporadic. I had met businessmen in the hotel that flew to Singapore just to make phone calls.

With a few days left in Jakarta I decided to take a car ride to Bandon, a neighboring city, a number of miles away. Halfway through my journey I had to pee really bad. I told my driver to stop at the next restroom. He immediately pulled over onto the grassy side of the road. As far as the eye could see were large rice paddies being tended by picturesque groups of people bent over planting, while wearing their typical wide-brimmed straw hats. I asked, "Where?" and he gestured to the standing palm tree next to me. I couldn't bring myself to become the morning show, so with a bursting bladder I made it all the way to town where the bathroom wasn't much better.

With a few days left Bud decided we should visit Bali, the next island over. We hopped a plane, Garuda Airlines, where I shared my in-flight breakfast roll with a giant cockroach. I couldn't argue with him; he'd claimed it first. As we were leaving the ground I spotted, out my window, about eight Russian MiGs all lined up in a row. I inquired about their use. The aircraft had actually been left by the ousted Russians, and were presently known as the Indonesian Air Force. The only problem with this group of fighter planes was that the Russians had also taken the pilots and mechanics, so the planes couldn't fly. They sure looked snappy and impressive for a grounded air force.

Flying over the blue water and landing in Bali was beautiful. This was paradise. We boarded a bus to our hotel. After leaving the bustling city airport and heading out of town, I found that *National Geographic* magazine was pictorially telling the truth. There, walking up and down each side of the roadways, were women of all ages with bare breasts. I eventually gave up trying to take it all in; it so makes one look like a tourist.

In a country where there is not a lot to do, I hired a guide to show me the local art bazaar and the burning of the monthly funeral pyre. For locals that can't afford a private cremation, their bodies were saved up for the monthly festival, to which tourists were invited. My guide, like some Mormons, had three wives, all living in different homes. He needed to stop for a minute at the house of wife number three before we visited the art bazaar. While he was inside I snooped around outside. In the backyard, half buried in the mud, was a wooden statue that sported a pair of wings and a tail. I asked about its significance. It was a temple statue called "Garuda" that wife number three had hauled across the island from her native village. Was it for sale? She shrugged her shoulders, and the husband said, "You don't want that; it's dirty. It was painted with natural fruit stains and they are faded—plus, it is old." My heart was leaping out of my chest in excitement. I asked, How much? She held up ten fingers. Knowing this was barter country, I held up five fingers, hoping that was five US dollars. The deal was done. They wrapped it in banana leaves and straw for safekeeping. My guide was not thrilled, as he expected me to purchase newly painted masks in the bazaar where he probably would have received a commission. I toted that ten pounds of carved wood along with me everywhere I went for the rest of the trip.

It was another month before I flew home. It seems the deal wasn't ironclad with the Indonesian group. So, Bud and I were asked to travel to Hong Kong to make sure everything was ready to manufacture the hair suits on the stretch material, and then wait. The studio was negotiating with a Japanese dance troupe in Tokyo just in case the deal with the Indonesian students fell through.

Hong Kong was fairly quiet and boring for me, and I was missing Marion. In my first three days in town I ordered two custom suits that came with not a lot of room for my butt, a dozen long-sleeved custom shirts that seemed short in the arms, and a vicuna coat for Marion that was short all over. One of the musts when visiting Hong Kong was to drive out to its border with China, climb up into a tower, and view the landscape of Red China. As a tourist on our side of the fence peering through a set of binoculars, you could almost wave at the Communist soldiers viewing you through theirs.

When we knew our stay in Hong Kong was being extended, we decided to move from the Hilton Hotel to the classier Peninsula, for three reasons. One, it seemed the Hilton was the major resort for US soldiers, there for rest and relaxation from the Vietnam War. It was noisy, with hot and hotter running women canvassing the hotel and the hallways night and day. All it lacked was New Year's Eve pointed hats and noisemakers. Reasons number two and three to move: the Peninsula's chocolate dessert served at dinner and the orange pancakes at breakfast.

Bud and I were wasting time one day walking down a main street when out of nowhere appeared hundreds of young people, marching and chanting praise to Chairman Mao while waving their little red books. It was his birthday. We stopped to watch for a minute as they passed by. We were unafraid, as it was all controlled by a very large Gurkha police force that lined each side of the street, each one carrying a club as big as a baseball bat. I talked with a concerned wife that evening. All that had been shown on American TV news was the march that looked like a Chinese riot in progress. I told her not to worry, and about the protective police standing in the shadows. Hong Kong was still a British colony at this time.

Uncle Bud loved to wear red socks with his short pants. Red was not a color of choice to be worn in a potential Communist country, especially with the Red Guard so active. With our stay extended, we needed to get some more money for our expenses. In the morning we went to the bank when it opened. In a hurry, Bud rushed through the front door and everything came to a very quiet halt. A uniformed guard mounted upon a stand behind the front door and another one at the rear had leveled his sawed-off shotgun at Bud. It seems you don't run into a bank unless you are planning to rob it. The next time we went for a little subsistence, both of us slowly walked in (and Bud changed the color of his socks based on political advice).

After a month's stay in Hong Kong, the studio struck a deal with Indonesia, I didn't have to go to Tokyo and do the castings all over again. The last thing was to check on the progress of the hair suits; hopefully they would fit better than my hairless ill-fitting custom ones. With my wooden statue under my arm, I could go home.

Once back at Universal Studios we sculpted and manufactured all the latex "Simian" foreheads and snap-on monkey teeth that we needed for filming *Skullduggery*, which starred Burt Reynolds.

ALIAS SMITH AND JONES, 1971: THE DEATH OF A FRIEND

In the early 1970s I was working on a television series called *Alias Smith and Jones*, one of the many cowboy shows that abounded at that time. (What can I say? Horses were cheap.) It was always hot and dusty, or muddy from the rain, with the smell of horse manure filling the air. It seemed that the horses either wanted to bite me or step on me; we had a mutual understanding to keep our distance whenever possible. Sadly the series didn't last long, as star Peter Duel took his life during a state of depression. Everyone could see it coming, even his sister. Peter would often say to me, "I wish I could live like you"—meaning substance-free, with a family and happiness. Often his girlfriend would come to me with a new black eye so I could cover it with makeup. She sure ran into a lot of doors. Peter was a rebel and I was a trusted friend. On another occasion the producer of the show, Joe Swerling, asked me to ask Peter if he would cut his hair, as it was getting too long. No one from production would confront him directly. I told him the request and Peter replied, "They can go f**k themselves." So, I went back to the producer and relayed Peter's message in his exact words. I guess that's what they did, because Peter's hair continued to grow.

Peter's troubled life ended on the floor with a smoking gun as he gazed up at the lights from under his Christmas tree. We never lost a beat. I was notified that Peter had shot himself about five a.m., and was told to report to work as scheduled. We were told to wait at work, as they were trying to cast a replacement less than twenty-four hours after his death. They decided Ben Murphy couldn't carry the show by himself, so they needed a second actor. We were told they approached Peter's brother to fill in, but he refused. In the afternoon we filmed scenes without and around Peter's character; by the next day Roger Smith had been cast to continue the role. It's all about time and money; no time to mourn. Someone probably said Peter would have wanted it that way. That's BS. Peter would have said, "Let's party." There's no business like show business. The show couldn't make it without Mr. Smith.

While working on the series, I had a surreal evening with the King of the Conga, Desi Arnaz. It was nighttime and we were filming around the horse corral on the backlot of Universal Studios. Nowadays these backlot areas are overrun with trams filled with tourists. We were ready to film, and the director had a last-minute suggestion: He wanted me to glue a typical Mexican bandito-style mustache onto our guest actor. That was a great idea, except my partner had packed up all our standby makeup supplies and gone home for the night.

When I was an apprentice makeup artist I was trained to think up solutions on the spot. Mustache . . . hair! I needed hair. I'm standing next to a horse corral and right in front of me is a horse with a shiny black mane and tail. Making sure no one was watching, I approached my equine solution with a pair of scissors. I gently grasped the long mane hair when a voice suddenly cut through the night, asking, "What are you doing?" The horse thief had been caught by the horse's caretaker, known in showbiz as a wrangler. I explained my plight, and he explained his: "You can't take it from the mane; it will [aesthetically] look bad"—as if anyone would have noticed a few missing hairs.

He went around to the back of the horse, lifted its tail, and swiftly yanked out a handful of hair. Needless to say, the horse reacted. Even though horses lift their tails to do their business, there is always an after spray, and my newly plucked hair smelled like it. With scissors, glue, and hair in hand, no time to clean it, I approached my actor. I painted his upper lip with adhesive and proceeded to hand-lay each hair until my mustache was complete. All evening the actor complained about smelling horse piss, but I assured him it was the chemicals used in the process to treat this special hair. Another lesson I learned as an apprentice: For the sake of saving one's ass, LIE! At the end of filming I cleaned up the actor and threw away the evidence. The next morning I got him a matching mustache from the makeup department.

Years later I felt compelled to admit my guilt and this entire story to his daughter, Lucie Arnaz, when she was a guest star on *Star Trek*. More amazing to me than the mustache tale were the stories that Desi Arnaz told me about his career as we sat together on a bale of hay most of the night.

Desi Arnaz brought his Latin style from Cuba. His drums and hot dancing, called the "Conga," took the United States by storm. It brought him recognition in the nightclub circuit, on Broadway, in the movies, as a television actor and comedian, but most important and impressive, as a businessman and negotiator. He and his wife, Lucille Ball, created a state-of-the-art studio in Hollywood called Desilu Productions. He was a power in the entertainment industry. By the end of our evening I was in awe of this kind, humble man on the hay bale sitting beside me with his smelly mustache.

WOLPER TRAGEDY, 1973

In 1973, Wolper Productions started to produce an ABC television series called *Primal Man*, the story of Australopithecus, a precursor to modem humans that lived in Africa some two million years ago. David Wolper was a prolific producer of excellent documentaries, and Wolper Productions was producing this film for the National Geographic Society. The finest laboratory makeup artists in Hollywood were gathered together to sculpt and mold all of the unique prehistoric makeup that would be needed. I was teamed up with Sonny Burman, who many years later supervised my *Star Trek* lab at Paramount Studios. Sonny and I worked as lab partners for several months; then, for some reason, it all came to an abrupt halt and we were all temporarily released to pursue other projects.

Months later I received a call that the filming was about to start up again, and they needed eight makeup artists to fly immediately to Mammoth, California. At that moment, I was working with my brother Monty on a film called *Doc Savage*. Excitedly I asked him if he would release me so I could return to *Primal Man*. My job with Monty at the time was applying dark brown body makeup to a lot of tribal people with a big sponge, not a particularly fulfilling endeavor. Wolper was to be filming in the snow, and I just knew that on weekends I would be able to get in some skiing at one of the best resorts in California. But Monty said he really needed me, because help was hard to find, and also my wife Marion didn't feel right about me leaving her and the children for a month. Two negatives convinced me to say, however regretfully, no thanks. The Wolper Production Company had to assemble a new team of artists, as most of us had committed to other projects. Our union membership at the time was not that big, so everyone knew everyone; old team and new, we were all friends.

A month later, on March 13, 1974, Marion and I were watching the eleven o'clock news when it was interrupted by a newsflash. The breaking news said a plane had gone down and an entire film crew had been killed in the Mammoth Lakes area. I broke out in a cold sweat. I couldn't stop pacing, and my heart was racing . . . Could it be my friends? As the story developed, we learned that a Corvair 440 Sierra Pacific plane, apparently overloaded with the film crew and equipment, had ascended from the small airport in Bishop and had had to fly around in circles to gain altitude. At 8:28 p.m., within several yards of the top, the plane slammed into the mountain, exploding into a fireball of debris that cascaded over the peak and into the opposite valley below.

All thirty-six passengers and the plane crew were killed. The writer, director, cameraman, actors, stuntmen, and all the technicians, including my eight makeup artist friends, were gone. I don't remember any funerals because there were no bodies to be found. Years later hikers in the area were still finding human bone fragments, some with animal gnaw marks. Today those fragments could be tested for DNA and old friends identified, but there has not been any call for such action.

To my knowledge, this is still the only complete film crew to evaporate in the line of duty. There has been speculation that they were flying visually, not on instruments, and that the dark mountains were not visible against an equally dark sky. There were no known mechanical failures. At the time, this incident was the worst air disaster in Inyo County history, but federal officials have never determined the cause. I have my brother and my wife to thank for me not being among the remains of this awful event.

THE GOLDWYN STUDIO FIRE, 1973

It's one thing for a film's box office to go down in flames, but not the major portion of a studio. At Goldwyn's studio in the heart of Hollywood, we were just starting our first day of filming on the second season of a children's show called *Sigmund and the Sea Monsters*, created and produced by Sid and Marty Krofft. This was the story of a young boy who lived by the ocean, and his friends, who lived in it. I had worked on other projects produced by the Krofft brothers, like *H. R. Pufnstuf* and *Land of the Lost*. The fantasy characters in this melodrama were humans that were zipped into all-encompassing suits—no way in or out without assistance, and with extremely low-designed crotches. The only way the performers could move was to waddle.

It was morning and everyone was on a break, as we were moving to a new set. The performers who were wearing the cumbersome costumes were all unzipped and resting. Another point to keep in mind: All the sets from season one had been shuffled around in season two, meaning our familiarity with the sets had been totally altered. For example, in season one if you went through the kitchen set you would find the fire exit. Now, leaving the same door, you would run into a wall.

The scene we were about to film was taking place in a cave that had been constructed with Styrofoam and painted with a shiny gloss lacquer to make it appear wet. As the crew was preparing the set, an electrician adjusting a small light moved it high enough that it made contact with the volatile surface of the cave roof. In a flash a small flame ignited in the cave. It spread as if it were burning gasoline on the ground. In another second the flames had leapt to the walls of the stage. The cast and crew stood mesmerized; no one was moving as the flames rushed up the stage walls. We were all silently asking ourselves, *Is this part of the scene, or a horrible accident?* Suddenly the hypnotic moment was broken when over a loudspeaker the director said, "*Get the hell out!*"

Everyone scattered, running for the exits that were not in their old familiar locations. To make our exit more difficult, the old insulation in the stage walls and ceiling was cotton or asbestos, and it was exploding from the heat. All around us were falling white puffs that resembled snowflakes. They were coming down in such abundance everyone thought we were trapped in a blizzard. I made a dash through the kitchen set only to find no exit door, so I followed the wall until I discovered a way out. Once I reached fresh air I turned to my right. Why, I don't know, because to my left in the next instant the entire concrete stage wall crumpled to the ground. Someone was able to partially open the huge stage door, and in so doing, the inward rush of oxygen imploded the entire building.

I ran into the closest office building, called my wife Marion, and said, "The studio is on fire; I'm safe," then, *click*, the phones went dead. I wanted to get as far away as possible, so I slipped outside the gate and across the street. Comedian Rip Taylor was one of our performers in the show, and he was dressed in a very silly costume. In Hollywood, no one notices. Rip and I stood together and watched the burning of Goldwyn's. When the fire was under control and our stage was reduced to a smoldering heap, I made my way back onto the lot and caught up with the rest of the *Sigmund* crew. I couldn't understand why they were so happy to see me. The reason? I was the only one not accounted for. Prior to my emerging from the ashes, Christa Krofft, our friend and the producer's wife, knowing the situation, had called Marion to ask if she'd heard from me. Marion replied, "I know about the fire, and Mike is safe." Both of them broke down crying, as the only thing Christa had heard was that I was missing in action.

By now the television news teams had arrived on the scene, and the one familiar face they gravitated toward was actor Steve McQueen. He had been driving by and decided to stop and watch the action. As the press bore down on him, asking question to which he had no answers, he was (unsuccessfully) trying to hide a young lady behind his back. It was Ali McGraw. Right behind them stood sixty crew members with blackened faces who knew it all. You have to love the evening news when it comes to a celebrity sighting.

When parking one's car on a studio lot, everyone is supposed to leave the keys in the ignition in case there is an emergency and the cars have to be moved. In the aftermath of the fire, expensive cars that were parked next to the stage with no keys were buried under tons of concrete and hot, twisted steel. One lowly crew member had parked next to the stage in an executive's space. Unknowingly Security had punished him by towing his auto away to a far distant parking lot. Result: executive's car—total loss; crew member's car—total save. Talk about one happy fella.

As I mentioned earlier, Rip Taylor and I watched the studio burn with many other onlookers. Rip was still in his costume, which consisted of pink pantaloons, green tights, a green silk cape lined in pink, and on his feet, pink swim fins that made running from the fire difficult. On his head was a green wig accompanied by green eyebrows, a green mustache, and on his waist, a large prop seashell, known then as a shell-a-phone. He was a sight to behold.

A very small lady holding two huge shopping bags, one in each hand, came up to Rip, looked him up and down several times, and inquired, "Are you working in a movie?" (In Hollywood the answer could have been "No.") Even more bizarre, when Rip returned to his hotel wearing this same getup (all of his clothes and personal effects had been destroyed in the fire), the desk clerk inquired, "Are you coming in or going out?"

Only in Hollywood.

LAND OF THE LOST, 1974–1975

In the early part of 1974 I was between jobs, which means, at that moment I was unemployed. My two children, Michael and Michele, were attending a small, private Episcopal school with other children from filmdom families. One person I knew fairly well from school was Marty Krofft, a producer who was making a name for himself by creating Saturday-morning children shows for television. I asked Marty what he was doing, typical showbiz talk, and he asked me the same. Marty said that he and his brother Sid were going to develop a pilot or test show with a new optical concept. It was to be titled *Land of the Lost*. Since I didn't have anything on my plate, it was a perfect match. Several weeks later a film crew met at the Krofft Factory, and we filmed a very simple test version of the story. The concept was accepted by the TV network, so we all went to work, creating and preparing for the first season.

It was a simple plot, and everyone was excited to get started. A father and his two children get thrown back into time and must learn to survive in a land dominated by dinosaurs, the dreaded humanoid lizards (Sleestak), and a race of humanoid ape-people (Pakuni). The family, aside from living and running to and fro from jungle danger, played a vast amount of the show filming in front of what was known then as a "blue screen" (also called a green screen). This technique allowed the optical crew to fill in the rest of any blank background with rocks, caves, trees, or even a dinosaur or two. It was much like today's CGI.

My first assignment was to re-create three very tall, green humanoid lizards with large black eyes. Next, I built three prehistoric humanoid monkeys. A sketch artist's designs had already been approved, and my job was to turn his drawings into reality.

There was a very limited budget, so I had to stretch the dollars to retain the quality, and my reputation. The young men that were selected to play the first Sleestaks were high school champion basketball players. Several of the people in the production office were USC fans, and they were hoping to convince the boys to commit to USC as their college. The first lizard, John Lambert, was already committed to the school. When their summer job was over David Greenwood went to UCLA and Bill Laimbeer committed to the University of Notre Dame. All three went on to successfully play professionally in the NBA.

In the beginning I had all three of them custom-fitted for latex diving suits with the zipper up the back. I had trouble convincing the dive shop manufacturing the suits that it was okay to place the zipper there (they told me the men wouldn't be able to get out). Not to worry, I said, as there would be a person assigned to each actor trained to unzip the suits. While the suits were being made I was busy sculpting and molding in my lab the oversized claw hands and the slip-on claw feet. Since one size had to fit all three of them, I made molds of the largest feet and hands (Laimbeer's; I don't remember exactly how big his foot was, but I think it was size sixteen). The giant head I sculpted in my dining room, in front of the air conditioner, as this was a very warm time in Southern California. The final pieces I needed to complete were the lizard's stomach, a small tail, and a large plaster sheet of scales, which when turned into latex would be glued all over the suits.

All of my lizard pieces were made out of thick latex on the outside and, on the inside, with urethane foam, to create a cushion. When everything was dry it was all assembled and ready for painting.

Painting was a challenge, as up to now most latex paint formulas used in the studio were a mixture of rubber cement, liquid benzene, and oil-based colored pigment. I didn't have the facilities to mix and spray this lethal concoction. I remembered that this formula was used at Universal Studios to paint the suit used in the famous *Creature from the Black Lagoon*, and that the actor had had to be submerged in water for days. I asked myself, *What would be the next best technique for coloring?* The paint had to be flexible, as there would be a lot of body movement and stretching. The color had to hold on well to the latex surface and not peel off. It had to be opaque and easily and quickly touched up if there was an accident. It was my wife Marion's idea to try Shoe Magic, a commercial spray paint that can be used to change the color of one's shoes when they become so moved. It was readily available in most shoe-repair stores, and it could be purchased in large spray cans. I found all the colors I needed and became a master at spray painting. Whenever there was a need for a touch-up, it was accomplished in seconds with a shake of the can and a push of the button.

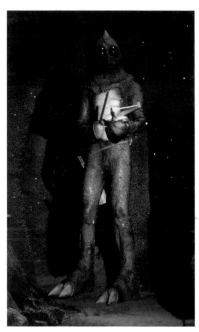

Frontal view of a Sleestack, *Land of the Lost.*
Sid and Marty Krofft Productions, David Rawcliffe photo

I purchased the Sleestaks' eyes from a craft store; they were half-round clear plastic shells about three inches in diameter. On the first day of filming I painted black makeup around the Sleestak's eyes so when their latex heads were pulled on, their eyes would appear solid black. Everything was ready; the lizards were all zipped in and the director sent them to stand on a fake rock ledge, eight feet off the ground. I felt uneasy about them being up there, as it wasn't easy to see through the heads. Slowly, from a distance, I noticed that their eyes were turning silver. I quickly climbed up the side of the rocks, whipped off their heads, and found the inside surface of the plastic domes covered in moisture, which was blurring the actors' vision even further. One step forward for any one of them and I would have lost a Sleestak or three. I spent the rest of the day continually taking care of my unforeseen eye situation, wiping out the condensation.

That night I took the three heads home to consult with my better half. We glued a piece of sheer black see-through cloth across the back of each eye, and this solved the problem. While wearing the suits, which was most of the working day, the boys would lose about five pounds. Not to worry, as this can be corrected with fluids. I think their fluid of choice was beer.

Lucky for the monkey budget, I remembered the hair suits that had been custom-made in Hong Kong for the film *Skullduggery*. Since they were of no current use to Universal, they were willing to rent us three at a very reasonable price.

Back when I was preparing the lizards I also had to sculpt and form the monkeys' three latex heads with a Neanderthal brow. Each head then had to be covered with a

A group of Sleestacks from the rear. *Sid and Marty Krofft Productions, David Rawcliffe photo*

Pakuni family from TV's *Land of the Lost*, 1974. *Sid and Marty Krofft Productions, David Rawcliffe photo*

long brown wig. When it was time for filming, the actors would slip into their hair suits and come to me for makeup. I would slip on their prepainted headpieces, which only covered their foreheads. I would then make up their face and hands with brown color and comb their long hair into the suit around the shoulders, blending the two together.

I don't know why I am so lucky to get shows with no budgets and no help. My daily job when filming the two seasons was to prepare one regular adult actor, two young people (a boy and a girl), and three ape people (one man, one woman, and one child), and to be responsible for dressing one Sleestak. Now that seemed normal enough to me, but when I didn't return for season three due to a movie conflict, they hired two people to replace me.

In 1976 I was nominated for an Emmy. The category was Best Makeup for Children's Programming.

A MAN OF MANY TALENTS

One of Hollywood's most famous photographers, Tom Kelly, was going to do some print work with David Bowie for his latest album cover, and requested me to be the makeup artist. Tom is most famous for his nude portrait of Marilyn Monroe lying on red silk.

For the album cover David wanted me to re-create a style from the 1930s. This technique had not been used in decades. I had to find a retired makeup artist that would teach me this forgotten method of a satin-sheen appearance. Since it was mostly applied with Max Factor cosmetics, I had to find them first. The secret to this flawless look was a bottle of glycerin water and a fine natural sponge. After dampening the sponge, the cake foundation, dry rouge, dry highlight, and dry shadow were gently patted over the face. When the water evaporated, the face was left flawless and glowing. I have never used this technique on anyone since then.

Standing by my lithograph by David Bowie, a man of many talents. *Courtesy of the author*

David was an amazing man, of many talents. In a large room in his Bel Air house, each corner was devoted to the completion of one of his endeavors. He created the "organizer" before there was such a thing. Hanging down the wall were lengths of tape facing sticky-side-out. There was a line for things to do today, tomorrow, this week, next week, and next month. David could stand there and with one glance know what he had to accomplish at any time in the near future. He was a singer, songwriter, musician, artist, an avid reader of history, and much more. As an artist, he created a series of five very small pictures, called *Arcana*. Each one represented a secret or a mystery of life, one for the stars, the moon, the earth, love, and death. The five pictures in brilliant colors were then turned into lithographs that are twenty-four inches wide by thirty-seven inches in height. David so loved this project that he even turned it into a limited edition set of personal Christmas gifts.

Around Christmas one year, I returned from the studio and Marion said David had stopped by with a present. He personally delivered a set of his lithographs to me, set number fifteen out of fifty. As far as I know, these all hang in private collections.

David and I worked together for quite a while; in fact, we were working together when his famous song "Fame" became world-renowned. The first time I heard him perform it live was on the *Cher* show. If you don't remember, the word "fame" is repeated over and over at different octaves. (I do remember thinking that it would make a great torture device.)

Because of my heavy schedule at the studio, I needed help with David. I needed someone who was both caring and good at what they did. Since Marion had been a model and a mother, she was both, so I pulled her out of "retirement" and she brilliantly took over! In the end David would call and say, "Can Marion come over?" I can't think of anyone better to lose a client to than my wife.

ROCKY, 1976

> At four o'clock, the makeup man, Mike Westmore, a gifted craftsman, knocked on my door, staggered across the room—no one was meant to get up this early— and proceeded to apply the makeup that he had built, piece by piece, for my face. It was brilliant. On several makeup tests before filming, I had gone home in full battle makeup, and never once did anyone detect that it was not for real.
>
>
>
> *The Official Rocky Scrapbook*
> by Sylvester Stallone
>
>

When the film *Rocky* appeared on the screen to millions of viewers, it had more historical significance than just being known as the latest feel-good flick. It pulled America out of its antihero gloom and doom. In 1976 Sylvester Stallone was only the third person to be nominated at the Academy Awards for Best Actor and Best Original Screenplay, following Charlie Chaplin for *The Great Dictator* and Orson Welles for *Citizen Kane*. Stallone personally lost both categories that night, but *Rocky* won Best Picture that year.

Sly, as he was known to his friends, took his father Frank's advice, when he told his son, "You weren't born with much of a brain, so you'd better develop your body." The advice was good for Sly's body, but Papa Stallone overlooked the brilliance of his son's mind. Sly's inspiration for *Rocky* was drawn from real-life events. United Artists and the producers loved the latest rewrites, but not him. The money for a buyout to have a major star play the part kept climbing, but Sly stuck to his guns—and I mean guns, as he had powerful ones connected to the end of each arm. In playful moods off-camera I would often be the recipient of a punch or two on my body.

The movie went into production with a budget of $1 million, and a man who had faith in himself. Forget the shoestring; this film was being made on half of a shoestring. So many times due to unforeseen circumstances Sly had to improvise new dialogue on the spot to fit the unexpected moment. It was also a family affair, as brother Frank appeared standing around a burning trash can as a street singer, and Frank Sr. rang the bell during the fights. Many people are familiar with Sly's mom, Jackie Stallone. She has a reputation for being a psychic, and she predicted her son's success, which was a million-to-one shot. When she visited the set to see how her boy was doing, we would sit and just talk. On one of those days, she stopped, leaned forward, looked me straight in the eyes, and said "Mike, I predict that someday you will be famous." Fame, luck, or good timing, *Rocky* was the beginning of my successful makeup career on the big screen. Sasha, his wife at the time, was always ready with her camera. She had a great eye for catching a particular moment in time. Even Sly's dog, Butkus, got into the act as a major player.

Prior to meeting Stallone I was working in my makeup salon in Beverly Hills. I received a call inquiring if I was interested in working on a small, low-budget boxing film. After my positive reply I was asked to meet with the actor in the Chartoff-Winkler Productions offices at MGM Studios. They also requested I bring my makeup case for a half-assed makeup test. Upon meeting the unknown actor, I laid out my makeup tools and went to work with nose putty and greasepaint to simulate a smashed and bruised nose and eye. The actor was pleased with my work, but had one final question: "How are you related to Frank Westmore?" I replied, "Tell me your story and I will tell you if I know him."

It seems that this unknown actor had had a small part in a Robert Mitchum film. It was late one night and everyone was starving. The film company was not delivering anything for the starving cast and crew to eat. Uncle Frank sent out for several hamburgers to feed a select few. The fledgling actor asked if he could have one and was flatly denied, like "Get lost." In show business you are supposed to be nice to everyone, as you never know when they are going to be on top, and it seems that no one ever forgets adversity. Back to the makeup test; I could tell that this actor was very anti–Frank Westmore, so my reply as to how we were related was, "I don't even know him!," which caused both of us to crack up in laughter. I was handed a script and skipped off into the afternoon sun.

The next day I dove into the script to discover there was going to be a fight manager. A dear friend of my uncle Bud, Burgess Meredith, had been cast in the role. He had to resemble an old retired pugilist with a broken nose, cauliflower ears, and small cuts over his eyelids. Rocky had to have similar cuts over his lids and take a traumatic beating during the final fight. Carl Weathers played Rocky's challenger, and he, too, needed to have the look of having undergone fifteen rounds of swinging fists. This became my first challenge in boxing. I had to choreograph a blow-by-blow progression of the constant beating.

Before starting my book research and designs, Sly invited me over to his one-bedroom apartment in Hollywood. I clearly remember the bleakness of the rooms. A punching bag was suspended from the dining room chandelier, and there was little to no furniture. He was Spartan in the true sense. This was the first time I met Sasha and Butkus, his bullmastiff. I would spend a lot of time with all three over the next few months. In the bedroom was a mattress placed on the floor where the two of us sat and watched Super 8 movies of old fights that contained brutal material Sly wanted to illustrate in his movie.

Touching up Sly's makeup in a gym scene from *Rocky*. *United Artists, photo by Elliot Marks*

Preparation

From watching the films I made sketches as to how the skin reacts to repeated punches. Slowly the initial bruises would begin to swell as the fight progressed. I could also see the color of the skin change from red during the initial smacking into an unrecognizable black-and-blue face. I studied the sweat as it trickled down and covered the fighters' bodies. When one received a sharp blow to the head, his neck snapped around and droplets of sweat flew through the air like rain blowing in the wind. Most of all I fixated on the blood. As I watched a cut on the forehead open up, the blood flowed in rivers, then branched out into tributaries following the sweat trails down the face, neck, and body, staining the fighter's trunks. All of this was very important to me, so I could re-create reality. When Sly was finished assisting me with my research, he took me to my one and only actual boxing match. We sat so close to the ring that I had the privilege of getting splattered with the real thing.

Now it was time to break down the script on paper. For the first three rounds, Sly and Carl exchange blows. One gets a little redness where the punches land, then the other. One eye starts to swell, then the other under the brow, back and forth. The swelling gets larger and more intense in color with every blow. Every time the swelling grew, it meant a makeup change to apply a more-pronounced appliance. Over Rocky's eye in one round the swelling has to be lanced in order to remove the pressure. The fight continues for fifteen rounds until both fighters have devastated each other. I drew for Sly what is known as a storyboard to display all that I had researched as each round progressed. This way there are no mistakes in communication.

Next, I had to take a plaster cast of Sly's face on which to mold, in three dimensions, my thoughts. My cluttered lab was located in my garage. I took him up to the house to cast his face in the kitchen. Sly sat down on a high director's chair. I turned on some calming music, mixed up my gooey molding material, and applied it all over his face. Years later Sly told me he wasn't quite sure of me at that moment, with all this lovely music and him being at my mercy, his eyes and mouth buried under goo and plaster. I also had to duplicate this same procedure with Burgess Meredith and Carl Weathers. From the plaster face and ears cast I sculpted in clay the designs that would be molded into latex and applied to the actors during filming.

Filming Begins

We began shooting on a chilly, overcast day on the streets of Philadelphia. Since this film had a small budget, we had a little trailer to house Sly, myself, Sasha, her camera, and Butkus, who had his choice of seats. The trailer also served as Sly's dressing room, a study room, a lunchroom, and a makeup area. On that first day as Sly sat in the makeup chair he pushed a button on a small tape recorder and a quiet voice began a motivational speech that would have inspired the world to greatness.

His regular makeup consisted of applying color and thin strips of plastic skin to the bone under each eyebrow that resembled cut and healed tissue. This is a look that real boxers and wrestlers develop when they have been hit and cut too many times. His makeup took twenty minutes to apply, and our inspirational message took twenty minutes to play. Then Sly dressed in his Rocky attire, popped on his hat, pulled on his gloves, and the four of us hit the cold morning air like *The Power Rangers* on their way to fight for justice.

During our stay in Philly we filmed the pet shop scene. It was located under the "L," the city's overhead train. During our evening filming, the crowds outside were restrained by the police. A young teenage girl became so distraught at the sight of Sly that she broke through the barriers and hit the pet shop front window like a wrecking ball, smashing against a brick wall. She began crying and screaming "Rocky, Rocky, Rocky." As the police tried to restrain her, Sly waved to have them bring her into the store. He took her aside for a few private words, signed an autograph, gave her a big hug, and sent her back out, a peaceful and happy girl. At this point I expected the entire crowd to hit the window for their reward. This is the kind and compassionate man that I know.

Since we only had a few weeks in Philly, we had to make the most of it, grabbing a scene here or there. Some of those moments really stand out in my mind, like Sly's brother Frank and some fellow vocalists harmonizing around a blazing trash container. The exterior of Rocky's training gym was located on an old street corner in Philly, but the interior with the fight ring was filmed in Los Angeles. One short scene was shot at Pat's, famous for their Philly cheese steak sandwich. Pat's is known not only for its sandwich, but also as a place frequented by celebrities when they pass through town. I once heard Johnny Carson praise it on his television show. It was a must on my list of places to visit. The night we filmed there they opened a special take-out window for the crew, and we could eat all the steak sandwiches we could consume. This was heaven on fresh-baked bread. Pat's has such a thriving business that they wouldn't let us return the next night to finish a small amount of uncompleted filming. The reason for the rejection: They lost too much money, as we interrupted their flow of business. I can compare the bustle of Pat's to Pink's Hot Dogs in Hollywood, where celebrity limos pull up day and night, and there is always a line of patrons extending into their parking lot.

One of the main reasons we went back east was to film the exterior scenes of Rocky's running and training. It all became an exhausting montage in the film. He ran by the wharf, through the outdoor market where someone throws him an orange; he ran through the Liberty Bell landmark, and the most famous run of all, up the stairs of the Philadelphia Museum of Art. I remember standing at the bottom of the steps, powdering Sly's nose, then off he went, bounding up the steps, one after the other. Upon reaching the top he raised his arms over his head and jumped for joy over his arduous run. That is the emotional beginning of the breathtaking end to the film. What the film viewers didn't know was that he had to do it several times.

Overseeing our city filming and safety was a friend of Sly's called Joe. I had lunch with Joe many times in mom-and-pop Italian restaurants that all seemed to have an autographed picture of Frank Sinatra strategically placed on the wall and tables covered with red-and-white-checked tablecloths. George Washington may have slept in a lot of places, but not as many as the places where Sinatra had dined. Another thing familiar to each establishment was the luscious smells that greeted you upon entering. The owner's mother always made her signature marinara sauce at home.

Joe's daughter was the young girl that Rocky walks home, only to be thanked with "Screw you, Rocky." We shot this in a rough Italian neighborhood and finished filming at two a.m. After being up all day and all night, we were invited into a local home to dine. This was an invitation we couldn't refuse. The last thing a tired crew wanted to do at two a.m. was eat, but we had to. It was the polite thing to do after we had disrupted the neighborhood. Upon entering the house we found that almost no one spoke English, and my Italian consisted of the word *pizza*. There was a woman in the kitchen slicing off hunks of meat and cheese to fill our sandwiches. Also, fresh-baked bread and bowls of pasta filled the table. Grandpa made wine in the cellar. It was the smoothest and tastiest home-brewed vino I'd ever had; I think that's what got me started liking wine. Upon leaving this unforgettable repast, cars were waiting to take us back to our hotel. The cars filled quickly, and I was still standing there, holding my makeup case. I said I would catch the next one available. A car door opened and Sly said, "Get in! By the time a car comes back for you in this neighborhood, all they're going to find on the street is a grease spot."

On one of our final evenings in Philly, at around ten p.m., a group of us went to Bookbinder's restaurant after filming. This place is historically famous for its seafood and turtle soup. Sly ordered me a bowl of clam chowder and a three-pound Maine lobster, and I ate it all. The next morning I arrived at work exhausted because I couldn't fall asleep all night. Sly laughed, and that is when I found out that lobster is a high-energy food that takes forever to digest, especially when drowned in a pound of melted butter.

Leaving the city of cheese steaks and the Liberty Bell, we flew back to Los Angeles to resume filming. The picture had such a low budget, I was the only makeup artist. Throughout the course of filming I had to make up Talia Shire (Adrian), Burt Young (Paulie), Carl Weathers (Apollo Creed), Burgess Meredith (Mickey), Sylvester Stallone (Rocky), and anyone else that had a speaking role. I mentioned that Sly and Burgess wore special makeup; it took about the same time to apply each one, twenty minutes. Whenever some production person asked how long someone's makeup would take to apply, I would always say twenty minutes. That's not too long or too short, and it kept everybody happy—unless it took forty. Sly wore his scarred eye pieces and Burgess wore a plastic cauliflower ear on both ears, a bump on the left side of his nose, and a small piece of plastic tubing shoved up his right nostril. Inserting the plastic tube wasn't a problem; it was the snot that trailed after it when I had to pull it out at the end of the day. This plug gave him the appearance of having an old, "S"-curved broken nose. The pieces didn't need a lot of makeup, as I pre-colored the plastic material with a scrape of color and a shake of mini red silk fibers. The pieces were all adhered with spirit gum and the edges were dissolved onto the skin with an acetone-soaked cotton swab.

Back in Los Angeles, Rocky's apartment was not a studio set but a real flophouse in downtown Los Angeles. It came with its own tribe of cockroaches. At night when the lights were turned off the tribe would scurry out of the walls and from under the baseboards. When the lights went on you could almost hear the thundering little feet scamper back into the walls, under the mattress and kitchen appliances. I was so taken by the herd of these century-old descendants, I kept a baby one alive in a Tic Tac box by giving him a drop of honey water every day. I don't remember what I named him, but he was my friend, my buddy. I didn't bring him home, but I did release him back into the tribe when we left.

How many people does it take to fill an indoor skating rink in California? According to our budget, none. After the cost of extra skating people was assessed, Rocky and Adrian skated alone to the sound of emptiness. Just another mishap that made this film more charming.

Where's the Beef?

Since Rocky, the boxer, couldn't afford to spar and work out in a gym, he pounded hanging sides of beef to prepare for his big day. One night we were scheduled to film this unique training technique, but didn't know how to go about it. Where does one find a whole side of hanging beef? At a slaughterhouse, of course. Off we went to a plant in Vernon, California. The USDA meat inspectors left the plant at five p.m., so unsanitary Hollywood arrived at six p.m. Upon entering the cool-down room, there were hundreds of full bovine bodies, looking like aliens, hanging down from their back feet on chains. Some of the more recently slaughtered continued to have steam rising from their shrouded bodies. All of them were waiting in line for the next step in processing. The rooms were so cold that odor was not a problem. Most of the herd we were surrounded by was slated for a fast-food chain.

The director and Sly selected the area in which they wanted to film. In the script Rocky is supposed to pound away on the meat while a little blood squirts in his face. Whoops! Dressed, cleaned, and processed hanging beef doesn't have any visible blood. I hear Sly's soft words: "Mike, I want blood to fly with every blow." I slathered down a carcass with a gallon of sticky, artificial blood, but that didn't work. From the caterer I got a small plastic bag. I shredded one side halfway down and filled the bottom of the bag with blood. Now, how was I going to make the bag adhere to the cow? Out of view of the camera I took two safety pins I had requisitioned from Wardrobe and pinned it through the meat. With the cameras rolling Rocky would hit the bottom of my little bag, forcing the blood to rise up, squirting him through my shredded holes. It worked perfectly. After the camera was put away my next job was to wash off all the fake blood with warm water and return the cow and floor of the slaughterhouse to their original state. When the inspectors arrived in the morning, no one would be the wiser. Who knows, maybe you ate a tenderized Rocky burger from a famous movie bovine; somebody did!

The Final Fight

My main challenge and the crescendo of the film was the final boxing match, the roar of the crowd and its immortal musical theme. The first day of our final match arrived. The ring was set up in the Olympic Auditorium, a huge sports structure in downtown Los Angeles. I was escorted to one of the large dressing rooms so I could set up all my necessary makeup tools. Since I was the only makeup artist and had to make up both Carl and Sly at the same time, I placed two high-backed captain's chairs next to each other. As the fight progressed I would have to be making makeup changes simultaneously. That sounded good on paper, but it turned out to be a nightmare, given the speed of filming and time within which I was expected to accomplish the impossible.

It is strange how mistakes can add charm to low-budget films, as there is no time or money to wait for corrections. On the first day of the big fight Sly's silk robe and the ring assistants' (or cornermen's) sweaters arrived late. The lettering on Sly's robe read "Italian Stallion," but instead of both words being placed on his back, the word *Stallion* swept across his butt. Since Sly was the writer, he wrote a line to cover the error. Next, the boxes of sweaters were opened for the cornermen. They were supposed to be red. Red cardigans were not available anywhere, so a local dye house insisted they could positively change the color of white sweaters to red. It was time to film, so we opened the boxes and got ready to pass them out. When Sly peered into the box, his eyes went wide and he was speechless for only a moment. Was this a trick? The sweaters were pink, and the dye company hadn't given us any forewarning. I forgot his exact words to express the future demise of somebody, but the show went on and the cornermen wore pink.

As we started filming I shined up their bodies with a rubdown of baby oil. During the second round they started to glisten a bit with a light spray of water. By the third round I had a spray bottle hanging from each pocket. By the fourth, water was flying everywhere as I had to spray one, then the other, all while hiding out of sight from the camera. I was never far away, as I knew when I heard my name, Sly meant, I need you *now!* As I sprayed down a nervous Sly, with all his pent-up energy, I became the local punching bag. He would smile and give me a knowing love pat with those large red gloves to my arm or stomach. By the end of the fight I came away well tenderized.

Once I had to start applying the latex swellings, it was all work. It started with a small piece under Sly's eye, and then both their faces continued to swell.

When I had to do both actors simultaneously, to save time after gluing and painting, I would hand my hair dryer to one to dry his face while I worked on the other. This went on for several days, changing and adding more swelling, bruising, more color, and more blood.

I watched Sly exhaust himself as he was creating his dream, punishing himself by absorbing punches that by mistake and misjudged distances really connected. Even swallowing all those raw eggs was disgusting, but he wanted to make the best fight picture ever.

One very important moment in the fight was when Sly had to have his eye cut because it was swelling shut. How to do it? Many of the effects and products that are used today hadn't been developed yet. How was I going to disguise a small plastic tube I could run blood through on his forehead? I awoke early one morning and a light went on! I had been an amateur magician, and knew the theory was always to fool the

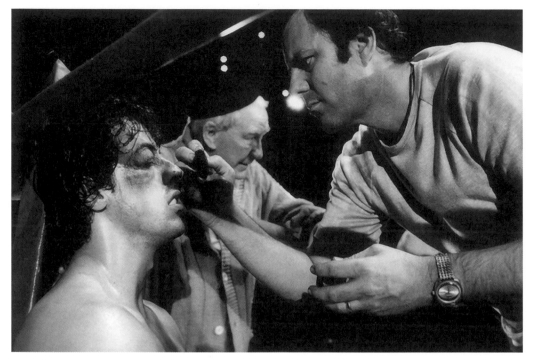

Rocky and Mickey (Burgess Meredith). This was a twenty-minute makeup application to create scarred ears and eyes, and a broken and misshapen nose. *United Artists, photo by Elliot Marks*

viewer's eye. The obvious is never expected. What if the blood came from the back of the razor blade instead of the latex appliance on his face? I dulled the sharp edge of a razor blade and rounded each corner slightly. A small metal tube was attached to the front corner of the blade that could be concealed by the holder's fingers and hand. Attached to the other end of the metal tube and hidden in the palm was a small rubber ball that was filled with blood, a ball much like the ones found at the other end of a squirting flower. Al Silvani was a real cut man in the world of professional boxing and played this part in the film. When Sly raised his head and said, "Cut me, Mick," Al drew the dull razor across the eye appliance and simultaneously squeezed the blood-filled rubber ball. Voilà! "Blood" squirted right on cue. Al's performance went so well that our trick was accomplished in one take.

At the end of round fifteen Sly's appliances were so soaked with water and oil they were falling off his face, and no amount of adhesive would keep them on. Again, my thinking cap had to be put on. I scooped out a big blob of petroleum jelly and smeared it under and over the falling appliances and squished them back into place. This quick

"Rocky"

LATEX BALL

- Rocky says "CUT ME" MICK"
- A small hollow Brass Tube is attached to the back side of a single edge utility razor blade
- The front edge of the blade is DULLED so it won't cut when drawn across the skin
- The small rubber ball is filled w/ Theatrical Blood
- The small rubber squeeze ball is SLIPPED over the long END of the Brass tube.
- squeeze the ball and the blood will flow from the front edge of the blade

My Geisha

EURASIAN latex EYE TAB

FULL ASIAN EYE Appliance

FACIAL Lift

Shelly Winters

ATTACHED THREAD

CLEAR MEDICAL TAPE

My notes from the famous "Cut me Mick" scene from *Rocky. Courtesy of the author*

trick made it possible to film the last scene of the movie without a major holdup. All of these little adjustments are done on the spot, with little time to pat yourself on the back. As a makeup artist, solutions on the spot are just expected.

The entire film had a shooting schedule of about twenty-eight days. After the principal photography had been completed, Sly needed some still photographs of adoring Adrian and Rocky wearing his after-fight makeup that showed his swelling and bruising. These photos, hopefully, would be used for publicity. Normally this is a very expensive process which includes a high-priced photographer, a studio, and a professional lighting crew. Sly called me requesting my makeup services, but there was a catch. There was no money left in the budget to pay for my services, let alone for a photographer. At this time I was working on another movie, one that was filming on location all night. Nevertheless, I was very proud of being part of the *Rocky* project, so I agreed.

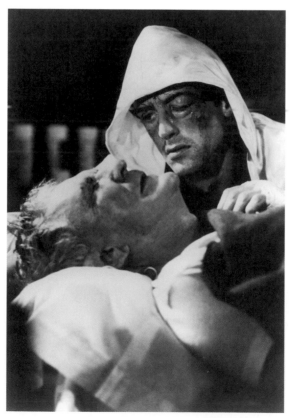

Mickey's death scene from *Rocky III*. *United Artists, photo by Elliot Marks*

We worked out a day and a time to meet at my house in Studio City. Sly and Talia arrived several hours before I had to leave. I applied her makeup and Sly's cut-eye appliances and greasepaint bruises. Meanwhile, Marion and Sasha hung a large black sheet outdoors on the side of our house; this was to be our background. Everything was ready. Sasha was set with her camera, and me, with a powder puff. I did a last look, powdered their noses, and left for my night job. The pictures turned out to be stunning, especially the hugging pose. That photograph appeared in magazines, posters, and publicity outlets previewing the new release of a boxing film that would set the world on fire.

A memorable moment in *Rocky III* is when Mickey dies on a table in the locker room. Burgess had to catch a flight back east and had to be gone by six p.m. It was in his contract. We got a late start filming because Sly and Carl had had to reshoot the running scene on the beach. Burgess lay on the table throughout the entire scene, even when he didn't have to, because it was so relaxing. The scene progressed with a distraught Rocky talking and crying at Mick's passing.

Throughout this emotional filming, whenever there was a lull I would hear "Hey kid, what time is it?" I gave frequent time updates all the way until six p.m. At the magic hour Burgess threw off his blanket, bounced off the table, and was out the door.

I went on to do *Rocky II, III*, and *V*—all with their own adventures, but with nothing like the pressure and challenges of *Rocky*.

ELEANOR AND FRANKLIN, 1976

Of all the television specials, miniseries, and movies of the week that I have worked on, *Eleanor and Franklin*—a two-part television special that aired in 1976—was among the most challenging and unique in my experience. The executives at ABC gave production instructions to spare no expense. The network wanted it to be historically accurate and beautiful. We were going to detail the life and times of the Roosevelts, a young couple who founded a relationship based more on political convenience and power than a great true love.

Stories abounded about Franklin's private life and Eleanor's often quite separate life. This show related as many of these events as possible without engaging in speculation. I worked on part one, in which the story is told through the eyes of an aged Eleanor as she takes us through her youth up to Franklin's first presidential election of 1932.

Daniel Petrie, a Canadian-born film director best known for his motion picture *A Raisin in the Sun*, was hired to direct this remarkable TV miniseries that would go on to receive excellent reviews and many awards. Jane Alexander, the great theatrical actress, was cast as Eleanor. She would have to appear to be eighteen and then age before our eyes to sixty years old. Edward Herrmann played Franklin. He had to age from twenty years old to fifty. Both leads were relatively young, so they had to go through a makeup transformation on-screen to show the effects of advancing time. Because of my prosthetic background and reputation, I was hired to create the metamorphoses.

The first several weeks I spent sculpting and molding Jane's aging facial appliances and constructing Eleanor's look-alike false teeth. I was working in the same lab at Twentieth Century Fox where John Chambers (my mentor) had created and supervised all the astounding simian masks for the original *Planet of the Apes*. I was surrounded by plaster ape molds and leftover latex ape appliances. Everywhere I looked I saw apes. In this special-effects makeup lab that had housed many technicians and their simian creations, I was happily all alone. The one thing that the rich budget and the orders to spare no expense did not provide for was time enough to complete my assignment in a leisurely fashion. There was a rush to test Jane on camera, wearing her old-age makeup. I worked feverishly from early morning to late at night for two weeks. I would have never seen my family if Marion hadn't brought me dinner every night.

On our first screen-test day I applied Jane's sixty-year-old makeup and carefully fit into her mouth the Eleanor Roosevelt teeth I had hand-sculpted from reference photos. Jane stood motionless as the cameras started to roll. I broke into a cold sweat because nothing was happening. She might as well have been wearing a pullover Halloween mask. I slipped onto the set, pretending to powder her nose, and whispered for her to do something—scratch her nose, smile, talk out loud—anything to become Eleanor.

Jane reacted promptly, and it was like standing in the presence of the actual Eleanor, brought back to life. Everyone was delighted, and I had learned a lesson that I've imparted to any and all appliance-wearing performers: Move!

While I applied her makeup during the main filming, she would listen to an audiotape of Eleanor giving a speech. This instilled intonation, cadence, and inspiration in her mind for the rest of the day. Once a day, Jane would become the embodiment of Eleanor Roosevelt. She was locked into her character, and no one would approach her during the day except for the director, hairstylist Jean Burt Reilly, her costumer, and me.

It was always fun to watch her go to lunch; she'd slip out of her padded undergarments, put on a summer dress, and walk off to the commissary in a sprightly fashion.

Makeup test for Jane Alexander as the elder Eleanor Roosevelt in *Eleanor and Franklin. ABC*

On these excursions she would cause numerous head turns and double takes because her youthful figure didn't have the face or hands to match.

Everything in the film was as authentic as the studio could possible arrange, right down to the flowers at their wedding. The particular flower from Georgia that had been selected for the real wedding decades earlier was now out of season and not available. A substitute was not historically thinkable. But they were in bloom in Europe, so boxes of them were flown in by the set decorators.

Aside from the studio lots, we also filmed at the Roosevelts' original Hyde Park residence on the Hudson River. For such a posh address, I was amused by how small the bedrooms were in that old mansion. We also located and filmed in Keysville, Virginia, where I got my first taste of racial segregation, especially in the restaurants. Whites sat in the restaurant proper in bright red Naugahyde booths. Blacks entered a back door and ate in the storeroom, where a wood plank spanned two wooden barrels. Even the drinking fountains had signs specifying who could drink where. I was taken aback when I first saw this.

At one point an elderly black woman who was working with us as an extra in the hot sun asked me for a drink of water. She explained that she couldn't overstep her bounds by taking a drink from the movie crew's water container herself. After I handed her a glass, one of her friends asked where she got the water. The friend answered, "The nice white man got it for me." The memory of being called the "nice white man" has stuck with me to this day, and I don't think of Keysville without the accompanying memory of the two thirsty women who weren't allowed to get a drink of water from the "white man's" supply. A liberal California movie crew, we had been told not to rock any boats.

On a few days when Jane and Ed both had to have their older-age makeup applied, I had to do both. It wasn't easy doing double duty, and it was very time-consuming—about two and a half hours in the makeup chair for each one. Production figured that financially it was less expensive for me to apply both and exhaust my butt than to hire an additional makeup artist. I used to wear jeans and sport shirts to work because the glue and the grease makeup were very messy. I basically took on the appearance of a farmhand before and after coming in from the field. My appointed associate makeup artist, when available, would dress in leisure suits and ties, looking like a producer. His main assignment was to apply a few simple makeups and keep up his long-standing friendship with the director. While I was slaving away, applying the special makeups, Production always wanted to know "How much longer?," even after the first five minutes. My dapper associate would pop his head in the makeup trailer and ask me, "Mike, how much longer?" After my response—which might be "Thirty minutes"—I would hear him outside saying, "We have about thirty more minutes." Suddenly "I" was turned into "We." This is not unusual in showbiz.

During anyone's career in the movie business, an incident always seems to occur that you wish hadn't happened, and here is one of mine. We were filming on some train tracks outside Keysville. Night was falling, and it had started to rain. Jane, Ed, Jean, and myself were not needed on the set, so we checked into our motel about six p.m. Dan was going to be filming until midnight with all the extra people that were portraying the multitudes that originally lined the tracks for FDR's funeral train in 1945. There were only four rooms adjoining at the motel and a single cabin across an open parking lot. I had been assigned the lonely cabin. Both stars were to be made up and coiffed in the morning in my personal room. Jane didn't think I should be so far away, as it meant that she and Ed would have to walk back and forth in the rain at four a.m. Jane made an executive decision and transferred Dan to the cabin and me into his cozy motel room. I knew in my heart of hearts it was wrong to do politically, but it was practical under the circumstances.

I went to bed early, as I had to be up at 3:30 a.m. to prepare the makeup. At 1:00 a.m. my phone rang; it was Dan, spitting mad. He was tired, wet, and downright nasty. My heart of hearts was right. I tried to explain, even down to the point of asking him to call and yell at Jane because she'd insisted on the switch. Dan replied that he wasn't going to wake up his star, but he would wake up the guy who had to stand for five hours, gluing and applying the special old-age makeup. The normally gentle, sweet Dan was pissed at me, and as far as I can tell, he stayed that way for the rest of his life. I don't think he ever forgave me, because he never hired me again.

Even so, with Mr. Petri at the helm, *Eleanor and Franklin* turned into a stirring visual masterpiece. It received seventeen Emmy nominations and won eleven, plus a Golden Globe. I was one of the winners. This was my first Emmy.

NEW YORK, NEW YORK, 1977

Robert De Niro was a genius at becoming the character he portrayed in all of his roles. I would watch in amazement as this chameleon would change his skin and morph into another persona. At the completion of a film he would shed the old character and reinvent Robert, the mild, quiet, considerate, artistic man that I knew. Every day was a new experience, because Robert always invented new challenges with every character. Robert gave each new character a flesh-and-blood personality that the viewing audience would believe was a living, breathing person.

Prior to filming *New York, New York*, Robert was taught how to play the saxophone by Georgie Auld, an internationally renowned musician. Georgie had a small part in the movie. He was always around to advise and practice with Robert whenever he desired. While Robert couldn't actually play in a band like he could have boxed semipro, he could purse his lips and press the correct levers on his instrument as Georgie's music filled the soundtrack. A musician watching the film would have believed he was really making music with his horn. Robert's mental concentration to perfect what other performers only consider props was an integral part of his position in time and space at that moment.

New York, New York was scheduled to film for three months, but because of the intensity of the big three involved—De Niro, Liza Minelli, and Martin Scorsese—the schedule was doubled. With the large budget that was projected for this film and the talented cast, many critics have said it is one of Scorsese's best directorial accomplishments. It took two days to film for every page in the script, so our 120-page script took approximately 240 working days to complete. I was forced to cancel other projects that I had committed to; one in particular was the sequel to *Eleanor and Franklin*.

The first morning I was introduced to Liza she exclaimed, "He's cute." *New York, New York* was as close as I would ever come to working on an old MGM musical. We filmed on their old soundstages, and Liza was right at home playing the part of Francine Evans, a big band singer. As the story goes, World War II was over and the entire world was falling in love again.

It is regrettable that every one of Liza's musical numbers was not viewed in their entirety, as each one was more amazing than its predecessor. The music, costumes, hairstyles, makeup, dance routines, and sets were all are based on the great MGM musicals of the 1940s. Liza was such a perfectionist that every hand gesture, tilt of the head, and foot movement was perfectly executed every time. She is known as a performer par excellence. These were long exhausting days for Liza, the dancers, and the crew. How did she survive those grueling fifteen-hour days? It would have been a great advertisement for Coca-Cola and Hershey's Chocolate. Liza's training in continuity was so ingrained that in the beginning of the film, especially in the nightclub scene, she had trouble adjusting to the freedom of movement and dialogue that Robert and Martin were so used to. It was an un-training lesson for the boys to get her to understand: You don't have to be perfect every time. With them it is okay not to duplicate every gesture and every movement. This thinking is contrary to most filmmakers but comes naturally to Robert and Martin.

I vividly remember two events. One day we were filming a huge nightclub scene, and an assistant director was responsible for keeping track of mealtimes. He got mixed up by a few minutes and allowed a thousand extras to go into what is known as a "meal penalty." That small slip cost the studio an extra $10,000! Needless to say, he was not back the next day for breakfast to pass out the thousand breakfast sandwiches.

The second event occurred during the first day of filming our nightclub scene. Our characters Jimmy (De Niro) and Francine (Liza) are entering the club. As the camera is rolling the two of them wind their way through the tables, filled with the party revelers. Out of nowhere a nonspeaking extra stands up on his own volition and throws a handful of colored confetti into Robert's face and hair and onto his wardrobe. For a split second it pissed off everybody, but then Robert and Marty went into a huddle and decided they liked the way in which the entrance played out. Marty yelled out, "Cut! Print!" This would be the master shot that everything would be based on for the next ten days. What that meant to me was that every morning after applying Robert's makeup I would have to glue onto his face, in the exact spot, the same color of confetti that "Jerko" had tossed at him. Upon accepting this action as part of the master shot, four Polaroids were quickly snapped of front, back, and right/left profile. This was my research for the next nine days, along with a tube of eyelash adhesive and a pair of tweezers, so I could duplicate and re-create continuity from day one.

One day we were filming a large exterior street scene on the backlot of the studio, where the characters would celebrate the end of World War II. I had hundreds of extras that had to facially resemble the 1945 motif. That meant red lipstick and stylized eyebrows on the women and short haircuts on the men. For hours prior to filming I combed the crowd for anyone hiding out; there are always a few. Our mega day was captured on film. The next day after work all the department supervisors gathered in a small theater to view the previous day's footage. The lights dimmed, the projector started, and on the screen as big as life in the front is an extra dressed as an Australian soldier with very long hair. I went crazy because I hadn't discovered him. He was a hider, which is not uncommon when an extra feels they are not getting paid enough to cut their hair. The producer calmed me by saying, "We will pretend he just came out of the jungle."

The most creative people were several extra girls that set up shop inside the fake storefronts that lined our fake city street. As soon as the rumor filtered around that the world's oldest profession was open for business, Security closed them down. Besides, wouldn't this be considered double dipping, as they were getting paid by the studio as extras to stand up, along with collecting additional nontaxable cash on the side (or should I say, on their backs)?

Robert was so into the time period of his character that he wanted to be surrounded with the vibes of authenticity. He requested a cigarette lighter from the 1940s as a prop that he could keep in his pocket. The prop person showed up with one that wasn't from the '40s, saying, "If it's in your pocket, no one will see it." Robert went ballistic, as he wanted to be able to feel the history in his pocket and to expose the historical lighter if he decided to take it out. This was a wonderful lesson in "Do as he asks, not what you think." A lighter from the '40s was soon found.

In looking back, I was privileged to work with the big three, but more so, to experience the birth of the song *New York, New York*. Liza had to belt "those little town blues" over and over again as we filmed the scene from every angle—high, low, close up, and far away. We all felt we were witnessing a moment in musical history, as Liza sent shivers up our spines on every single high note. In the final sequence of the film there's a number called "Happy Endings," and it really was.

PARADISE ALLEY, 1978

My behind-the-scenes adventures on this film were as strange and challenging as the story. Sly Stallone was enamored with the many production hats worn by Orson Welles on some of his early projects. In 1978 he decided to wear different hats for writing, directing, and starring in *Paradise Alley*, based on his own original screenplay. Basically, he was going to control all the creative aspects that would make up this film. After seven years I was returning to work at Universal Studios as an outsider. Since Sly was in total control we didn't live under Universal's rules, we worked by Sly's—even down to the excellent food that was catered throughout the day.

The movie storyline became as complicated as Sly's imagination. The film was set in the 1940s in the Italian slums of New York. It tells the story of the three Carboni brothers who collaborated in an attempt at success. One of the brothers was a wrestler, another a promoter, and the third a con artist. Within the script Sly's creative concepts came fast and furious. One problem with the final film was it seemed to have three different genres. Instead of the story going in one direction, it appeared to go in three: one was serious, another humorous, and a third fantasy. It was confusing, even on-set, unless you had a playbook.

There were many strange fantasy scenes that never made it into the first screening of the movie. The first run did have Nazi zombies and a dead hooker in the morgue that kept making money off drunken clients. In a barroom scene playing the piano and crooning is the famous Tom Waits, also known as "Mumbles." On the top of the bar nestled in a large basket of peanuts is the head of a war veteran known as "Legs," played by actor Ray Sharkey. The rest of Legs's body had been blown away in the war, but his head survived. Patrons sitting at the bar would shell the peanuts and feed them to Legs as they all chatted away about whatever. Who could pay attention to the dialogue when you're fascinated by another mind-twister? Included in the cast were twenty-five professional wrestlers, and Sly had appropriate names for each of them, along with the entire cast. Can you imagine being known as "Fat Lady," "Burp," "Bunchie," or even "Hooker #2"?

Over the many years I was with Stallone I could never get enough of his humor; most of the time the one-liners flew over everyone else's heads, but I appreciated them. I would break into a subtle grin and have to walk away. Sly had a mind that didn't sleep. He always seemed to be trying to improve and enhance his storytelling ability. I suppose *Paradise Alley* coulda, shoulda, woulda—if only Universal had left the original story untouched.

In preparation for the movie I had to create special fight makeups for two of the main characters, which meant they needed scars, bruises, and swollen faces. At that time my lab was at my home. The first to arrive was Frank McRae, a former NFL player; in the movie he was "Big Glory." The door to my lab was open and lying by it was our 140-pound German shepherd, Max. As Frank approached, Max grew curious; not being scared of the 300-pound former lineman, he decided to go on the offense. I restrained my snarling puppy by grabbing his huge tail as he lunged at a terrified Frank. The second to arrive for a face cast was Terry Funk, a professional wrestler. Terry held the NWA World Heavyweight Title. In his professional world he was known as "Chainsaw Charlie," and in the move his title was "The Thumper." Max took up his guard dog duties as usual, but Terry gave him a casual glance and said, "Shut up, dog, or I will kill you." Max licked Terry's hand and peace broke out.

One morning on the set while we were preparing to get everybody ready, an actor refused to have his hair cut in the period style that Sly had requested. I told the actor to wait in my barber chair and reported the refusal to Sly. This is when I found out that Sly had missed qualifying for his barber's license by just a few weeks. He came with me to my station and picked up my electric clippers. The speechless actor went wide-eyed as Sly said, "This is what I want." The actor wasn't getting a Beverly Hills hairstylist, but Sylvester Stallone. Sly shaved a two-inch-wide bald pathway from the back of the thespian's neck to his forehead, then handed me the clippers and softly said, "This is the style I would like, Mike; please finish it." The tearful performer watched in silence as I continued to shear off the rest of his long hair as Sly left to make another decision.

While filming, our stage was very tightly closed to visitors, as Sly didn't want anything to be revealed. At this time the national magazines were trying to probe into anything of interest, including gossip about personal lives. A reporter pursued me for an article on Hollywood makeup tips. An hour after my discussion of printable chat, the interviewer said, "Well, I guess we're finished." She closed her notebook and continued: "Off the record, tell me about the actors' and actresses' personal lives, especially Stallone's." My wife Marion (who I could call "Brains") had warned me of this, and I came off as the dumbest in-the-know makeup artist in Hollywood. My article never made it into the magazine. They tried it a second time, and this interview didn't make it to print either. Of course I knew what was going on in everyone's personal lives; all makeup artists do. Did they (the magazine) think I wanted to perform hara-kiri via my boss? As the rags were still hinting at rumors, they tried a third time. At this interview I expounded on unheard-of new techniques like gluing eyelashes on upside down while standing on your head and using green eye shadow for cheek blush. Wouldn't you know it, this time I was published! My peers thought I was crazy, and my only reply was, "They printed it!" I, who could have been nicknamed "Closed Mouth," was never bothered by a tabloid again. My wife will admit, my life can be as strange as *Paradise Alley.*

CAPRICORN ONE, 1978

After viewing my work on *Rocky*, Peter Hyams, who wears many hats—camera operator, director of photography, director, and producer—called me to inquire about my services for an upcoming film that was going to require a number of special makeup effects. Peter was the one man in control of everything, so he had all the answers, just like directors/producers Norman Jewison and John Huston. The film *Capricorn One* was based on a theory that our real moon landings never occurred but were faked on a secret movie set in Hollywood. Due to a faulty rocket, our actors/astronauts are whisked away to a soundstage and the manned mission to Mars is a hoax. The astronauts are then forced to pretend they landed on the red planet. When the cover-up is exposed and the NASA program is in jeopardy, the government must do away with the evidence, and the astronauts. Realizing this, the men escape. A chase ensues across the desert. This is when I get to open my bag of makeup tricks.

The cast was very impressive. It consisted of James Brolin, Sam Waterston, and O. J. Simpson. They had to show the ravages of a desert crossing, which included dehydrated, sunburned, and blistered faces. Jim was the brave one; at one point he let a scorpion scamper across his face, and there was no way to de-stinger the little menace. In another Brolin scene I was handed a large, dead, gutted rattlesnake. My job as chef was to fill it with raw catfish that had been coated with an edible blood. In a ravenous moment he pretends to slice open the snake, take a large bite out of its bloody insides, and chew it up. We were filming the reality show *Fear Factor* before Hollywood ever thought of it.

The second desert astronaut was Sam Waterston. When we were filming around Red Rock, California, Sam had to climb up the sheer rock face of a canyon wall while reciting a poem. The scene was designed so that when he reached the top of his climb, the poem would be finished, with freedom presumably within his grasp. One catch: His captors were waiting for him.

The third astronaut was O. J. Simpson. On our first meeting at my lab I had to mold a plaster cast of his face on which to create his deteriorating desert image. Usually it is behind closed doors and under the plaster that one gets to observe the real person. O. J. settled into my large barber chair. I placed a cape around his neck and over his clothes to catch any falling mess. Throughout this preparation he was talking on the phone. I told him it was time to hang up, and he nicely told me to start the process and he would hang up when it became imperative. This was the pre–cell phone era, so it had a cord attached that I had to wrestle with.

I mixed up my gelatin-like molding material and started to apply it to the top of his forehead. It slowly flowed down his face, covering his eyes, cheeks, nose, and phone. I said, "You're going to have to say good-bye." I took the gooey phone from him and the molding material continued to flow over his mouth, chin, and neck. Thirty minutes later I removed the cast and O. J. exclaimed, "That is the longest time I've ever had to keep my mouth closed and be awake at the same time!" Every morning on the set O. J. would check the sports page, rapidly flipping through it then tossing it aside. Finally, on one occasion I asked him if he was going to read it. His reply: "Why? There's nothing about me."

Hal Holbrook was also a member of the illustrious cast, and he performed a scene that I have never forgotten. Hal recited the longest monologue that I know of where a movie cast and crew had to stand silent and motionless for eight minutes. During this time period there were no cuts and no camera movements or interactive dialogue with the other actors who were sitting around a table. Peter filmed this scene twice, and Mr. Holbrook performed each take perfectly. Peter must have had him in mind when he cast the part, as Hal is one of the few actors who could not only pull off that perfect recitation, but also keep your interest at the same time.

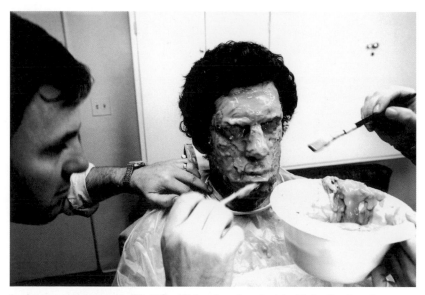

Applying casting material to Elliott Gould's face to make a stunt double for *Capricorn I*.
Warner Brothers, photo by Bruce McBrown

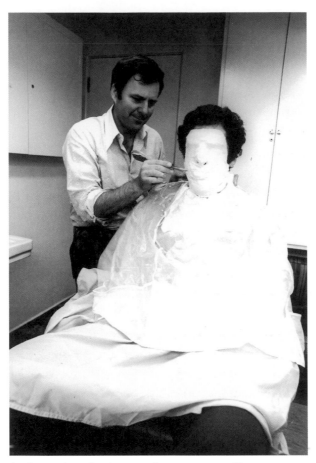

Applying a plaster bandage over the casting material for support.

Warner Brothers, photo by Bruce McBrown

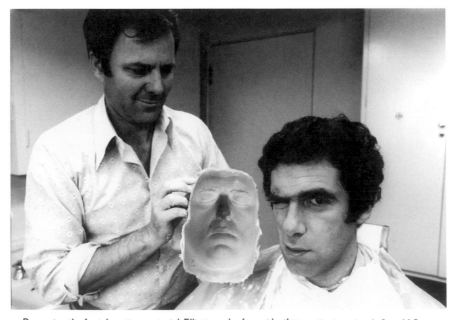

Removing the facial casting material. Elliott, you're free at last! *Warner Brothers, photo by Bruce McBrown*

I had to make plaster face casts of Elliott Gould and Telly Savalas so that I could construct latex stunt masks to be used at a later date. I remember that Telly had been hired for one day at the extravagant sum of $25,000, and there was a time limit as to the hours he would film. We didn't finish all the day's work with Telly. Begging him to stay didn't accomplish anything. Peter had me hastily take a plaster cast of his face before the six p.m. contractual deadline. The stuntmen who wore these masks as they performed death-defying airplane maneuvers were more concerned about my wife Marion, as she was about to deliver our third child. Marion would drive out to our distant desert location every Friday night and take Michael and Michele back to school every Monday morning. As the weeks went by she continued to grow, and had become the sweetheart of our stunt group. What was so concerning to everyone was that there were no hospitals nearby.

The stuntmen didn't feel qualified to play doctor in the event that she went into labor, and Brolin had only played one on TV. By the time we finished the movie Marion was still carrying McKenzie, much to the relief of everyone. My ace in the hole was that Peter had offered me the services of one of our helicopters in case McKenzie decided to start her acting career early in the desert town of California City.

TRULY TRUMAN

Lisping, whining, giggling, slurring. Truman Capote had such a strong physical presence, and made a striking impression. He was a compelling, colorful character who you could not easily forget. Oh yes, the man was one of a kind. Call it karma or fate, our paths would cross on several occasions, and I feel I've been connected to his persona at least three times.

In 1978 I was making up actress Marsha Mason, known for her performance in *The Goodbye Girl*. At this time she was married to playwright Neil Simon, whose plays *The Odd Couple*, *Barefoot in the Park*, and countless others had entertained the world. Marsha was performing in one of her husband's plays that had been adapted for television, called *The Good Doctor*. One morning Marsha informed me that Neil was dropping by the set to visit, and she wanted to introduce me. I knew that this would be an entertaining experience! Neil arrived without the fanfare you would expect from one of the world's most commercially successful playwrights. He sat down and we had just begun to make small talk when in walked Tennessee Williams. All of a sudden my mind switched from Neil Simon's comedies to thoughts of *A Streetcar Named Desire* and *Cat on a Hot Tin Roof.* Tennessee seemed to be a bit nervous, and had two or three cigarettes going at one time. He joined in the conversation with his heavy Southern drawl and unmindfully covered himself with layers of ash. I was just settling down into a somewhat normal conversation when none other than Truman Capote walked into the room, electrifying the air with his singular presence. I was circled by three literary geniuses!

Truman had recently starred in Neil Simon's movie *Murder by Death*, and apparently wanted to be part of this gathering. He pulled up a chair, and before long the conversation was quite lively. I must admit that Truman was leading it. It was well known that Truman loved to be the center of attention, and was even known to stretch the truth a bit or embellish a story if need be.

There he was, waving his hands in the air, telling anecdotes about his life. As he talked and I relaxed, I couldn't help but notice that he had the softest-looking skin I had ever seen. (Keep in mind, I've laid eyes on some of the softest skin in the world.) This is something only a makeup artist would notice. He was just like a character out of one of his books, and all I kept thinking about was what an amazing character he would be for an actor to play someday.

His best friend, Harper Lee, who played a major role in his life, was also the author of the classic book *To Kill a Mockingbird*. The movie version of this book was one of the first films I was assigned to work on in 1962. It is, in my opinion, one of the best films Universal Pictures ever made. Not only was it well cast with Gregory Peck, Ruth White, Robert Duvall, and the child actress Mary Badham, but the studio was also wise enough to stick fairly close to the novel, so it turned out to be a great success. On the set of the movie I assisted in molding and making a special makeup for Ruth White (who played Mrs. Dubose), and had the opportunity to meet Ms. Harper Lee.

Fast-forward to the early 1990s: Robert Morse was playing none other than the one and only Truman Capote in the one-man show *Tru*. I had worked with Robert in the 1960s on an experimental musical television series called *That's Life*. At night after filming, Robert and I took Red Cross diapering classes together, since Marion and his wife Carole were both due around the same time.

For Robert's portrayal of Truman, he wanted a small dental wedge to fit between his two front teeth to close a little gap. He felt this might be distracting, and unlike Truman's teeth. As a favor, Marion and I got seats to see him perform in the play. We arrived early and chatted away with Robert as his makeup artist prepared him to become Truman. We laughed and reminisced about old times, and brought each other up-to-date. We talked all the way to curtain time, and Marion and I had to run out the stage door and around to the front of the theater to avoid watching it from backstage. We plopped into our seats just as the curtain was rising. I like to think that Robert held the curtain a couple of minutes just for us. After spending time with Robert, it was quite startling to see him walk out onstage as Truman Capote, just as I remembered him. We were mesmerized for several hours. Robert had captured the true essence of Truman. I wasn't at all surprised when he won the Tony for his performance.

I would have thought that this would be my last encounter with Mr. Capote, but then I saw the celebrity biopic *Capote* (2005). As I watched Philip Seymour Hoffman portray Truman Capote, exact in all aspects of mannerisms and personality, it brought back the unforgettable man to me once again. Although I didn't work on that film, I feel I was part of it, as Truman's spirit has crossed my life several times.

Ah, Truman! Even after all these years, his flamboyance and wit are still irresistible.

I CALLED HIM "DAN THE MAN," 1927–2006

I would like to introduce you to a man that breathed fire but was filled with compassion. He was Dan Curtis, producer/director. He was a man that slipped under the radar in Hollywood's Walk of Fame, but was a unique driving force in the entertainment industry. When I first met him at his office for a job interview, his first question was, "Do you know Dick Smith?" Dick was a well-known and respected makeup artist on the East Coast. My reply was, "Yes!" Dan picked up the phone in front of me, dialed Dick, and asked him the reverse question. Dan hung up the phone, looked me in the eyes, and said, "You have the job."

Dan's early directorial fame in New York came from his vampire soap opera *Dark Shadows.* He is famous for his wooden-stake-through-the-heart shots. He would set the camera very low with the lens pointed upward at a steep angle. Below the lens and out of sight was a large bag of sand. The stake-driving actor would kneel in front of the sandbag with the sharp stick in one hand and a hammer in the other. They would place the point against the bag and hit it with such force that it would drive the shaft into the sand. If the actor didn't hit it hard enough for Dan, they did it again and again, until he was satisfied. To see this scene on film, you knew that was going to be one dead vampire.

I was hired by Dan for my special-effects background in 1973. He was making one of the first ninety-minute, late-night movies of the week that premiered at midnight. They were filmed in three very long days and were low-budget productions, of the kind that I'd never worked on before, or since. There could be as many as fifteen to thirty performers that needed makeup. I had one makeup table, and I was the only makeup artist. Dan would film up to thirty or forty pages of dialogue a day. Presently a one-hour television show produces ten to fifteen pages a day, and features might film as few as one to four.

How was this impossible challenge accomplished? Dan plugged in a TV monitor next to my makeup table so I could watch the set from afar and told me to keep slapping it on; then he took a box of tissues to personally blot off any perspiring performer. This was my introduction to "Dan the Man."

Following in this genre, we did remakes of *Frankenstein*, *The Picture of Dorian Gray*, and various vampire stories. Many projects preceded his claim to fame, but two television miniseries epics, *Winds of War* (1983) and *War and Remembrance* (1988), made history. The two plots took place prior and during World War II. Dan was one of the first people given permission to bring a film crew onto the sacred grounds of a German concentration camp.

On both films I was hired to create the period looks of the performers before the filming commenced. In between the speedy movies of the week and the epics, Dan and I had bonded in mutual respect for the parts we both were to play. In 1975 he produced and directed a pilot show entitled *Trilogy of Terror*. It consisted of three individual stories that would fill a one-hour time slot. The final concept didn't sell as a series, but this one-hour show became a cult classic, starring Karen Black in all three stories. The most famous star of the three is a wooden Zuni fetish doll. In the story it comes to life to pursue its victims to the death. What would be simple computerized movements today were handmade, hand-manipulated special effects of the day.

Karen, our mostly naked leading lady, is pursued around her apartment by this bloodthirsty, knife-wielding doll, and that is the plot. Dan was such an innovative director that he always chose unique camera angles. He decided to get the personal view of the doll as it scurried around the apartment rooms in pursuit of Karen, who was running for her life. Trying to escape, she enters the bedroom and slams the door shut. To achieve this effect Dan had the camera operator and the camera mounted on a four-wheeled sled that was just inches off the ground. A second person standing behind was responsible for the starting, stopping, and speed of the mobile cart. The timing of this effect was crucial; it had to be perfect. The operator lay down on the cart and pressed his eye onto the camera eyepiece. The pusher had to be able to stop on a dime, but in all the excitement, he crossed the stop line on the dime. Karen slammed the bedroom door with such force that a chain reaction occurred, pushing the entire camera rig back into the operator's eye. The crew groaned, and take two was filmed with a very leery, black-eyed operator.

To make the doll appear mobile, the floor of Karen's apartment was elevated more than five to six feet from the real stage floor. It was high enough for the special-effects people to comfortably manipulate the doll's movements from underneath. As the doll slashed Karen, she became bloodier. The fake blood was formulated with a sweetener which made it nontoxic and edible, but it was sticky like honey. In the final scenes Karen subdues the doll, and in so doing, she has to roll around on a gold shag carpet. After the first take Dan called, "Cut!" Karen arose, her body heavily covered in curly gold carpet fibers—one of those aftereffects never anticipated. I had to arrange for buckets of warm water and towels to remove this gold fur from her body so there could be a take two.

In the final scene the camera zooms in on Karen's face as she hides behind a door. As her grin widens, she exposes the false "piranha"-like teeth I'd made for her, which matched the wooden teeth of the doll. She had become the embodiment of the little Zuni.

In 1977 Dan directed and produced another thriller called *The Curse of the Black Widow*, starring Patty Duke. Patty played the part of a woman who transforms into a black widow spider. During her transformation the red hourglass of a real black widow appears on her abdomen just above the pubic bone. Patty wasn't naked; she was wearing panties. I constructed a very thin, clear plastic appliance shaped like an hourglass with a long thin tube extending down from an opening in the bottom. One end of the tube was inserted into the appliance and the other end was connected to a syringe filled and ready to deliver the red liquid. After gluing the appliance in place, I had to hide the length of tubing by taping it to her inner thigh. To achieve the right angle and keep me out of camera sight, I was lying on my back, looking up between Patty's spread legs. On cue all I had to do was pump the syringe and her hourglass would turn red. Today a computer would have taken all the fun out of creating a practical process that worked. I do remember Dan's strong words after Patty and I had settled into position, as this would have been the perfect moment for catcalls and comments. "EVERYBODY SHUT UP!" he shouted. The stage went deathly quiet. Dan the Man had spoken.

On another of his projects, a horse and buckboard driven at high speed by a stuntman accidentally overturns on a curve, throwing the driver out onto the ground. The buckboard and horse proceed to roll over him. Hollywood stuntmen, like all stuntmen and -women worldwide, are brave, and a little death-defiantly crazy. They will do anything for a challenge, or a buck. As the buckboard finished its roll he jumped up. The rest of the cast and crew ran to his rescue as he stood there, proclaiming the stuntman credo: "I'm okay, I'm okay." Nice red blood shot out of both nostrils like a fire hydrant had blown open. "Okay—I'm not okay," he said as he sat down.

The last time I saw Dan he was sitting alone in a cafe near Paramount Studios sometime in the mid-2000s. He looked tired. He had given it all to Hollywood. Aside from the normal chitchat, he told Marion and I that filming in the German concentration camp was a most difficult endeavor—not because of the demands of the film, but because of its history and all of its ghosts. The presence and pressure of death and evil were everywhere, and I could see that it was still playing on Dan's mind and soul. I will never forget the man with the large white teeth and black curly hair who breathed fire and directed with emotion. He passed away in 2006.

The Eighties

Before Neverland, Michael Jackson, the King of Pop, resided in Encino, California. Where he lived was no secret or surprise because when you pulled up to the guardhouse at the front gate, a multitude of fans would line the wall right across the street, waiting and hoping to catch a glimpse of him. Unfortunately, Michael was a prisoner on his own estate. To have wild animals and be able to call it your "zoo," with your own candy store—he created what others can only dream of.

My purpose for visiting was certainly not for the animals or candy, but to help him leave the premises of his estate without his personal entourage, and to be able to enjoy the "free" world without being recognized. After I created different disguises for him, I was told Michael was able to slip out into the night to enjoy his personal and business life.

While I was at Michael's estate, I did have the opportunity to meet "Bubbles," his chimp, up close and personal. Bubbles had the most perfect face for a chimpanzee; if he didn't move, you would swear he was a toy. On one of my visits, I took my daughter, Michele. She was a giant fan but said she could act cool about it. By the time we left, Michael was asking Michele for tips on how she got her spikey hair to stand up.

On another occasion, as Michael and I were having a conversation about makeup application, I was leaning on the doorjamb with my arm outreached. Bubbles immediately thought he had a new bar from which to swing. With no effort at all, he launched through the air, grasped onto my arm, and commenced swinging back and forth. Since Michael didn't tell Bubbles to get down, I didn't want to drop my arm, so we continued what I thought was a serious conversation as I was being used as a jungle gym.

RAGING BULL, 1980

Many people consider *Raging Bull* one of the best films of the 1980s, and the greatest sports movie of all time. The film is so expertly crafted, so tight, and the acting seems so natural and effortless, that it's easy for fans to not realize that many months of meticulous planning went into the production.

I had created the makeup for several *Rocky* films and had become quite an expert at creating realistic cuts, bruises, swelling, and sweat. It was because of this talent and experience—making a boxer look authentically beat-up—that the producers of *Rocky* asked me to be part of their next boxing film, *Raging Bull*, based on the autobiography of ex-middleweight champ Jake LaMotta.

I was excited. I immediately knew this was going to be something special, because the film was to be directed by Martin Scorsese and would star Robert De Niro. What an opportunity! By this time they had already collaborated on classics *Mean Streets*, *Taxi Driver*, and *New York, New York*, and it was thrilling to think I'd be working as part of this amazing team.

I must say, however, I was shocked when I read the original first draft of the script. To tell you the truth, I wasn't even sure I wanted to do it anymore. The Jake LaMotta book had been adapted into a screenplay by the talented writer Paul Schrader, who wrote the masterpiece *Taxi Driver*—but this draft of the LaMotta story read like a clichéd B-movie. Basically it was a bunch of scenes about a broken-down boxer strung together with a lot of four-letter words. Other than the talent that was involved with the project, I couldn't find any redeeming reasons to be part of the movie. I later learned that the producers must have felt the same way, because they called the LaMotta character a "cockroach," and didn't see how any audience would be able to relate to him. Marty and Robert set off to rewrite the screenplay, and in just a few weeks, they had put their legendary stamp of genius on the script.

When I received the next version of the screenplay I was blown away. It still had the rapid-fire dirty dialogue, and the stinging physical and verbal abuse, but *Raging Bull* was now not just about a boxer in the ring; it also told the story of LaMotta's relationships, especially the intense passion this complex athlete felt for his young and gorgeous second wife, Vikki LaMotta. Although still unsympathetic, the Jake LaMotta character was now multidimensional, seething, and obsessed—filled with passion and anger, ambition and jealousy, and, most of all, rage. He brought all of these emotions with him into the ring, making him an exceptional fighter. His self-destructive behavior made him more sympathetic to an audience, and his decline had an almost Shakespearean quality to it.

Because of the success of *Rocky* there were many boxing films in production during this time. I have read that Martin Scorsese decided to film *Raging Bull* in black and white to distinguish it from the others. Maybe that's partially true, but I think there was more to it than that. Black and white would also set a certain mood, give the film a noir-ish feel, and be another way to draw the viewers into LaMotta's dark tale that unfolded mostly during the 1940s and '50s.

Turning De Niro into LaMotta

Since the first part of my job would be to turn Robert De Niro into Jake LaMotta, I flew to New York to make a plaster cast of Jake's face. That's where the makeup process would begin.

There are several steps in the process of making a cast of someone's face. First, you have to set the person down and try to make them feel as relaxed and comfortable as possible. A bald cap is placed on their head to protect their hair. Next a coating of Vaseline is smoothed over the eyebrows and eyelashes. Now it's time to use a product called alginate, the same material dentists use to take a cast of teeth. It comes as a powder, but when mixed with water, it forms a flexible, rubbery paste. The paste is then smeared over the face, leaving holes through which to breathe. After five minutes the alginate sets. The next step is to take plaster bandage and cover the alginate mask, wrapping the person like a mummy. It gets a little warm, and you always warn the person being cast not to worry about that. When the plaster sets, the entire piece is removed from the face. You now have a copy of the actor in negative form, but you need a positive version to work on. So, you plug up all the holes and fill the cast with plaster. After one hour it sets. Then you peel away the alginate and have an exact copy of the person's face.

I met Jake LaMotta at the Third Street Gym in Manhattan to give him the details of what I was going to do. After I explained the process, he wasn't at all comfortable with the idea of getting an entire cast of his face. Many people aren't because they feel very restricted and claustrophobic. It's funny, because it seems the more macho the man, the

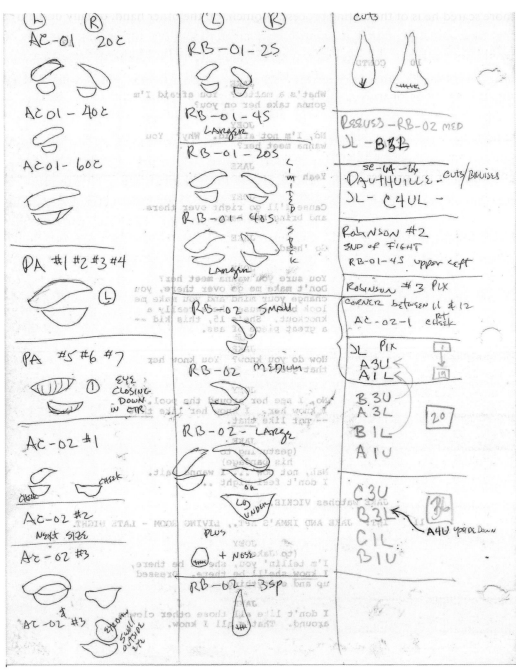

Pencil layout for *Raging Bull*, drawn on the plane from Los Angeles to New York to meet Jake LaMotta. This is the order of how I would swell the faces of the individual boxers. *Courtesy of the author*

more scared he is of the casting process. Women, on the other hand, usually don't give me any trouble. No matter how much I explained to him that the process was safe, he would not consent to having his face cast. Eventually, I talked him into letting me cast only his trademark nose. I assured the ex-champ it wouldn't hurt a bit. I even promised that if I was lying or tricking him, he could beat the living daylights out of me.

Robert De Niro was the total opposite. I made a cast of his face without any problems at all . . . except, umm, maybe his snoring. Perhaps because he knew of my reputation from the *Rocky* films, he was totally at ease. He was an exception to the "macho guy afraid of the process" rule. I didn't even have to promise him anything. Maybe it was because we got to know each other from a series of interviews before we started. When I made a cast of his face he was cool, calm, and very relaxed. He came to my house for the process. My wife was out with the kids and the place was dead quiet. When Robert was fully encompassed in the molding materials and plaster, I heard this deep breathing coming out of the two little holes left open for the nostrils. Robert was so comfortable with the procedure that he fell deeply asleep and began snoring inside the cast. From this cast, I made Robert into Jake.

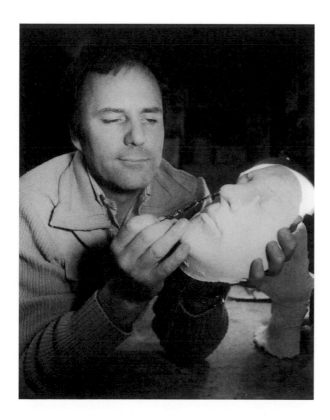

Sculpting LaMotta's nose on the plaster cast of De Niro's face. *United Artists*

Unlike the *Rocky* films, Robert had to wear different latex noses and eyepieces throughout the film, as well as different bruises, cuts, and bandages that would follow each fight. For eight months prior to filming, I had to create and test over a dozen different noses and eyelids. Every one of the sets I made was scrutinized and filmed and then suggestions were offered to change them for the next test. The early tests were taped in my living room and sent to Marty for his opinion. We did so much testing in my living room that I started to keep Robert's favorite foods in my refrigerator. He practically became a member of the family, heading straight to the fridge every time he came to the house.

Months before filming began, Robert began spending a lot of time with the then-unknown actor Joe Pesci. The two actors who would be playing brothers were building up a closeness and chemistry that would come across on-screen.

As the makeup tests continued over the eight-month period, Robert made friends with our two-year-old daughter, McKenzie. In between tests, he would sit on the floor and play games with her. Marion said to me, "Watch, Robert has something in mind." How right she was! Lo and behold, Robert asked us if we would let our little doll play the part of his daughter in the movie. It was only natural for this consummate actor to want to build up a relationship of tenderness and warmth with the little girl who would be portraying his daughter in the movie. As I said, every detail in the film was planned out way in advance in order to give every frame of the film a feeling of authenticity. Robert realized that the affection between him and McKenzie would come across on-screen and make them more believable as father and daughter. We gladly agreed to let McKenzie appear in the film—her first performance, and the beginning of a successful acting career.

When the day came to screen the final makeup tests for Robert, I slipped a copy of the latex nose into my pocket and headed for the screening room. I knew it was perfect, but I also knew that at this point, they were looking for something beyond perfection. After the test, Bob Chartoff had one last request: Could I shave a little more latex off the end of the false nose? I pulled out the nose and held it up to the light for him to see. The end was already as thin as tissue paper; there was nothing left that could be shaved off. This convinced him. Now, everyone was satisfied, and we were one step closer to filming.

Casting Vikki

On this film I wasn't just in charge of transforming Robert De Niro into Jake LaMotta and taking care of all the boxing makeup effects. I was actually the supervisor of all the makeup, and it was my responsibility to make sure everyone had the right period look, right down to the color of lipstick worn by the actresses. I was flown to New York with the understanding that I would be doing the makeup for seven or eight actresses who would be testing for the choice role of LaMotta's second wife, Vikki. The real Vikki LaMotta was still in her teens when she married Jake, so they needed an actress who was not only young and beautiful, but also had the acting chops to hold her own with De Niro. I was never told who would be testing, but it was my understanding that several big-name actresses were up for the part.

In Hollywood a lot has to do with nepotism and networking, and who you know, but Cathy Moriarty was to get her big break the old-fashioned way—by the sheer star quality of her presence. The story of her discovery is on par with Lana Turner being discovered sitting at a soda fountain. Actually, Joe Pesci had seen Cathy at a beauty pageant being held at a local bar in New York, and he was bowled over by her magnetism. She had real charisma, along with a striking resemblance to the real Vikki LaMotta.

Pesci introduced her to Scorsese and De Niro. They thought she was absolutely perfect: her age, her look, her voice. The two were so taken with her that they started working with her on the script to see if she was able to "act." The day of the test I made her up and they put the smoldering seventeen-year-old in front of the cameras— and that was it. It was unnecessary for them to test any other actress; they had found their Vikki. It kind of reminded me of the search for Scarlett O'Hara in *Gone with the Wind*, when an unknown Vivien Leigh beat out every big actress in Hollywood for the juicy role.

Makeup Challenges On-Set

When filming started, on a daily basis I would apply "Jake's" nose and scarred eyelids. Robert would sit down in the makeup chair and I would lay it back like a surgery table. He would go to sleep and I would go to work like a surgeon, carefully gluing down the latex, blending the edges, and then coloring. When I finished, I would gently wake him up. He went to sleep as Robert De Niro but woke up as Jake LaMotta.

The fight consultants said that Robert had trained so diligently for this film, he probably could have entered the real ring and won a few matches. Jake LaMotta himself said that he would be proud to be De Niro's trainer and manager. At lunch, there was no eating for De Niro. He spent his time continuing to train.

Robert got his body in such great fighting condition that we spent the first month filming the fight sequences. I had to devise appliances with tubes running everywhere.

This way blood could be spurted out of his nose, forehead, cheeks, and mouth. You may have heard that because *Raging Bull* was filmed in black and white, the blood used in the boxing scenes was actually chocolate syrup. It's true that in the days of black-and-white movies they used chocolate syrup instead of fake blood, because the dark liquid photographed better. For *Raging Bull* I added a twist. I actually mixed fake blood and the chocolate syrup together to give the sticky substance a reddish tint. It actually looked like fruity dark blood, and made it more realistic for the actors and director while the scenes were being filmed. A fight scene was never accomplished in one take, so I would have to clean Robert up and we would go again.

Director of photography Michael Chapman, De Niro, and I confer in the ring during filming. *United Artists*

De Niro makeup with latex nose and scarred eyelids.
United Artists

De Niro makeup with swelling and blood. *United Artists*

In the ring, he needed attention all day, which meant keeping him oiled and wet, and keeping all the latex edges in place. At the end of the day, I felt as if I had spent a few rounds in the ring myself (which I had, in a sense); but if I was as exhausted as Robert, it was a good exhausted, because we were accomplishing what we had set out to do.

Nothing was shot in sequence, so I had to keep meticulous records and photos of each scene. One day we would film open gashes and fresh swollen bruises. The next scene in the sequence of the film—showing the aftermath of dried blood, bandages, and dark swollen bruises—would be filmed many months later. My entire script was laid out for me and orchestrated on a daily basis, as the makeup for the aftermath of the fights was as important as that done for the fighting matches themselves.

Jake and Vikki

Marty had been very precise in researching the fights, studying the actual matches, so it was all very real. But Jake would invariably say, "Nah, it didn't happen like that . . . he never touched me." Even boxing legends have a way of remembering history the way they want it to be remembered. But eventually his version of the facts became so distracting that it was decided it would be better off if he remembered them off the set. I'm not saying he had a screw loose, but let's just say that I've seen enough television documentaries about the body to know that the brain can only take so much battering around; after so many concussions, something is going to turn soft.

LaMotta had a huge head. It was said that he had very weak hands and didn't like to be hit below the neck. As a result he took many of the blows to his head. It's impossible for a head to be battered around like that so many times without it having some sort of impact on the normal thought process. (Maybe this is a good time to add that LaMotta is a boxing legend, and was a pretty nice guy to me.)

The real Vikki LaMotta, on the other hand, was always welcome on the set. She was a very nice lady, and talk about a knockout! At the time of filming she was in her fifties, but she had a terrific body, beautiful face, and gorgeous blonde hair As a matter of fact, after the film was released, she caused quite a stir by posing for *Playboy*.

Robert is one of those actors that fully dedicates himself to each role he plays, and that included when the time came for him to play the aging, bloating LaMotta. Production shut down for several months while Robert gained weight. To play the scenes at the end of the film when Jake is in broken-down middle age, Robert's weight had to go from 152 to 215. To help accomplish this goal, Robert started eating pasta at a restaurant in Santa Monica. It was a real, old-time New York kind of restaurant with authentic Italian cooking. Once you entered, you were hit with the smell of gourmet Italian cuisine that sucked you in to staying and eating! I guess it was easy for Robert to pack on the weight.

There was also a Thai restaurant he liked, although he didn't go there quite as often. Still, he had a special reserved table there that no one else was allowed to sit at, just in case Bobby decided that he was in the mood for Thai that night.

After a night of eating, every morning Robert would also show up on the set with a dozen glazed donuts. He's such a nice guy, he would always offer one to me, but I never took it. I didn't want to interfere with his "training." Actually, a friend of mine, Bob Norin, created a large rubber stomach for Robert to play the middle-aged Jake. It was unnecessary. Robert's overeating ballooned him larger than the fake stomach.

Adventures while Filming

Whenever I spent much time away from home, I liked to have my family with me. During this film we lived at the Mayflower Hotel in Manhattan, which has since been turned into condominiums. At the same time, the Russian Ballet was also staying at the hotel. Every time you passed them in the lobby or elevator, they would be accompanied by a chaperone that looked more like the Gestapo. Every once in a while a rumor would circulate the hotel that another dancer had defected. We all lived in fear that one day a dancer would approach and say, "Help me escape." If it had happened it would have made our stay at the hotel a James Bond adventure.

The hotel was across from Central Park. One Sunday afternoon, I was strolling through the park with my family. We came across a man surrounded by a group of rather attractive women. They were having what looked like some sort of beauty conference or seminar. The closer we approached, the clearer you could hear the young man imparting his wisdom and knowledge to his young students. As we got even closer, his lecture became apparent. This young man was a pimp schooling his latest crop of prostitutes in the art of the world's oldest profession. I was in awe. Marion told me not to stare and reminded me to close my mouth as we swiftly moved our children away. This was one sight they didn't need to see and one lesson they didn't need to learn.

When we were filming back in Los Angeles, Cathy Moriarty had her own brush with "professional ladies." During production they put her up in the renowned Chateau Marmont on Sunset Boulevard (back then, this street was still a popular area for "working girls"). Now, one thing you must understand: Cathy Moriarty was a real beauty with a very voluptuous body. Some of the uncouth apes on the set would joke that when she walked, it looked like a bag of squirrels fighting to get free. Actually, her walk was more like a strut. So when she'd amble down the boulevard to get groceries or something, the prostitutes viewed this nubile beauty as some new girl trying to infringe on their territory. Cathy had to quickly make friends with the ladies and explain that she was an actress in town working on a film.

On the last day of filming, I went into the makeup trailer and was met by two people who were not on the call sheet. I had never seen either of them before. The man told me he was Robert's stand-in, and then he casually added that the woman was the fluffer. Not expecting either, I went in search of someone who could tell me what was happening, and more importantly, what the hell was a fluffer. Eventually all of my questions were answered. Apparently, in Jake's real life, he believed a fighter should refrain from sex before a fight. The story as told to me was that when Jake became aroused the night before a fight, he ran into the bathroom where there was a glass of ice water. He then gave his penis an ice bath. This was a scene Marty wanted immortalized in cinema history. The stand-in was cast for close-ups of parts of the anatomy Robert didn't want photographed.

On the other hand (pun intended), the fluffer was cast to help the stand-in keep standing. It seems that in the porn industry, when making a porno, someone is hired to keep the actor in the scene aroused in between takes, while new shots are being set up. In other words, the fluffer on *Raging Bull* was hired to make the ice-bath scene as realistic as possible.

Needless to say, no makeup was needed for either one of them, so I opted out early. I have never seen this part of the movie, but I'm sure it appears in some foreign version somewhere.

Aside from being one of the greatest adventures of my career, there was one more surprise in store. Because of the popularity and controversy over the film, and my special period makeup, the film was heavily and well publicized at Oscar time. The film was nominated for eight Oscars, including Best Picture, Best Director, Best Supporting Actor for Joe Pesci, and Best Supporting Actress for Cathy Moriarty. However, at this time, there was no Academy Award for makeup. Even though I was submitted for a special Oscar, all special Oscar requests were turned down, except for *Star Wars* and a lengthy presentation to Henry Fonda for his lifetime of work. (In fact, he hadn't made *On Golden Pond* yet, and as of that date, had never won an Oscar.) There are a number of great actors that have been nominated but have never taken home the gold. Greta Garbo and Cary Grant are two examples.

In the end, *Raging Bull* won two awards. Both Robert De Niro and film editor Thelma Schoonmaker were rewarded for their outstanding work. It seems like a crime that a movie so highly regarded and influential in cinema history did not win Best Picture or Best Director.

TRUE CONFESSIONS, 1981

Working with Robert De Niro is always an exciting roller-coaster ride, because he so fully embodies every character he ever plays. In this motion picture he had to portray a Catholic priest, and my assignment with him was to subtly apply an aging makeup. He was so into his character that he memorized the Catholic Mass, in Latin, with all proper procedures and movements. He probably could have performed the service in any church on a Sunday morning, and no one would have been the wiser. When the director wanted to change or substitute certain moves for the sake of camera angles, Robert disagreed for the sake of reality, and for all of the worshippers worldwide that would eventually see the film. Robert won.

Part of the movie was filmed on Olvera Street, a historic center in downtown LA. During the day Robert was always attired in his black priest costume as he walked from his hotel room close to the filming set. Along the way he would pass by many Latinos that lived around this neighborhood. When seeing a priest pass by so close they would say, "Bless me, Father." Robert felt very uncomfortable ignoring their request, and we talked about how they must feel, being ignored by the Church. In a quandary, he asked our technical adviser priest for direction. The priest's advice was to bless them. If you'd been one of the lucky ones lining the pathway, you too could have been given the sign of the cross by Father De Niro.

Robert's dressing room in the local hotel was an elevator ride up several floors. A few times a day we would make the journey up and down and the other riders never recognized him for the star that he is. He was only recognized as being a man of the cloth. As the elevator doors would open, the loud and talkative riders would go into hushed silence, and would remain that way until we left. Robert was able to use all of this human reaction in his priestly role.

The film included a little bit of everything about life in Los Angeles in 1948. The whorehouses frequented by the rich and famous, ambition, cynicism, and murder were all at the plot's core. We had a former madam along with a priest as technical advisers. I came prepared with a lot of what I thought would be whore makeup, only to be informed by my technical adviser that the mistresses of the rich and famous didn't wear makeup, perfume, or anything that would leave a telltale sign that a client might wear home to his wife.

What amazed me most about the cast of this film was the number of well-known professionals that were assembled. All of them were great performers in their own right. It was a privilege to stand behind the camera and watch Robert De Niro, Robert Duvall, Charles Durning, Ken McMillan, Ed Flanders, Cyril Cusack, Burgess Meredith, and many more. I had worked with all of them on separate projects. You can just imagine what it was like when this group of Irishmen all got together between scenes. And I thought working on *Ocean's Eleven* with the Rat Pack was a trip. On *True Confessions* there were more than a few toasts to the Old Country and the wee folk.

One of my most interesting career stories is connected to this film. I was asked to create a duplicate body of the live girl who was cast to portray "The Porn Star." Later in the film she's very dead, and cut in half. Although the storyline was not supposed to parallel the famous LA "Black Dahlia" murder, this part of the plot comes very close. The script called for a dead female who had been severed in the middle and dumped onto a weed-strewn lot in Los Angeles. Casting finally selected our actress/victim, and I met her along with others at the sculpting studio of Lia Di Leo in the San Fernando Valley.

Lia was an expert in the art of sculpting and casting wax figures. I decided to create the figure in wax instead of rubber because of its lifelike qualities. With all the studio executives standing around, our dead girl to be was asked to remove all of her clothes and lay on the floor in the dumped position the director desired, so she could be photographed for future reference. At that moment, the girl who had graced the pages of *Playboy* magazine adamantly insisted that only the man with the camera hanging around his neck be present for her nakedness. I happened to be the man with the camera. Everyone left and I circled her, capturing every detail of her body, positioned faceup with crossed legs and outstretched arms. Later I had to endure comments like "It's a dirty job, but someone had to do it."

I handed over the photos and a hair-color sample to Lia so she could start her work. I met our girl at my lab the next day so I could cast and make plaster copies of her head, face, hands, and feet. Lia duplicated my plaster body casts in wax and then attached them to her wax body, which at that moment looked like a Greek statue with parts missing. For Lia's final touch she inserted glass eyes into the hollow sockets, and with a hot needle, punched real hair into the head and crotch of our victim. And then the *coup de grâce*: She sliced the body in two.

Now it was my turn. I took the two halves back to my lab for coloring. To retain the skin's luminosity, I brushed and stippled the surface with tubes of artist's oil paints as if I was painting a picture on canvas. Each half took a day to paint and dry. One other small detail: Since she had been cut in two, her intestines had to be falling out. With a soldering iron I shaped and created the entrails out of the solid wax that filled the inner body. As I painted this pile of trailing melted guts, my children would watch and expound with "Gross, Dad." (This is an overall view of the story, and my kids all grew up to be normal.)

Now, let me take you back to where it all started: in the Los Angeles morgue.

When it comes to making a movie, no wishes are impossible to achieve. Mountains can be moved. One of my makeup challenges in the film was to duplicate a medical examiner's autopsy closure on our girl, so I needed to see a real one up close and personal. Soon after my request to the movie production office, I was snuck into the Los Angeles morgue with my Polaroid camera hidden under my coat. I was escorted through a large metal door into a very cold room. *Funny,* I thought to myself, *I am the only one standing; the other four hundred are all covered with a wrap and a tag around their toes.* Oh! I forgot; one was sitting in a chair in the corner, as that is how they found her. She may still be sitting there, waiting to be claimed.

The wax body torso from *True Confessions*. *United Artists*

The wax body legs. Note tattoo on upper hip. *United Artists*

As an attendant uncovered the corpses, I was able to do all the research I needed. I found out that cameras don't work well under forty degrees, and neither did my stomach. My tour of the facilities also consisted of meeting two dozen fresh bodies lying in the hall on gurneys, waiting to be processed. January is a busy month in Los Angeles for shootings, knifings, and suicides. I guess there is not enough room in the newspapers to cover the demise of all these poor souls.

As I completed my research for cutting, opening, and sewing up corpses, my parting gift from the coroner were several sturdy, five-inch-long, "S"-curved needles which I was told were great for sewing up a Thanksgiving turkey, and a roll of wax-coated thread that wouldn't absorb "juices." This research was all done for a scene in the movie morgue where our real, live dead girl had been examined and sewn back together. Needless to say, when my wife Marion and I had lunch at a nearby Mexican restaurant after this visit, the burrito didn't set well.

One of the clues to the identity of our dead girl in the morgue was a rose tattoo discovered on . . . shall I say, discreetly, her butt. The tattoo is also discovered in a scene where the police are watching her perform in a pretty bad copy of a porno film. Someone puts two and two together, live girl / dead girl tattoo, to solve this brain-twister. While our girl was still breathing and performing in the porno, it was also my job each day to hand-paint the rose tattoo on the naked backside of this former *Playboy* bunny. This was another makeup assignment that somebody had to do.

It is very common for makeup artists to have their creations recognized. It's good for the ego and better for your reputation. Before we started to film, producer Irwin Winkler took me aside and asked me not to publicize my beautiful wax body, as it wasn't a major story point in the movie. When on camera the body laid in the dry weeds, waiting to be discovered by our actors. I would bring it out in the morning, put it in place for the day, and then lock it up at night back at the studio. One afternoon the body "finished" early, so I transported it back to the studio's secure lockup. I placed the two halves in the back of the production manager's station wagon without a cover and drove off. As we sailed down a fairly open California freeway in the middle lane, my driver and I were discussing lunch when an extremely tall semi pulled up along our right side. The truck driver had a great view down into the back of our car. He appeared wild-eyed, like his eyeballs were going to pop out of his head. I thought to myself, "What's his problem?" We slowed down and dropped behind him so we could shoot off at the next exit.

The following day two men showed up at the vacant lot wearing black shoes and white socks with a tie. Who else could these two plainclothesmen be but real police detectives from Homicide? They were here to investigate my traveling meat market. They wouldn't take my word or anyone else's that my *Sweeney Todd* dummy wasn't real. I had to personally escort them back to the studio, unlock the box, and proudly show them my handiwork. After our show-and-tell, the detectives complimented me for my work, and then told me the truck driver had had a loaded gun. He'd planned to run us off the road and hold us until the police arrived, but we had foiled his plan by dropping back and exiting before he could do so. He had managed to get our license number before that, and had contacted the police.

The next morning the Los Angeles newspapers exclaimed that the sighting of the traveling torso had been solved. It seems that other drivers had also reported seeing the bouncing body, but due to shock, no one else had reported the car's license number, or had had sufficient nerve to confront these two wild and crazy guys with a hacked-up body. The unpublicized corpse got enough press without me opening my mouth.

For Robert, I had to create a subtle aging makeup that wouldn't appear as an obvious transition. All my highlights and shading were applied first. Then, to create the fine lines around his eyes, I needed a material that would dry and shrink the skin. I knew that Duo adhesive would work, but when dry it leaves an opaque latex skin that is difficult to conceal with makeup, so I mixed Duo with K-Y Jelly and small red fibers; this mixture dried clean and clear, so no cover makeup was needed.

Robert's temple hair and eyebrows needed to be grayed, but he hated the available products because they photographed chalky and blue. My solution: I inserted individual short lengths of curled white hair into his natural brows that had first been dipped into glue. The same procedure was applied to his longer white temple hair. To add liver spots to his forehead and the backs of his hands, I painted them by hand as was the normal procedure. Everyone thought it looked great, but it still wasn't acceptable to Robert. In reality, liver spots are irregularly shaped, and are visible in multiple shapes and sizes, in varying shades of brown. To do this by hand would be extremely time-consuming. Robert insisted on both speed and reality. He and I put on our thinking caps and it was all resolved with a small stiff brush, multiple shades of cake makeup, and a custom stencil. I hand-cut small irregular holes in a three-inch piece of plastic. I could quickly move it around his forehead and hands as I applied the shades of makeup through the little holes. The completed aging makeup on De Niro took two and a half hours to apply, and was so subtle that it was overlooked the first year the Academy Award category for makeup artists was established.

ESCAPE TO VICTORY, 1981

My next adventure with Stallone was in Budapest, Hungary, in 1981. The plot was about Allied POWs preparing for a soccer match to be played against a German national team—an event that Hitler was going to use for propaganda. The game was to be played in Nazi-occupied Paris. Prior to the game the POWs from the French Resistance and captured British officers strategize an escape plan. Most of the world-renowned soccer players at this time had been signed up as actor/athletes for this film. It was a very international cast, which included Pele from Brazil, Bobby Moore from England, Osvaldo Ardiles from Argentina, and many more from Belgium, Poland, Norway, Holland, Scotland, Denmark, and Ireland.

Before leaving on my long flight over the North Pole, I was asked to take with me several necessary items. The production company figured they could barter their way through Hungary with boxes full of American blue jeans, since they sold there for an exorbitant price. I was asked to accompany several boxes that would be left outside my departure building. Upon my arrival at the Los Angeles airport, I noticed stacks of boxes lining the outside wall of the terminal; upon closer examination, my name was written in big letters on all of them. The boxes held a thousand pair of American blue jeans. I made it to Budapest, but the boxes didn't. Somewhere between here and there they disappeared and were untraceable. Along with the pants, one of the producers had asked me to personally carry in my luggage a large supply of his personal "aspirin," which I agreed to do. Two things I learned later: This producer had a reputation for sniffing powdered substances, and Hungary was the "aspirin capital" for the Soviet Bloc, until Russia moved the plant across its border. This was like me, as they say, "carrying coal to Newcastle." I'm glad no one investigated my luggage, as I still might be in a Hungarian jail.

A number of the American crew that arrived in Budapest were missing personal items and luggage which contained clothes, cameras, and a guitar. I was met at the airport by a short, round, smiling official who kissed my hand by accident, as I was standing at the end of a line of women who were receiving his official welcome. My room at the Intercontinental Hotel wasn't very large, so I knew I would have to make other arrangements when Marion and the kids arrived. Stallone had been offered a nice split-level suite at the Hotel Gellért, which was on the other side of the Danube River. After investigating his surroundings, he preferred the multiroom suite at the top of the Intercontinental Hotel that had been reserved for Brezhnev, then current premier of Russia. Sly moved up and I moved across the Danube to his suite at the Gellért. For our relaxing pleasure, beneath this hotel were public baths that date back to the Roman occupation.

At this time Hungary was under Russian occupation, and the Olympics were about to commence in Moscow. This caused the great disappearance of limos, caviar, and "aspirin" from our city, as they were spirited away to Moscow. Our film was only the second Western movie to be filmed there. It was the only way Pepsi could get their worthless Hungarian money turned into real dollars. Make a movie there and pay for everything with the local currency, *forints*, then take the movie outside and play it around the world. We were told to be very careful and obey all the rules. On the first US movie project that had been allowed behind the Iron Curtain, one of the actors kept espousing the evils of communism to the common people. In his room he kept a canary as a pet. Upon returning to his room one night after work the cage door and window were open. He became enraged with the hotel staff and the front desk until he opened the door to his freezer. Lo and behold, his bird was so smart it had been able to open its cage door, climb into the freezer, and close the door. For everyone's safety this particular actor was on the next plane out of Budapest.

Daily Living Behind the Iron Curtain

The cement walls on the old city buildings were scarred with the bullet holes and tank shell reminders of the unsuccessful Hungarian Revolution that occurred in 1956. For the people's pleasure, Budapest is filled with lush public parks. We were told not to let our children run and play in the bushes without checking first. Due to overcrowded housing, it was the best place for young people to be alone and have sex. Having this knowledge, it was my duty to check under all the bushes. When I arrived, the weather was still cold from winter. The store shelves were filling with merchandise. As time wore on and spring arrived, tourists from different countries visited the city on the Danube. They came by plane, car, and boat. Three months later when we were preparing to leave, it was time to purchase some souvenirs. There was nothing of value left on the shelves. I looked for a set of Heron fine china for twelve, manufactured in four different colors; not a single set was left to purchase. There was no such thing as "in stock"; you had to buy it when you saw it, or forget it. Unlike America, all manufacturing was controlled by the government as to the quantity produced every year.

Hungarian is not a language a non-Hungarian can understand, or even pronounce. The only word I recognized in the local dictionary was *grapefruit*, and they didn't have any available. Bananas were another missing fruit, as it was only delivered in December with an exchange from Cuba. I once repaid a helpful operator at the telephone exchange with oranges that Sly had imported from Vienna. In many places Americans were not looked upon with favor. I once stood on the corner of a busy street asking for directions and no one would speak to me, even though they had all taken English in school. Privately and behind closed doors they would converse, but in public, hate and fear were their motivation for silence.

The only place in the city to get a decent all-American hamburger or hot dog was at the American embassy or the American Club. The embassy was always fun to visit. Upon arriving you could always wave to the man in the box with the blacked-out windows that was located directly across the street from the entrance. The Russians always knew who was coming and going. The club had a three-hole golf course on the side of a very steep hill. The greens were formerly the backyard of an old, privately owned stately mansion before the Communist invasion. Only people from Western countries were allowed on the club's premises, and conversations had to be very guarded.

Not knowing how I was going to survive on Hungarian cuisine, I quickly discovered there was plenty of fried chicken, roasted venison, and caviar to be had. That became my diet. There was always a lot of seasonal fruit, and we were there during cherry season. In the market, unlike in America, you didn't pick out the fruit and bag it yourself, as my daughter Michele found out. As she filled a bag with the best and ripest, a woman who was four feet tall and four feet wide with a scarf on her head started to scream. Between unintelligible phrases was heard the word *Ameeerican*. Marion decided this was not good, as activity at the market was coming to a standstill. With kids in hand she made a hasty beeline down the street.

On another occasion while filming in the countryside, the film company decided to take a break. We were working on a train, and right next to the tracks was the largest old cherry tree I'd ever seen. It was so big we had to hoist each other up into its branches. We proceeded to fill ourselves with beautiful red cherries, when suddenly someone said, "Uh-oh!" Coming through the golden wheat field with a huge pitchfork in hand was another of those four-by-fours. Lucky for us she was a sweet lady, and told us in her native tongue to enjoy the fruit. I'm sure glad she was agreeable, because that wooden pitchfork was bigger than her.

Back in the hotel we were told the rooms were bugged, but we never found one. I do know that whenever we verbally discussed a desire or need to have something fixed, or mentioned that something was missing from our breakfast tray, there would be a knock on our door and our request was magically fulfilled. One day while walking by the side of our hotel, we noticed a door was open, probably due to the extremely hot weather that day. A quick glance revealed that the room was filled with cots and men sitting in T-shirts and wearing earphones, next to what looked like large radios. We quickly looked away and continued down the street, although given my son's interest in electronics, he would have liked to join them.

One leisurely Sunday while crossing a well-traveled bridge that spanned the Danube River between Buda and Pest, out of nowhere our little four-year-old daughter McKenzie started to recite the Pledge of Allegiance. We didn't know if we should laugh or run; in fact, we didn't even know she knew it.

Most all the Hungarians I met always seemed to be under stress. There wasn't an abundance of money to go around, and it was only spendable within the country. There was a black-market exchange rate in Vienna if you could get there. My additional money was paid to me in *forints*, so it went to pay for food, clothes, souvenirs, and entertainment, like the circus or opera.

This was one of the slowest-paced films I have ever worked on due to our director, the great John Huston. Every morning, Monday through Friday, I would meet Sly at the studio and hand-apply a sword tattoo on his upper arm, for his character. His costar was Michael Caine, a wonderful and generous human being. He was always giving his Hungarian money away to the less fortunate. In between setups (the preparation time needed for a new scene), the world-renowned soccer players would choose up sides and have a go at it in the dirt fields of our make-believe POW camp. When the onlookers started to shout, Pele would perform his famous upside-down kick and everyone would go wild. Watching this group play sandlot soccer would be the equivalent of attending a match today with ten David Beckhams competing against each other. Since the soccer squad and my family stayed at the same hotel, I rode to work with these stars every day and got to know them quite well.

We spent a lot of time filming the movie's final match at one of the Hungarian soccer stadiums. The production company hired thousands of Hungarian townspeople to fill the stadium. I don't remember whether they got paid, but hopefully they at least received a free lunch. As I mentioned, Sly has a wonderful personal side that the world doesn't get to appreciate. Without any warning there are always comments and actions that occur spontaneously. We were walking down a bustling stadium hallway when for no reason he grabbed my son Michael and threw him into a very crowded women's lavatory. It was one thing to toss him in, but then Sly blocked the door with his body. When he finally let him out, Michael appeared all red-faced and embarrassed, leaving behind the echoing, indecipherable shouts of the women potty-goers.

On another occasion in the stadium, a policeman approached us and started a serious conversation about our youngest daughter, McKenzie, which translated into "I want to buy your little girl; how much?" This sincere gesture was frightening and made us hang on a little tighter to our adorable four-year-old Shirley Temple.

How the Other Half Lives

Michele, our oldest daughter, made friends with the young daughter of our company cook. They were about the same age. She invited her to their home for a weekend. We thought it would be a wonderful enlightening experience. Off she went with two books under her arm. One was *Hungarian to English* and the other, *English to Hungarian*. Since the young girl didn't speak any English, the two conversed and played the entire weekend with sign language and the help of the two books. Michele learned that her new friend attended regular rifle practice and was capable of breaking her AK-47 apart and cleaning it, which she did daily. This girl's second duty to country was to learn how to run the local train, the reason being that if the West invaded and adults were needed to fight, the children and two adults would take over its operation. I will let you imagine why the children were given weapons and trained in how to use them.

Sunday night Marion and I started to worry, as we had forgotten to get an address or phone number as to where Michele was staying. Needless to say, we didn't get much sleep until we saw Michele's smiling face and heard all about her adventures the next morning. With the local citizens, you never knew what to expect in reply when you asked a question. Once I asked why there weren't any Chinese restaurants in Hungary, and the response was: "Because they want to make war." I guess if we all used that philosophy the world could be a thinner place.

On weekends Sly liked to break up his Hungarian experience by flying to Germany. Late one Sunday night there was a knock at my hotel door. I opened it to a tired Sly standing there with an outstretched arm holding a package. He said, "Here, I bought you something." That something was a Sea-Dweller Rolex watch, and I have worn it ever since. The next day Sly accidentally broke his watch, so he asked me if he could borrow my now-retired but trustworthy Timex. I don't think he wore it with the same pride with which I wore my shiny new Rolex. (Hey! I never got that Timex back.)

I hadn't seen our director John Huston since 1963, when he'd directed *The List of Adrian Messenger* with Kirk Douglas at Universal. He was a favorite acquaintance of my family, and used to call my uncle Bud, "Buddy." John didn't like to get up early or film late, and never worked on a Saturday or Sunday. This made working in

Hungary more like a vacation than a movie location, where you typically worked six days a week, before sunrise to after sunset, and longer. John had just published his autobiography, so every day a literary interviewer from somewhere around the world would be escorted onto the set for a private meeting with the legend. It wasn't really private, as he would huddle with them out of doors in the middle of where everyone was working, so we all got to hear the same questions asked over and over. John, in his deep voice, was a master at making you think that this was the first time he had been asked that same question.

Due to this daily book distraction, every once in a while an event would occur in the background that would force us to reshoot the same scene over again. Once a brand-new Mercedes drove by, and another time a 747 flew overhead and nobody caught it. I was most impressed with John, because he was the voice of a cartoon character in the animated version of *Lord of the Rings*. In a moment of silence I would slip behind John's director's chair and whisper, "Do Gandalf." He would oblige, reciting a few lines for me. During the course of my career, it has been a thrill to have been in the company of some of Hollywood's real legends.

All good things must come to an end. We packed our bags and were taken to the airport for our return to America. Before flying all the way home we would make a quick stop in England to visit relatives. (That's another story, which I'd call "The Westmore Nose," mentioned in "The Sixties" chapter.)

Back in Hungary the same man who'd kissed my hand upon arrival and had stood in the shadows while we were filming picked us up at the hotel. The citizens of this country were not legally allowed to accept tips or money of any kind. We were told it would throw their economy out of balance. In my pocket I had an unused wad of forints which were useless to us outside the country. At first he refused to accept them, so on our drive to the airport I slipped the money into his coat pocket. Nothing was said, but the smile on his face showed his appreciation. As the game is played, he never officially accepted the bills; they just magically appeared in his pocket. When we arrived at the entrance to the airport, it was hell, in the sense that it appeared as if every Hungarian in the country was trying to leave that day. It seemed like there were hundreds or thousands of people waiting to board or pick up acquaintances. I never thought we would make it onto the plane.

As we exited the car our mysterious driver started to shout in Hungarian, and the sea of humanity parted. You would have thought we were with Moses. At the same time the crowd was shouting at us. I asked him, "What are they saying?," and he replied, "You don't want to know." The Hungarian language has been rumored to contain more swear words than any other language in the world. We arrived at the check-in counter with bags in hand. Our main man spoke a few words to the official and our luggage was tagged and whisked away. Our bags were never opened for inspection, which was a good thing, since Marion had hidden some small antique pieces in my socks and shoes. (It was illegal for antiques to leave the country; anything old was considered a national treasure.) We were then escorted to a window for a passport check. Again our man slid our papers and several cigars through a small window to the inspector. They had a pleasant chat. The passports were stamped and returned to us. While in Hungary we had to relinquish our passports upon arrival and couldn't get them back until our departure. We were once again American citizens. Within thirty minutes we'd said good-bye to our driver / government official and were escorted onto the plane.

The movie was a victory; the filming went well, we'd had a new experience, and Pepsi had gotten their money out of Hungary. Remember the producer who'd asked me to escort a thousand pair of jeans into the country and bring him some "aspirin"? When I was about to leave he asked me to bring home with me an old rug that had been used as a prop in the movie, adding that I should just leave it if I encountered any trouble. I later learned that it was a very expensive antique rug.

BLADE RUNNER, 1982

My brother Marvin supervised the makeup department for the film *Blade Runner*, a futuristic sci-fi thriller set in Los Angeles, California. He asked John Chambers and me if we would create and construct specific, specialized makeup effects that were called for in the script. We met with director Ridley Scott to discuss what he had envisioned. Because of Ridley's reputation, we knew it was going to be a bumpy ride. It has always been a pleasure to work with Ridley or his brother Tony, as they have the ability to squeeze the creativity out of every pore. Each one of the following four effects was an individual challenge.

First, John and I constructed an exact, elaborate copy of Joe Turkel's head so Rutger Hauer could crush it in his palms.

In another scene Rutger pulls Harrison Ford's hand through a hole in a wall and methodically breaks two of his fingers. The arm was created by first having Harrison plunge his own arm into a bucket of jelly molding material. After removing it, the cavity was filled with plaster to create a duplicate of his hand and forearm, based on which we were able to develop a latex copy. A copper wire skeleton that included the fingers, wrist, and forearm was inserted into the glove. This metal armature allowed the wrist and fingers to bend at any angle. I filled the remainder of the glove with very fine sawdust to give it a very flesh-like feel. The final touches included painting and adhering false fingernails and hair. When the arm went to work, all Rutger had to do was reach through the hole in the wall, grab the fake arm (which was being held on the other side), and yank it through. Rutger bent the fingers back to resemble breakage. Everyone on the set groaned. In the film, sound effects added a crunching sound to complete the illusion.

Harrison and I spent several hours together while I was working to develop the arm. I realized later that we never discussed showbiz. He had been a builder, so we talked about all aspects of construction; he actually gave me many useful hints that I used and passed on.

My favorite effect is when Rutger gets the tip of his ear shot off by Harrison Ford and blood pours out on cue. Today this would be designed in a computer, but we did it practically. To start the makeup I glued his ear to the side of his head and then attached the two-piece latex ear over it. Small tubes were inserted into the back of the appliance to deliver blood on cue. A long piece of clear fishing line was attached to the top piece, and the other end of the line, to the tip of a fly-fishing pole. The two pieces of the ear were joined together with a water-based gel so they would separate easily and go back together just as quick. When the camera was rolling and Ridley gave the signal, the upper part of the ear was snatched off faster than the eye could follow. Simultaneously a plunger filled with fake blood was depressed, causing the red liquid to flow up the empty tubes and squirt into the air. After a little cleanup and ear replacement, we were ready for take two.

In another scene, when Rutger has his hand pressed to a wall, he stabs a large nail through the back of his hand, causing blood to squirt out in all directions. Since he wasn't in favor of using his real hand for the scene, I created a fake one. The palm of the latex hand was rigged with blood tubes facing outward in all directions. Once the camera was rolling, the fake hand was pressed to the wall. Rutger would then jam the nail through the back of the latex hand with his real hand. As soon as the nail pierced the latex skin, blood (under pressure) was forced through the tubes, spattering all over the wall. That is how it was originally designed, as Plan A. At the last minute, however, Ridley wanted to change the effect to Plan B. He wanted Rutger's palm to face the camera so the audience would see the nail coming through the skin as he forced it from the back side. Yes! That's great, but it meant more money and more time. The studio said no, so we went with Plan A.

It is said that the story raises more questions than there are answers. The ambiguity of the movie is the reason for its success. For all the hours and creativity John and I contributed to the success of the film, we are uncredited. Nonetheless, it was a great ride—especially to the bank.

FIRST BLOOD, 1982

I had been working as Sylvester Stallone's makeup artist for several years by this point. He had decided to take some time off and let his body heal from the blows inflicted during the *Rocky* films. Not wanting to sit around, I accepted the assignment of being the makeup department head on *The Best Little Whorehouse in Texas*, starring Dolly Parton. A week before I was to leave for Texas I got a call from Sly, and he said, "We're going to Canada!" I replied, "I can't; I've accepted another assignment." Then he said, "Perhaps you didn't hear me. We're going to Canada."

We went to Canada. Perhaps it was the convincing Italian tone in his voice that changed my mind. I was looking forward to this adventure because it called for some very exciting makeup effects that I had to create on the spot.

The story of *First Blood* originates from a book about a peaceful but soon to be rebellious Vietnam veteran called Rambo. Because of an early-on altercation with the police, Rambo is on a race for survival for the rest of the story. The ending of the movie and some of the milder police encounters are quite different than the novel, because the producers saw the potential of additional sequels. Hence, Sly becomes the action figure known as Rambo. This film has been looked on as one of the greatest action films ever produced, and set the bar for action film stars to follow.

After scouting many different wilderness locations, the producers of *First Blood* found the perfect setting in Hope, British Columbia, Canada. There had to be sufficient housing and places to eat, as the crew consisted of approximately one hundred people, mostly Canadians. We were there in the cold of winter, but Hope was a summer vacation town that attracted fishermen. This meant there were enough motels and simple eateries to accommodate us all (but you really had to like pizza and beer). The town was transformed into Rambo Country. The sheriff's office with the large breakaway glass windows was constructed on the lawn of the District Hall. A make-believe gun shop and gas station were built specially for the movie. We ended up burning down the gun store and blowing up the gas station.

Kirk Douglas was hired to play the part of Colonel Trautman. Kirk arrived one morning and went straight to his rented house on the river. There was some kind of tension in the air; no one wanted to talk to him. Like a show-off, I said, "I've met him; my uncle Bud has worked with him many times at Universal Studios, and I personally worked with him on *The List of Adrian Messenger*." So, instead of the powers that be greeting one of Hollywood's most famous stars, I was appointed to welcome him to beautiful downtown Hope. Turns out Kirk had a conflict with the script; he wanted Sly's dialogue. When this idea was rejected, Kirk disappeared so fast, you would have thought he was on David Copperfield's stage. Within a day Richard Crenna was cast, packed his bags, jumped on an airplane, and was working on the set as the new Colonel Trautman.

I was probably in the best shape of my life at this time, because Rambo was always climbing and running, and I had to be right behind him with the baby oil to shine Sly's body and squirt bottles containing water to resemble sweat. I had to carry everything in a backpack so my hands would be free to scale the cliffs and jump over rocky river bottoms.

We filmed at all hours of the day and night. One early, ice-cold morning around two a.m., a slightly disoriented girl stumbled into our midst. From what I could understand, she asked if we needed a cook. I told her we didn't and she disappeared. Suddenly I felt a punch on my arm from Sly's bodyguard, "Little Tony," who said, "Dummy—she asked if you needed any *coke*, not a cook."

My finest hour (or minute) in the film was when Rambo was lying on a frigid riverbank in the bottom of a canyon, sewing up a cut on his bicep. For the sake of reality I had to keep the blood flowing from the wound as he proceeded to sew it closed. The plastic cut I had glued to his arm was rigged with several feet of intravenous tubing. How small was the tubing? So small that when a grain of sand from the riverbed got caught in the tube, it impeded the flow of the blood. Both of us were lying next to each other so I could pump and he could perform. The air was damp and our hands were frozen, but Sly slowly maneuvered the grain of sand out of the tubing with his thumbnail. He proceeded to sew up his arm with the fishhook and thread. At the same time I was pumping blood and praying for no more sand. Sly had to wear this wound throughout much of the film, so a new one had to be made, applied, and removed each day.

On another occasion the scene called for Rambo to jump from a mountain ledge onto the top of a pine tree and slide down through the branches until he reached the

I'm preparing Stallone's arm scar for the stitching scene. *Carolco/Orion Pictures, photo by Joseph Lederer*

ground. A stuntman did the initial jump, but Sly completed the scene by hitting and sliding through the last few branches. These were not little tree branches; they were small logs. It appeared that he hit the last branch so hard it cracked his rib. He was then shuffled off to the hospital for a checkup. The doctor was more concerned about tending to my blood-splattered plastic scar than he was with treating the more-painful cracked rib. (This same scenario occurred again when Sly took me to Europe for the movie *Escape to Victory.*)

One of our scenes in *First Blood* called for a prison, and Vancouver had just the right setting. Down by the river was an abandoned prison with thick concrete walls and guard towers in each corner. It was right out of a 1940s gangster film. In an area where we weren't filming was a unique cell block. Here the prisoners were allowed to paint the inside of their cells. What did they paint? In many, the three walls were covered in outdoor scenes, with mountains and water. Some had ceilings painted in blue with white, puffy clouds. One unique ceiling was painted dark blue to resemble the night sky; then it was adorned with the moon and a galaxy of stars. These were the cells of the men who were in for life. Not all memories are happy.

In one scene Rambo is being beaten with a rubber hose. Sly and the director discussed the intensity and brutality of the scene, and Sly decided to take a few hits for real. We filmed the beating once, twice, three times, and the director wanted more. Each time Sly was hit with the rubber hose, red welts would appear on his back, and as an extra touch he was sprayed, full pressure, with a fire hose. Because there had been some disagreement between the two early on, Sly assumed this was being done on purpose. I could see anger and strength boiling in him. He was becoming a madman ready to kill, a real Mr. Hyde. Tom Bronson, the costumer, and I were standing close by, right next to the jail-cell bars. Sly's back started to look like *The Last Temptation of Christ*, so Tom and I made our move. I wrapped my arms around Sly and held him close to the bars and Tom did the same. We held on to the bars for dear life as our knuckles turned white. All the time Sly was writhing trying to get loose. Finally the anger passed. Better judgment prevailed, and we stopped filming for the evening.

In a police station scene Rambo makes his escape by throwing a policeman through a large glass window. To keep everybody safe the producer ordered special breakaway glass. It was so expensive that he only ordered two panes. Once it was placed in the window, everyone was ordered to stay far away. During the rehearsal Sly accidentally tapped the window with his elbow and it shattered into a million pieces. One thing was certain: We knew it would work. Sly gave a sheepish grin and said, "Oh well, that's one."

How cruel can I be? On a long and boring afternoon outside, the crew was setting up a simple scene with Stallone, Brian Dennehy, and a young, naive Canadian actor named Alf Humphreys. An evil joke crossed my mind. I could tell by Alf's excitement and muttering that he was nervous and wanted to perform at his best with these two Hollywood stars. I had just met our young Canadian a few days earlier, as it was my job to apply his makeup. He was playing the role of a deputy sheriff. The entire scene and dialogue didn't take very long to film, and Alf did very well. Now it was my time to strike. I waited just long enough for the camera to be turned off and moved away, then casually slithered up to Alf and hissed in his ear, "When the director films this scene, aren't you going to act with more emotion?"

Wide-eyed and panicked, Alf replied, "That wasn't a rehearsal; we shot it!" His second thought: "Was I no good, eh?" It seems "eh" is a Canadian word that goes on the end of every Canadian sentence; that's what makes Canadians different from the rest of the English-speaking world. Now was the time to strike again; with a blank look, I shrugged my shoulders, made a small apology for saying anything out of line, turned, and slowly walked away, leaving Alf to ponder his acting career. This was the beginning of a friendship that still exists today. We still laugh at my *Gotcha*, which made my boring day, "eh."

When Rambo is first stopped and searched by the sheriff, removed from his person is a "Ramboesque" bowie knife. Stallone made three duplicate copies of this unique knife. The blade was long, wide, and sharp as a razor. In the scene, the sheriff (Brian Dennehy) withdraws the knife and examines it. Without watching what he is doing, he plunges the knife back into the sheath. Whenever viewing this scene I cringe. Watch Brian's face carefully, as the point of the knife slices through the heavy leather and buries itself into Brian's palm. He doesn't flinch or stop. He continues with the scene. No one knows that he is hurt until the director yells, "Cut!" Then we all heard "&#%!@?!" As Brian opened his blood-soaked hand, we saw a sizable slice in the middle of his palm. The next yell was "Medic!"

It's always good when difficult stunts go well. One scene called for Galt, the antagonistic small-town deputy, to fall a hundred feet down from the skid of a hovering helicopter onto a boulder in the bottom of a canyon. In the sequence following the fall, the camera zooms in on Galt lying spread-eagled on his back, on the boulder. To film this stunt the canyon was filled with giant airbags. Galt's stuntman, whom I presume was paid very well, performed a swan dive off the helicopter, flipped over onto his back in midair, and landed among the cushioning bags, safe and well. Then we cut to a close-up of the real actor, Jack Starrett, spread across the boulder, his crushed, lifeless body surrounded by pools of blood. (When traveling with Sly, I could never carry enough fake blood and sweat.) To make an unplanned event more believable, Jack's body temperature was so warm and the air so cold that a foggy mist was rising like vapors from his body, as if his spirit was leaving.

In another stuntman sequence, Bennie Dobbins was not so lucky. His assignment was to drive a car up a ramp and fly through the air. Bennie launched his car so high that the camera never caught him coming to the ground. His car continues to exit the right side of the screen, still climbing. What goes up must come down, and the car practically did a nosedive back to earth. It hit so violently that it crushed Bennie's spine. He had to be airlifted back to Los Angeles, and his career was mostly over. This is a perfect place to exclaim, "Why do bad things happen to good people?"

This was the last night of filming before our Christmas break, and the reason our family got a late start driving up the snow-covered mountain roads to the Christmas hotel. This also happens to be one of the best stories of my career. In this scripted scene, Brian Dennehy, the sheriff, was stalking Rambo. Brian was on the roof of the sheriff's station near a skylight. Rambo, inside the station, decides to shoot up the place, skylight and all. Our sheriff falls through the glass and onto the floor. Before filming the scene I had to prepare Brian's face for the aftereffects of falling through shards of shattered glass.

I covered Brian's face with a multitude of liquid scars, creating them by painting random strips of flexible collodion on his forehead, cheeks, and nose. As collodion dries it shrinks, pulling the skin into a depression, thus giving the appearance of a deep cut. My father used this same technique on Paul Muni in 1932 for the original *Scarface*, and I created the prosthetic scar for Al Pacino in the 1983 remake. After the collodion dried and had done all its shrinking, I laid fresh blood into each depression, and with a squirt of water it ran in bloody rivulets down his face. He now looked like Carrie and Frankenstein on a bad day. I told Brian that I would wait for him in the makeup trailer to remove all our damage, as these scars don't come off easily. I told my wife I wouldn't be long.

I went to the makeup trailer to wait for Brian. Fifteen minutes went by, thirty minutes, forty-five. I started to look for Brian out in the pitch-black night. Now more than an hour had passed, and there still was no sign of Brian; in fact, there were no people at all. Everyone had left. Our car was packed—Marion, the kids, Christmas gifts, and a tree tied on top—so with guilt in my heart, we left. We had a great time, but I couldn't stop thinking about Brian and where he disappeared to.

On the first day of filming after the holidays, I was in the makeup trailer and heard off in the distance someone shouting my name in a loud bellow: "WESTMORE!" I knew it was Brian coming for the kill. As his story goes, after we'd finished for the night, he went, makeup and all, to share a lot of cheer with our director, Ted, in his trailer. Brian, feeling very good, changed his clothes and forgot he was wearing his goulash face. From Hope he was driven to the Vancouver airport for his holiday trip home. As he entered the airport terminal, he couldn't understand why people were rapidly parting like the Red Sea. He said people looked at him in horror as they fled. By this time some of his reason was returning, so he went into the men's restroom and looked in the mirror. Gazing upon his bloody, mutilated face, he realized what all the panic was about. Before boarding the plane he washed off the blood and tried to remove most of his scars, but they held on pretty tight. I'm sure he met his family with a little of the residue still in place. I have worked with Brian several times since that night of horror, and each time it brings a chuckle between the two of us.

Most writers start off with "On a sunny day . . ." I don't think we had many sunny days in Hope, so I can start with, "On an overcast and dreary day," a Vietnam vet heard about our film's plot through the news. He decided to assault this renegade soldier and save the township of Hope from his terrorist attacks. He was dressed army-style. The reason for his arrival in town quickly spread, as he was asking questions. Someone forgot to tell him we were only making a movie. It wasn't long before the Royal Canadian Police rounded him up and escorted him down the Trans-Canada Highway. In his mind, I'm sure he felt the desire to save the residents of this innocent town (and I use the word *innocent* loosely).

We were filming at night, so we didn't arise until noon. Breakfast was usually a sandwich around lunchtime at the local deli. I was sitting at a table in the deli's window one day when for the second time, the real Rambo passed by. The hair on the back of my neck rose, as I realized the Vietnam vet was back. I literally levitated from my chair and snatched a phone from the wall. The proprietor helped me call the local police, who scrambled into protective action. Our potential killer and town savior was never to be seen again. As we all know, Rambo lives again and again and again . . .

THE DAY AFTER, 1983

The television special *The Day After* was a real first—but a first in what, exactly? Was it just a scary fantasy dreamed up by a science-fiction writer, or an implausible "What if"? What was the world facing and thinking about at this time?

In reality, the world was facing a lot more than what the general population was aware of. Nick Myers, the director, had some idea of what we had in store. He wanted to wake up and shock the world. The final project was only half as disturbing, because the network reduced the six hours of film to three. Missing was a lot of character development in the first (pre-bomb) half and much of the (post-bomb) survival and death in the second half. Rumor had it that it was deemed too scary for television.

The plot was centered in Middle America—Kansas City. On a clear day there's a shock wave, and a mushroom cloud rises above the landscape, evaporating agriculture, animals, and people. The blast was based on a two-megaton bomb that would annihilate everything within a two-mile radius. That thought is devastating, but in the real world this bomb was already obsolete, as the warheads mounted on the missiles at that time were twenty megatons. Across the United States in secret locations, buried deep underground, were giant silos with missiles prepared to retaliate against any foreign aggression. In the Arizona desert there is still a silo, which is now a museum. When we were there filming *Star Trek: First Contact*, the museum docents were some of the real people who had manned and cared for these missiles from hell. If you see the movie, you will have a glimpse of this hole to the devil's chamber. Four men, two officers with launching keys and two enlisted men, were responsible for igniting these behemoths into the sky at just a moment's notice.

While Nick, our director, was scouting for a location similar to the ones housing real silos, he found a large barren plot of land surrounded by a wire fence that was at least twelve feet tall. There was a small, nondescript house right in the middle. As he tried to rouse someone to inquire if we might film at this perfect location a man emerged. I don't remember if he was dressed as a civilian or military. Nick was told to get lost, no discussion. I guess we had really found one of the real sites. We heard that the deep concrete silos were constructed next to the houses, as I saw in Arizona, or built directly under the house to avoid detection. Not a good place to be sleeping if it was time to blast off. Nick ended up having this perfect setting duplicated and reconstructed elsewhere.

This was a time when optical printing and special-effects makeup shared the spotlight, and that is why I was there. It was my time to create makeup magic in a most horrible and realistic manner. This was not a fantasy thriller. To work on this film, everyone had to assume a cut in pay, as the budget had to be large enough to accommodate the new optical processes. This was to be a labor of love, not financial gain, and everyone agreed to be a part of it.

The word *optical* means to create an effect for the screen visually instead of practically. For *The Day After*, it meant we had to create the illusion of a bomb exploding over Kansas and people evaporating. Today this technology is used for a range of special effects, from re-creating dinosaurs to simulating world destruction or heroes flying through the air.

Prior to filming I found as much research as I could on the effects of the atomic bomb on Japan. I was prepared to simulate a few nasty burns and blood. Just as we were about to start filming, the United States government released the postwar footage of the Japanese people who had been close to Ground Zero, but survived. As soon as it was possible to enter the radioactive locations, American photographers were sent in to document the effects of radiation on humans. We all thought we could learn something to improve our contributions to the project. The lights dimmed, and we were exposed to film footage that I have never forgotten. Hairstylist Dorothy Long kept breaking down and periodically having to leave the room, sobbing. When the lights came up, I had compiled two pages of notes on all the different conditions that exposure to radiation can cause. I saw bleeding sores, burns, welts, melted skin, blisters, hair loss, etc. On some women the radiation was so intense that their bodies appeared to be tattooed with a design, when in reality, it was the pattern of their dress that had been burned into their skin. The research was overwhelming.

The first half of *The Day After* for me was lipstick and powder. The second half was the bomb. Our first special effect in the film went wrong, and it could have ended the production, and Jason Robards. In the scene Jason is driving down a busy freeway on his way home; there is a flash of light and then the windshield implodes. The idea was to have the glass rigged with an explosive charge that would simulate the power of the bomb's force. At first it was thought Jason could duck beneath the dashboard and the glass would fly overhead. Cooler minds prevailed, so it was decided to remove him from the car. Thank God! When the scene was filmed, the explosion created a fireball that engulfed the interior of the car. Anyone inside would have been incinerated.

In another scene a farmer is standing outside as the mushroom cloud ascends into the sky. He's hit by the blast and his body starts to smoke, then evaporates. The smoke is mine, and the evaporation is optical. To simulate the smoke, I was using a corrosive liquid, which, when it comes into contact with the moisture in the air, would react by creating dense smoke. I proceeded to apply a barrier cream on the actor's skin. Using a long cotton swab, I quickly laid a line of the liquid up his forearm, onto his shirt, and across his shoulders. This chemical was so volatile that I was the only one allowed to apply and store it.

The cameras were already rolling as I stepped out of frame. The actor was smoking so well, it looked like he would ignite into flames. When the director said, "Cut," a special-effects (not makeup) apprentice appeared out of nowhere and threw a bucket of water on the actor, thinking he was on fire. Why? To this day, no one wants to 'fess up or take the blame. When this toxic chemical comes into contact with water, it instantly generates 300 degrees of heat. The actor's shirt across his shoulders was melting into his skin. Without thinking I grabbed his shirt and stripped it off. To make matters worse, we were out in the middle of a cornfield, and the so-called medic we had there to save our lives in case of accident had no burn ointment, and the caterer had left, so there was no ice available. Into a car went the actor; he was taken to the closest hospital, which wasn't very close. That particular chemical has since been banned for any use in the United States.

As Rod Serling of *The Twilight Zone* once said, "Picture this." The script called for a typical Kansas farmhouse to burst into flames and explode, much as we've all seen in atomic bomb tests filmed in the Nevada desert. To hasten the burning process a special-effects team tried in vain to pre-spray the structure with green-tinted rubber cement. The rubber cement was too thick, so they resorted to randomly throwing buckets of the slime here and there on the exterior walls. As I stood watching this scientific application of goo, I wondered why they didn't just blow it up. The rubber cement was ignited and the fire quickly spread. After what seemed like forever, the wooden structure slowly began to burn, cameras rolling all the while in hopes of catching the magic moment. I was standing close enough to feel the intensity of the heat on my face as the house finally made liftoff. This was one of those Hollywood moments when theory didn't equal the reality of what was supposed to happen. The hours of waiting turned into seconds on the screen. This was a great lesson for me, as I have never taken any makeup or special project to the filming set without knowing the immediate visual results ahead of time.

As the film progressed, we created the walking dead during the post-bomb time frame, with our burns and blisters. On our biggest day of extra actors, my makeup and hair crew had to burn up and dirty one thousand of the local residents; everyone wants to be in the movies, no matter what they look like. We had a very long trailer, and the extras would enter one door for makeup, move down for messy hair, and then get hit with dirt bags on the way out. It was an assembly line for burns, blood, and dirt. A thousand people to make up, and all we had were three makeup artists and three hairstylists. This was going to take a miracle.

My teenage son Michael and my friend Zoltan Elek were with me, so I knew we could do it. We started in the morning at five a.m. People lined up for what appeared to be a mile-long procession. The burns we simulated with warm gelatin, and it was Michael's job to formulate the goo and keep us supplied. Using spatulas, Zoltan and I would smear and texture the gelatin onto everyone's face and hands. When it dried we didn't use regular makeup; that would have taken too long. I purchased different aerosol colors from an art store, so a couple shots of color, and they were off to the hairdresser. We couldn't spend any more time than a few minutes on each person. We never stopped for lunch. The production assistants kept passing us hot dogs to shove down our throats so we could keep going.

Michael had become such a help that the producers wanted him to stay and be put on salary, but I said, "No; he has to get back to high school, as summer is ending." I hated to put him on that airplane, and missed his company.

The scene we were preparing for was a post-bomb hospice that had been organized in a high school gymnasium. The thousand made-up extras were to fill the floor, but it was impossible to have them all ready for the first shot. Nick started with the principal actors and the first wave of a few background people surrounding them. As we finished more extras, the circle became larger, and the camera pulled back. Twelve hours later, at five p.m., everyone was ready. The director was able to film a wide sweeping panoramic shot of the entire inside of the building, the floor covered with the desperate and dying. This is known as a master shot, which is usually laid out first. I'm glad I didn't have to clean up everyone. That night there were a lot of dirty bathtubs and showers in Kansas.

When the film was completed, Marion and I attended a special screening where people from all walks of life were in attendance. There were network executives, the film's cast and crew, doctors, lawyers, the clergy, and people interested in saving the world. Following the film there was to be an intellectual discussion on the importance of *The Day After*'s message. The lights came on. There was silence. There was no discussion. I have never seen such a somber mood prevail over an audience. No one was going to dinner, very few talked; everyone wanted to go home and hug their children. I know that we sure did! If half a story could make such an impact, I couldn't imagine what our entire story would invoke. This was my tenth Emmy nomination.

MS. B (AND THE "B" DOES NOT STAND FOR BETTE)

When you think about movie icon Bette Davis, a lot of things might pop into your mind. The arresting Southern firebrand of *Jezebel*, the flamboyant theatrical diva of *All About Eve*, and the demented has-been of *What Ever Happened to Baby Jane?* The Bette Davis I knew was all of these characters combined, with a few qualities she never portrayed on-screen thrown in.

In the 1930s and '40s, Bette Davis was the Academy Award darling of Warner Bros. Studios, one of the most famous actresses in Hollywood. Her personal makeup artist was my uncle, Perc Westmore. They had a star/artist relationship that moviegoers outside the motion picture industry don't understand. It's like this: You have a studio family and a personal family. Bette and Perc were very close. Most people don't think of Bette Davis in an erotic way, but in the early days, she preferred to have her makeup applied while lying on a couch totally nude—that's right, buck naked—and handsome Uncle Perc was the artist to fulfill her desire.

In the later years of Bette's life, when the aging star was being presented with a multitude of awards and working on her final screen projects, I became her makeup artist. Since she always liked to be made up at her apartment in Hollywood (thank goodness, not in the nude anymore), I would have to pack all my equipment, carry it up the stairs, and set up in a little dark room. I referred to it as the "Dark Hole of Calcutta."

It was so dark I always had to take additional lights just to keep from sticking a brush into those "Bette Davis Eyes."

One of her last television films was *Right of Way* in 1983, costarring Jimmy Stewart and Melinda Dillon. I was hired to make up Bette, and my uncle Frank was hired to do Jimmy. Frank had to drop out due to health reasons, so he asked me to handle Jimmy too. I asked Bette if it was all right with her, and she replied, "Of course, darling."

The very next day, however, I found out that Bette had replaced me, so I ended up handling Jimmy and Melinda. Little did I know, this was a blessing in disguise. Every morning I would make up Melinda and then head over to Jimmy. After he was made up, he liked to center and hold his hairpiece while I glued it down and combed it into place. During those mornings, Bette would storm into his trailer with her personal rewrites and script changes. Because his eyesight was failing, she would read them to him. He would sigh and then agree to anything she wanted, or should I say, demanded. Ms. B would then descend on George Schaefer, the director, and announce to him that this is what she "and Jimmy" had decided to do. The wonderful and compassionate George would also agree to her changes. I must say, Jimmy Stewart and George Schaefer were two of the most wonderful artists you could ever meet and work with. Melinda was also a warmhearted pro.

Ms. B controlled everything for everyone. Melinda, thirty years younger than Bette, was playing the role of her daughter. Bette even changed poor Melinda's wardrobe because it looked too good. By the time she had exercised her power over Melinda's clothes, Melinda's character, a well-to-do bookshop owner in Carmel, California, was dressed like a librarian in Kansas at the turn of the twentieth century.

There were times when Ms. B would even accuse Melinda of drinking, an accusation Melinda always denied. But on the other hand, who could spend ten to twelve hours with Ms. B and *not* have a drink! Melinda and I had lunch almost every day, and sometimes, yes, we did top it off with a glass of champagne to help us endure the rest of those final hours.

At the end of the film, everyone who had worked on the movie wanted to have Ms. B sign their scripts. Signed scripts came pouring out of her trailer, with inscriptions such as "Let's do it again," and "You're so wonderful." When mine came out, it said in bold letters scrawled across the entire script cover, "BETTE DAVIS." Are you still wondering how I coined the name "Ms. B"?

This film was made shortly after *On Golden Pond*, a movie in which much of the charm derived from the warm chemistry between Henry Fonda and Katharine Hepburn, playing a long-married couple. *Right of Way* also concerned an elderly couple. Charming, kooky, elderly people were "in," and I think that they were trying to do a television version of a devoted septuagenarian couple. The plot, somewhat ahead of its time, was about euthanasia. Bette and James Stewart play Mini and Teddy Dwyer. When Mini learns she is terminally ill with a blood disease, the couple decides to commit suicide together.

If the producers were trying to re-create the tender chemistry of Fonda and Hepburn, they were very disappointed. Bette Davis's sour personality during the period of filming came through in her performance, which made the film less poignant.

At the private screening, the film, with its rewritten dialogue, was so poor that at the end there was only a smattering of applause. Everyone tried to sneak out as soon as possible and flee into the night before someone could ask the eternal question, "How did you like it?"

I guess Bette didn't hate me as much as I thought, because I ended up having one more shot with her. My phone at the studio rang one day, and it was my wife, who in her soft voice asked, "Guess who called?" She paused for effect and then answered her own question: "Bette Davis!" These were not exactly words I had been dying to hear, but still—I couldn't resist the nostalgic challenge to respond to dear ol' Ms. B.

As it turned out, Bette was going to guest on Bryant Gumbel's talk show, *Today*. The day before the shoot, I realized that I didn't remember the exact time Bette had requested me to do her makeup the following day. I hesitantly called her apartment in Hollywood around eleven a.m., only to be greeted with a resounding, "WHAT?" Let's just say she didn't sound happy . . . or awake. But she certainly sounded loud. When I asked her my question, she mumbled something like, "One-thirty p.m., and don't ever wake me up in the middle of the night again!!" *Slam* went her phone. All I could say to myself was "Be strong, Michael—be strong!"

Needless to say, I arrived exactly on time. I even stood out front for a few minutes looking at my watch. Bette swung open the door and a cloud of smoke greeted me. As almost any film aficionado knows, Bette was a smoker, and one of the habits she'd acquired from a lifetime of lighting up was that she would strike a match on anything that was close by. Because a craving for a cigarette could pop up at any time (and for her, they popped up every few minutes), she had jars of wooden matches all over her apartment so she could light up on a whim. A lot of her antique furniture had strike lines across them. The first time I saw her do this, I was horrified that she would mark an antique this way. Picking up on my reaction, Bette cast a huge billow of smoke in my direction and shrugged.

After I arrived that day, I realized that I hadn't packed the extra lights I needed to brighten her "Black Hole of Calcutta" apartment. I suggested we do the makeup in the one beautiful, bright, sunlit room in her place. "No such thing," she roared, as if she was Baby Jane and I was Sister Blanche. "Go get the lights!" Half an hour later, Marion returned with my lights. I started my cosmetic artistry, which included coloring and blending her cheeks, brushing on mascara, and creating those oh-so-beautiful, arched, Westmore-styled eyebrows. When I announced I was finished, she demanded a hand mirror to review my work.

"OH MY GAWD!" she screamed.

"What's the matter?" I asked. It sounded like she might be having another stroke.

She quickly spat out "NO! NO! NO! I need more color in my cheeks, and the eyebrows are all wrong!" She grabbed a tissue and began violently wiping away all of my work.

I could have been insulted, but I realized that at this point in her life, her eyesight wasn't the greatest, so she was one of the last people who should be criticizing my work. Besides, she was nuts.

She picked up a sponge and the pink crème rouge. My heart sank as she dug into the rouge and rubbed gobs of it up and down her cheeks. She then seized an eyebrow pencil and crudely drew three intersecting half circles above her eyebrows onto her forehead. It reminded me of a toddler playing with a magic marker.

When she had finished her handiwork in about three seconds flat, she looked like she could have been the prototype for Bozo the Clown. I gulped, smiled, and politely asked which circle she wanted me to complete, and she staunchly commanded, "You figure it out!" As long as it was a high-arched semicircle above the eye, it was fine with her. She didn't care how high up her forehead it went. I wiped away two of the circles while she smeared on some red lipstick, took a deep drag on her cigarette, and informed me that we were ready to go.

Bette had had a stroke earlier in the year, so she had to be transported in a wheelchair. There I was, pushing the legendary Bette Davis through the studio, and she was looking even scarier than when she had played Baby Jane. The unintended consequence of her makeup job was to make her look deranged.

Bette had an agenda for doing the interview. She was there to defend herself. Her beloved daughter had just written a scathing memoir, *My Mother's Keeper*, which revealed what it was like growing up with Bette Davis as a mother. As the interview progressed, Bryant Gumbel would respectfully ask her questions about her career and all of her recent accomplishments. Bette would completely disregard the question and charge in with a comment about her estranged daughter. The result was like something out of an absurdist play.

When the show was over, Bryant asked me if I understood any of the interview. How could I lie? I politely told him I didn't understand a word of it. He nodded and vowed never to interview her again. I said, "If you promise never to interview her again, I promise I will never do her makeup again." We shook hands on it!

As I wheeled "Baby Jane" out of the studio, I kept thinking to myself, "You are getting well paid for this, so suck it up; it's almost over."

Bette called me again, but alas, I was true to my pact with Bryant, and never set foot in "Calcutta" again. Come to think of it, Bette once said to me, "You're not at all like your uncle!" I never cared to find out what she meant by that.

I must say, Bette was loved by many! She still is, and her movies from the Golden Age continue to entertain new audiences. But I'm sure God has his hands full. By now Ms. B has probably tried to rewrite the Bible and reorganize heaven.

UNCOMMON VALOR, 1983

How would you like to travel to Hawaii? Stay in a resort with your family? Enjoy the balmy nights and the warm blue water, and get paid for it? When you work in the film industry you never know where it will take you; sometimes it's downtown Los Angeles or Philadelphia. My brother Monty asked me to join him on his film, *Uncommon Valor*. This dangerous and violent adventure was about a group of Vietnam War veterans uniting to search for and rescue prisoners of war who were being held in a jungle compound.

Aside from occasional blood and guts, the director wanted the stealth soldiers to wear the typical army camouflage makeup. To add a touch of realism, my brother went to an army surplus store and purchased the real thing. It was not as easy to apply as regular cosmetics because it contained a lot of wax. Soldiers wearing it in the humidity during real warfare couldn't afford to have it melt in their pockets or run down their face. We found some great research photos of soldiers in action, so we were ready.

The star of the show was Gene Hackman, and he didn't want to sit that long to have that &#%!@?! stuff painted all over his face. Gene played it with a few smudges. It's a good thing he wasn't in a real war, as a clean face glows under the light of a tropical moon. The technical adviser told us that a bright face makes a good target. But we were filming make-believe.

Our youngest soldier on the squad was a kind and gentle soul, always prepared and on time. It was a thirty-one-year-old Patrick Swayze. There was no dancing here; all his footwork was running with a gun.

My main charge was Fred Ward, who wanted a full, multicolored camouflage face. On the first day that Fred was on-set, I free-handed the colored patterns. I started under his right eye, and it seemed to take forever, as I interlocked each color. The second day it took a little longer, because I worked from photos taken the previous day. After several weeks I decided to apply Fred's patterned face without my research. As long as I started in the same spot each time, I could duplicate my patterns and brushstrokes. In a rush one day, I started under the left eye and soon found myself questioning where to paint next. "Memory, don't fail me now"—but it did. Back to the photo!

Our most colorful character—not in makeup, but in personality—was "Tex" Cobb, who was more of a professional boxer than an actor. In the beginning of the film he was placed near the front of our squad as it traversed the jungle paths. One day Tex couldn't be roused from his second-floor apartment. When the door was opened by the manager he was gone, but the window was open and a sheet was hanging down the side of the building. Tex had escaped paradise. He was found headed for the seaplane that hooked Kauai up to Honolulu. Tex had decided he needed a day off, not realizing this was showbiz and he was an integral part of it. After his infamous stunt he was moved to the rear of the squad, just in case he had to be replaced.

I found Hawaii to be another world as we worked behind the tourist scene. Prejudice and strong-arm business control was everywhere, plus the lack of a good Mexican restaurant, which is a necessity to a Californian. We were told that under no circumstances should we venture up to the mountains from our valley location, as it contained one of the island's finest marijuana fields. They were known as "gold" and were heavily guarded, as one of our crew members found out.

Some days I would take my son Michael to work with me. He had bonded with my Samoan driver Cyril, who would take him on truck runs for supplies. On their adventures Cyril would always stop at a stand by the side of the road for the greatest-tasting hamburger, called the Ono Burger. The secret to its flavor: salt and pepper. Everything tastes better in paradise, including guava sherbet.

I had Sundays off, so I took the family for a trip down the Nā Pali coast. On this adventure we would straddle the sides of a rubber boat and explore the reefs and caves along the shoreline. That day our boat had just one functioning motor, so the captain was debating whether or not to cancel the trip. The water was calm and the sky was beautiful. What the heck, we thought; let's go. There were so many caves; our guide wanted us to experience a trip into at least one of them.

The one he selected was a very large cave that went deep into the cliff and had a very high ceiling. As we motored near the rear of the cave with our backs to the entrance, someone noticed, with alarm, a high wall of water bearing down on us. I looked at Marion and said, "You go with Michael Jr. and Michele." (The three of them were wearing life jackets.) I said that I would take McKenzie with me, as there were no jackets small enough to fit her. To add more stress for our guide, our one working motor had conked out. Fortunately, it restarted just as the wave hit us, lifting our boat so high that I knocked my head on the rock ceiling. The wave passed by us to crash on the rear wall. We wasted no time and quickly headed out to sea to spend the rest of the day snorkeling. Our guide had no explanation as to why a twenty-foot-high rogue wave was hitting the shores of Hawaii at this time.

On subsequent days we spent time hiking Kauai's "Grand Canyon of the Pacific" (yes, Hawaii has its own version, called Waimea Canyon) and lounging in the clear, blue lagoon where the musical *South Pacific* was filmed.

My brother Mont with his infectious smile was always known as a fun and caring individual. He was a prankster as well as a master makeup artist and teacher. Midway through a day in Hawaii the film crew, including us, was moving from the lower lush jungle to a windy mountain ridge. Extending along the ridge the studio had constructed a Vietnamese village, dressed to appear as if Agent Orange had destroyed both the village and its population. Mont and I had arrived before anyone else so we had time to snoop around in all the little thatched huts. One of the open-air businesses was a barbershop with a skeleton sitting in the barber chair. Mont looked at the skeleton and thought for a moment. That was bad! He then asked me if I had any loose hair with me. It just so happened I did. He strongly suggested we glue some onto the skeleton. I was horrified. Mont won; we pulled out the loose hair, some glue, and a pair of scissors. Quickly working together, our skeleton soon sported a full head of wispy hair. The film crew started to arrive. We walked away, not mentioning our dirty deed to anyone. The crew had laid dolly tracks that allowed the camera to slide by as it took in the panoramic view of everything in the village. As the camera slid past the barbershop, it captured our masterpiece for posterity.

THE THREE CONS

A makeup artist's career takes many turns, as mine has from the beginning. You never know who is going to be on the other end of that jingling phone and what that unknown voice will ask of you. Over my many years there have been several seemingly innocent voices with requests that developed into unforeseen adventures. The following all started as challenging special-effects makeup projects and ended in exercises that showcased unimaginable human nature. The final result always had a monetary goal. Come with me and share some of my best work that never made it to the silver screen.

Aiding and Abetting

The voice on the other end of the telephone said, "Hello, I'm an actor, and I need several character makeup changes for a film I'll be starring in. It's a low-budget operation, and you probably wouldn't recognize any of the other actors."

My makeup lab was at my home, in the garage. I didn't have any assistants, so everything I created was very personal and private, which actors preferred. The man I came to know as Ken arrived at my lab soon after our phone conversation so I could take plaster casts of his teeth and face, on which I would mold his makeup pieces. He had a wonderful Eurasian face to transform. The menu of pieces I created included different sizes and shapes of noses, dentures, assorted colored contact lenses, cheeks, scars, moles, and plumper (a plastic piece that fits inside the mouth against the gums to push out the shape of the exterior jawline). He already had a collection of expensively styled wigs, beards, fake eyebrows, and mustaches made by one of Hollywood's finest, Mr. Z. Everything we made was to be identifiable with a specific character.

Ken was a young man in his early thirties with the mind of a supercomputer. It seemed strange when he asked me to teach him how to apply everything, as most movies have a professional makeup artist on staff. He said the film was so low-budget, they couldn't even afford to pay a makeup artist. Ken soon became proficient in the application and gluing of all the pieces, including basic makeup to change his overall skin tone. At the end of our session, Ken collected all his materials, paid me an unexpected bonus, and disappeared.

A year later I was working on *Raging Bull*. One day an actor sitting ringside shouted up to me, "Didya see your name in *Sports Illustrated*?" I couldn't believe I would be mentioned in a sports magazine. A cold chill went up my spine on that hot summer day as I read and realized that Ken Uston, my phony stage actor, was none other than a professional gambler. He was one of the most, if not *the* most, famous international card counters in the game of blackjack.

Later Ken told me he had decided to hang up his cards because he had been physically beaten and almost killed by a group that didn't appreciate his card-counting talents and all the money he was winning from the casinos. As the monetary success of each of his made-up characters grew, so did the group's surveillance, meaning that he would soon have to abandon that character. He finally ran out of characters.

Like all performers who seek recognition, on his way out he decided to give a three-part interview to *Sports Illustrated*. I guess playing cards is sort of a sport. Unfortunately, his story included me—ME!—as his disguise guru. And as he most generously wrote, "I couldn't have done it without him."

There's a New Champion in Town

I received a phone call from a man who had written a book on "how to beat the IRS." He called me because he needed special makeup. His book had become so popular that he had been asked to be a guest on several television talk shows. He wanted the disguise because he had used a pseudonym, and didn't want to be recognized. He explained that I hadn't written anything illegal, but the book did provide information that someone could use, as he said, "to stretch the rules."

The makeup consisted of a typical disguise, which included a wig, colored contacts, eyebrows, mustache, false dentures, and a latex nose. I finished the makeup early so we had extra time to wait for his car to come pick him up and take him to the television station. While we were sitting in my living room, he spotted a chess set on the coffee table and asked me if I would like to play a game. I told him the set was only there for decoration; my game was backgammon. In a very bold and cocky voice, he said, "You don't want to play me in a game of backgammon. I make a living playing in backgammon tournaments all over the world." He had now piqued my interest, so I decided to go up against this self-proclaimed champion.

As our game continued, the rolls of the dice were coming my way, one right after the other. It was obvious he was becoming more and more frustrated as I swept around the board, eventually beating him at his own game. I figured the odds of me beating him were about a thousand to one, and needless to say, he didn't take it well. We didn't have time for a second game, as his car had shown up. He vowed to return to avenge his loss and prove his title. I was looking forward to our rematch, but the champion never returned.

To this day, I remain the champ of our game together. I forgot to buy a copy of his book, so I just pay the taxes my accountant tells me to.

What Happens in Vegas Doesn't Always Stay in Vegas

While at Universal Studios a man called my uncle Bud and said, "I am a multimillion-aire, and I am going to a party in Texas. I need to be disguised. All the invited guests will arrive in disguise, but first we ante up $1,000 each. The last guest to be recognized wins $15,000." He would pay us $1,500, and we had to prepare it ASAP.

The man soon arrived from Canada with his wife and two children, a family man from all appearances. After taking impressions John Chambers and I worked fever-ishly while the man took Bud on a drive around town. They drove by expensive prop-erties that he claimed to own. Bud was impressed, but John and I thought something was fishy. Several days later he came back to the studio with his family for his makeup test. To jump-start his change, he had shaved his head bald, shaved off his distinctive mustache, and gained fifty pounds. He also said he had obtained a position at the gala event as a waiter. With this disguise, he felt sure he'd win.

On a Friday, we packed up his makeup kit, he wrote us a check for $1,500, and then he drove off in his convertible Cadillac with family on board. Saturday night he called Bud to say, "Don't cash the check; I won first prize, and I'm going to split it with you." We were all so excited, because that meant $7,500 in our pockets. Weeks came and went, and John and I figured he'd never come back with the money. Finally we talked Bud into depositing our original check. Not only were the funds insufficient, but there was no such bank. One day two FBI agents knocked on our door at Universal request-ing an audience. They were holding a somewhat faded and poor-quality picture of our winner without any makeup.

They requested that I reconstruct the disguise on the plaster mold of his face. This is because we had disguised a man who was on the FBI's most-wanted list. After leaving us the man had headed to Las Vegas, where he applied his makeup and held up a casino. We were told he dumped the makeup into a toilet and fled the country. Bad news was, we never got paid; good news was, several years later he tried to sneak back into the United States and was sent to prison for theft. Upon his release he returned to the scene of his makeup crime and had lunch with us. Oh! By the way, the wife and two daughters were rented for the day. That's Hollywood; it's all make-believe.

2010, 1984

I still don't know how I was nominated in 1984 for the film *2010*. My creative input was for two old-age makeups on actor Keir Dullea, on-screen for less than three minutes. Peter Hyams was the director and a master of many talents. If he'd known how to do makeup, he would have done that too. We had a star-studded cast including Roy Scheider, the only man I know that mooned the White House (and I have a picture to prove it). Even Arthur C. Clarke made an appearance. My assignment, other than supervising the makeup, was to design and construct Keir's sixty-year-old makeup and re-create the original aged makeup created by Stuart Freeborn in the first film, *2001*.

For the sixty-five-year-old makeup, I made plaster casts of Keir and sculpted pretty much at will the sags and wrinkles that were necessary to make this makeup convincing.

The challenge came with the re-creation. All references to the original *2001* makeup had been destroyed. This was ordered by the first director Stanley Kubrick. Nothing was left to steal or copy from the first film. Peter had several frames of the original film lifted from the print and made into eleven-by-fourteen-inch photos. This was my research. Keir as the aged Bowman lying in bed was never filmed in close-up or straight on, only in profile. It was up to me to create my interpretation. To the average moviegoer an old-age makeup in one piece would have been acceptable, but I wanted to make my life difficult and try something new to me. Dick Smith had attempted this very successfully with Dustin Hoffman in *Little Big Man*. Instead of a one-piece latex pullover, the makeup consisted of individual pieces. I had a nose, upper lip, lower lip, chin, upper and lower eyes, throat, jowls, ears, and backs of hands. The bald head, back of the neck, and forehead were all created in a large, seamless silicone mold.

I remember some of my colleagues' amazement that I was able to make a seamless latex appliance. I think I was too naive to realize that this had never been accomplished before. The makeup was too complicated and too involved to try a test first, so on the day of reckoning I was ready. A small camera was mounted beneath the makeup counter and aimed directly up at Keir's face. The camera took a photo every few seconds. Later when this film was processed you could watch a five-and-a-half-hour makeup application take place in one minute. The final touch was to insert cloudy contact lenses into his eyes and a set of aged plastic teeth into his mouth.

Keir was skeptical about reprising his role because the original makeup had taken Stuart eleven hours to apply. I guaranteed him half the time with the aid of my brother Mont, Bob Norin, and hairstylist Vivian McAteer. Keir is a master at yoga and meditation so he put himself into an awakened trance. When we had completed our trying

Scuplting in clay Keir's old-age makeup for 2010. *MGM Studios*

Applying Keir's old-age makeup. *MGM Studios*

Keir in completed makeup. *MGM Studios*

five-and-a-half-hour makeup ordeal he jumped out of the chair just as relaxed and calm as when we'd started. The filming progressed nicely, but I'm sure Keir was tired after an hour of removing all the latex, a wig, chipped false fingernails, false teeth, white contact lenses, and eyebrows. This scene had to be filmed in one day, and after eighteen hours we all got to go home. This work earned me my first Academy Award nomination.

WHY ME?, 1984

In 1984 I was approached by Lorimar Productions to create the makeup for a television movie entitled *Why Me?* The catch was I only had two weeks to create everything needed for the production.

The movie was based on the true story of military nurse Leola Mae Harmon, who was stationed in Alaska. Driving down the highway she was hit head-on; her car was thrown off the road and ended up in a ravine. What made her story different was the nature of her injuries. As her steering wheel was spinning out of control she fell forward into it. The damage left her with torn lips and broken jaw. The inside lining of her mouth and gums were totally destroyed, and most of her teeth were chipped or knocked out. The film is based on two years of her life as she progressed through many surgeries. During this time she formed a bond with Dr. James Stallings, her reconstructive surgeon, which would later end in marriage. What made this story so unique was

that it was the first time vaginal tissue had been used to reconstruct facial features. It was the closest tissue to the inside lining of Leola's mouth and lips. All of the other attending doctors at that time were against the procedure, but Stallings persisted.

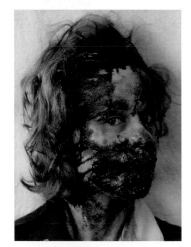

Why Me? the accident. *Lorimar Productions*

I never met Leola except through a photograph, but I did meet Dr. Stallings. Since the entire story takes place under military care, there were no pictures or references available. Between the doctor's verbal guidance and my sketching, I was able to re-create the different stages of the reconstructive progression. I met Glynnis O'Connor, our actress, and started my two-week marathon of facial casting, dental casting, sculpting, and forming foam latex facial appliances. When production started Dr. Stallings sent his surgical nurse Judy from the Midwest to act as my technical adviser. Judy would guide me as to the proper skin colors for postoperative appearances and the proper knots for surgical stitching.

At one stage of the real surgery Leola's mouth was totally closed with an overlapping skin graft. I had to duplicate this look for the film, but I couldn't let Glynnis go for days without eating or drinking. I created a small hole in the corner of the latex appliance that we could slip a straw through. There was still no way she could eat for several days while wearing this stage of the makeup. I made a pact with her that I wouldn't eat either; we would only drink chocolate malts. (Little did Production know, this was my favorite.)

Early on, Glynnis, being the consummate performer, wanted to experience what it would be like to have to mingle in public with just such a partial deformity. One morning after the makeup was applied, a driver took us to a supermarket. It was fascinating to watch the reactions and expressions as adults would glance at her and then look away before Glynnis could catch their eye. Children were more curious. They would stare and question the lady with no mouth.

Glynnis gathered a few items and we approached the checkout counter. The clerk completed tabulating, bagging, taking the money, and returning her change. She never made eye contact, although Glynnis stared at her the entire time. Our actress had done her homework. She knew what it was like to walk in another's shoes.

The entire production took twenty-one days to film. The number of sleepless hours I spent preparing and filming seemed twice as long, but my reward was worth it when I received an Emmy nomination. That year I was up against the popular miniseries *V*.

Skin graft operation. *Lorimar Productions*

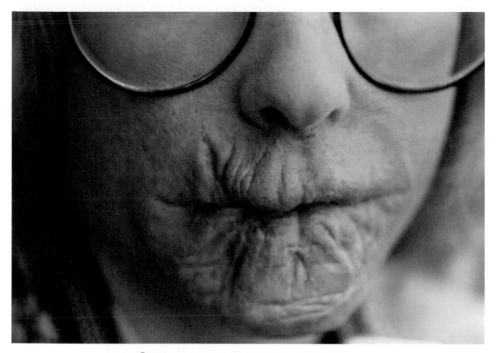

Beginning reconstructive surgery. *Lorimar Productions*

Post-operation recovery. *Lorimar Productions*

On that special evening Marion and I were sharing a table with the makeup artists from *V.* Everyone expected them to win. The winner was announced: "For Best Makeup, Michael Westmore, for *Why Me?*" Marion and I literally screamed in amazement. I graciously accepted my second Emmy Award and made the rounds of photographers.

ICEMAN, 1984

The film *Iceman* starred Timothy Hutton, Lindsay Crouse, and a multitalented unknown actor named John Lone. It fell into my lap by chance. I was contracted to do *Staying Alive*, but as deals come and go, this one had fallen through. At the same time director Norman Jewison and his partner Patrick Palmer were producing the film *Iceman*, and hired me to create the Neanderthal look and all the special makeup effects for John Lone. This was an assignment of a lifetime, as I was offered more money than I had requested; my own personal car (when there was a road to drive upon); upscale living conditions, which included a kitchen; and since I was to be gone for three months, airline tickets for my wife Marion to visit whenever we were in Vancouver, British Columbia.

After testing many actors, John Lone was the only one who could not only act but could also withstand all the physical strain that was part of this character's role. He had the ability to squat all the way down to the floor and then spring straight up and land on top of a table. John had been trained as a youth in the Chinese theater, so he had the physical ability to do all that was required. Remember, this was filmed before the advent of computers. The actors and stuntpeople risked their lives for the motion picture industry, and this project was no exception.

The story starts with the discovery of a Neanderthal man frozen in an ice cave. A block of ice containing his body is chipped out and flown to a laboratory to be thawed and studied. While in the laboratory, he comes to life. The story poses the question: How would an individual understand and assimilate into a world when "awoken" thousands of years later?

From Prosthetics to Glacier Safety

At my lab in Los Angeles, months before we started to film, I had to create a brow-ridged forehead, a broader nose, oversized teeth that would broaden his cheeks from the inside, plastic scars for his body, a long and straggly wig, a beard, a mustache, eyebrows, and all the special makeup effects the script called for—all items that John would wear for the coming months. Michele Burke, my associate, joined me on our quest north. To complete John's daily makeup application, it took Michele and me working nonstop for three hours every day.

Our first location was in Churchill, Manitoba, a town located right in the path of the migrating polar bears as they headed south. We were told that if we were charged by a bear, we should curl up into a ball and let him sniff and play with us, but not move or cry out. Usually we knew when one was in the vicinity, as the town bell would ring, which meant stay inside. Glad to say, none of us had the opportunity to play sports with a bear.

Another day we were filming a distance out from land on the frozen sea shelf that covered Hudson Bay. You could actually hear and feel the tide beneath our feet as it surged in and out. As I was talking with the script supervisor, there was a loud snap, almost like a gunshot. A large crack like Harry Potter's forehead scar shot through the ice and directly between her outstretched legs. Our guide said it was time to go. We were whisked onto a helicopter and flown to solid ground. Another piece of advice we were given: If you are standing on a piece of ice and it breaks away from the land, stay on it, because, if you jump into the freezing water, you won't last more than a minute.

We always had to walk exactly where our guides told us, especially when traversing a glacier. Prior to us walking over any ice, the guides would mark a pathway on solid ice with a line of red string attached to small metal rods which had been hammered into the glacier's surface. To step a few feet to the right or the left could mean falling down a snow-covered crevasse, only to be discovered a few thousand years later when the glacier receded.

At the end of the movie, John Lone, the iceman, was to be filmed flying off over a glacier, holding on to the landing skid of a helicopter. John actually did this death-defying stunt himself—no dummy, no stuntman. Twenty of us were flown to the side of a glacier bowl. There was nowhere to stand on level ground until a small patch was shoveled flat. Our guide always had the authority to tell us what and where, and when to do it. Near the end of the day he said it was time to leave. Our director Fred Schepisi had another idea for one more shot. Fog had started to roll in, and again, the guide reiterated that it was time to leave. After ten more shots we were finally enveloped in pea-soup fog. There was no way out, and this was Wednesday. (Every Wednesday night I would place a long-distance phone call from the hotel to my wife; remember, there were no cell phones yet. I could just hear the hotel operator telling Marion, "I'm sorry, your husband hasn't returned from the glacier.")

Back on the glacier, it looked like we were going to have to spend the night there. I hoped the guide had brought s'mores and songbooks. All of a sudden a small patch of sun broke through the fog. With that we scrambled into the small helicopters and barrel-rolled amusement park–style as we lifted off the ice and shot down the valley to dry land. The guide later told me he had emergency gear available for us all to spend a comfortable night under the stars, sleeping on the side of our outdoor refrigerator.

There is a wonderful scene in the movie where the iceman is being chased by Timothy Hutton, the doctor. To fly the crew to the top of Bear Glacier we again rode in helicopters. On this trip I was riding with Fred, the director; Ian, the director of photography; and several other men much larger than myself. As we flew ever higher to the sheer mountain and glacier wall, the helicopter faltered due to the thin air. It kept laboring, trying to rise to the top, only to fall back time after time. I decided to slip on a headset to listen in on the pilot's conversation. He was talking to the ground crew, saying, "There's too much weight; I can't gain altitude." As a chill went down my spine, I thought, "Who are we going to throw out?" And with that, a strong updraft scooped us up and deposited our group on top of the glacier.

There's never a dull moment on a movie set. As I stood on the top of Bear Glacier in Western Canada, a helicopter was revving up its motors not too far behind me. The spinning blades created more wind force, as it was about to lift off. Between me and the flying bird was the helicopter's door, which had been removed and stuck in the snow. The door had been removed so a camera could be mounted in its place. With all the swirling motion the door was picked up like a leaf in the wind and slammed into my back, pushing me facedown into the ice. The crew all came to my rescue, asking "Are you hurt?" I could honestly say "Yes," although I wasn't bleeding. It felt more like the Incredible Hulk had hit me in the back, so my recovery was quick. I'm glad the door hit me full on, because spinning on edge, it might have cut me in two.

I was back on my feet, sufficiently recovered to continue with the scene where the doctor is chasing the iceman. John was placed on one spot of ice and Tim was placed on another, about twenty feet apart. Between them there was nothing visible but a field of snow, under which had been planted explosive charges. On the director's signal the explosion opened up a huge crevasse that had been covered with snow and ice for thousands of years (something Hollywood could change in a matter of seconds). Both John and Tim, destined to be separated by this new hole, were just a few feet from its edge. One error in judgment, and one (or both) would have seen the inside of a glacial cavern up close and personal, all the way down.

In another scene, from the iceman's perspective, he is floating in space. This scene followed our adventure on the glacier when the iceman grabs onto the helicopter skid and flies up into the sky. Suddenly, the iceman decides to let go. I guess nobody told Neanderthals they can't fly. This was not a stunt that John was going to participate in. Dar Robinson, one of the world's greatest and most respected stuntmen, was hired to take his place. After applying iceman makeup and wardrobe, Dar and associates were flown several thousand feet up into the air. When they reached the prearranged altitude, Dar and his buddy dove out and away from the helicopter. Dar's associate had a small camera mounted on the top of his helmet to get close-up photos, and also to assist if anything went wrong. He was Dar's lifeline. In freefall positions, both of them hurtled toward earth. At a specific altitude, by the pull of a concealed cord, the buffalo robe that Dar was wearing split open in the back and a small parachute was released to slow his descent. His buddy with the helmet camera was wearing a larger chute, so it was possible for him to skydive over to Dar, allowing the two of them to land safely.

Dar was famous for all sorts of miraculous stunts. He even jumped off the top of the Seattle Space Needle with a bungee cord attached to his foot. He told me he left nothing to chance, and scientifically calculated every death-defying maneuver. Dar's life was eventually taken, not performing one of his amazing screen moments, but on a motorcycle, where the odds had not been calculated.

Colder than . . . It Needed to Be

How cold is cold? The script called for another shot of the doctor chasing the iceman. Fred decided it would be great to film this just as the sun was rising over the horizon. We all arose in the middle of the night to prepare for this shot. Michele and I had to get up three hours before everyone else to get John into makeup, and then we were driven to the location, an actual ice floe. The outside temperature had reached minus-sixty degrees. This was one of those times that you question your own sanity. I asked myself, *What am I am doing here?* I wasn't going to take my hands out of my pockets to do anything. Even my snood, which is a long furry cone that protects your face and nose, was covered in hanging icicles due to my breath. After the morning filming was completed, warm never felt so good.

Not everything was filmed out of doors. On a set that looked like a laboratory from a *Star Trek* movie, the Neanderthal man was defrosted from his tomb of ice. It was up to me to figure out how to do it. Ira the mad scientist, who had a supply store in

Burbank, California, was always my go-to man for a think-tank meeting. After several experiments I finally developed a look-alike for melting ice. I made a thick clear jelly from a chemical called Methocel, which is also used in wallpaper paste. Into this I slowly blended shiny, small mica flakes. Since the material is nontoxic, I could spatula it all over John's naked body and face as he lay on the operating table. Due to the applied thickness and shine, it gave the illusion of ice. When the camera was rolling I would spray the Methocel with warm water, and this would look like the ice was melting right in front of our eyes.

For some psychological and physiological reason, John, our iceman, wanted to restrict himself to eating just once a day, and that was dinner. After filming every day it took an hour longer to clean him up after the film crew had left and turned out all the lights. The latex forehead had to be removed carefully, along with the chest scar, wig, beard, fingernails, and teeth. Everything had to be cleaned and prepared for the next day, which I would do as John showered off all the brown body makeup and dirt. Since I was provided with an automobile, it became my responsibility to return John safe and sound to our hotel, but on the way back each night, we always stopped for dinner. We had two favorite restaurants: one called Bridges in the Granville Marketplace, which served continental French food, and another in Chinatown. In Chinatown we ate in a small annex where all the local Asians dined. John would eat anything and everything. I told him to order it all, and if I didn't like the look or smell of something, he could eat it. There were a few dishes that squished, oozed, burped, and were not recognizable in the animal world. I passed on consuming these.

Every other night we ate at my choice, Bridges, where we were treated to flute and harp music and ate recognizable fare. We actually dined there so many times that when we walked in the door, they knew to bring us two different specials of the day, since we had tried the entire menu (twice), plus a chilled bottle of Hunter Valley Chardonnay. John and I had one problem at Bridges: After our main courses arrived, mine always looked better, so bites were always in order. Between the giant slug in black bean sauce and steamed chicken feet, I did prefer coq au vin and pot de crème. During our many nightly meals John and I were able to solve all the problems of the world.

John and I became such food aficionados in Chinatown that everyone wanted to have dinner with us on Sunday evening. We would arrange small dinner parties, and the conversations always turned to trashing the Hollywood film community. Three of our favorite regular dinner guests were Lindsey Crouse; her husband David Mamet, the famous playwright; and their baby Willa. Little did we know he was taking notes on us and our Chinatown dinners. We were celebrated in his book *Writing in Restaurants*.

Applying makeup to John Lone, *Iceman*. *Universal Studios*

There was a time in the movies when makeup artists had to create scars or swelling with wax, latex, or acrylic that was squeezed out of a tube like toothpaste. John would lie on the cold floor of the makeup trailer every morning and, using a stencil, I would draw a primitive bird design on his chest with a red makeup pencil. From a tube, I would create a worm-like line of plastic over the red outline. John would lie there for about ten minutes while the gooey stuff dried. After coloring my creation with brown and pink makeup, John's raised Hollywood scar resembled the native scarification you see in pictures of primitive tribes today.

During our filming we were helicoptered back into the Canadian wilderness, over jagged peaks and through snow-covered valleys, until we reached a cavernous opening in the side of a mountain. This is where the iceman is discovered. While working inside this cave, the size of a huge ballroom, we were all given a warning. Our guide said, "Look up; see the huge crystal ice chunks adhered to the rock ceiling? Noise, vibration, and heat can cause them to come loose and without warning crash to the cave floor." Then he asked for us to keep our voices to a minimum. Here was a movie crew that would be making sounds as heavy equipment was moved in and out of the cave and hot lights turned on to illuminate the set. I guess three out of three isn't good.

The first day went just fine, but I had an uneasy feeling about being in the cave when I wasn't needed. I would go outside and enjoy the scenery and wish my wife was with me to enjoy this untouched white wilderness. The next morning we all arrived bright and early, and there on the frozen ground in the middle of our cave sat a chunk of ice that weighed several tons. It had fallen from the ceiling during the night, right where we'd been working the night before.

Several times we worked right at the face of a glacier, so close I could press my nose onto it. There were many things to observe: The glaciers were receding as a constant stream of water poured from its translucent blue base down the valley. Smooth, round rocks would be found at the base of the glacier as its movement would tumble them over the centuries, like a gemologist polishes his stones in a polisher. Way above our heads on the side of the valley mountains, I noticed a road, and inquired as to why it was built so high up; what was it used for? The guide replied that several decades ago, that road had traveled alongside the top of the glacier. It was impossible to try and calculate how much ice had melted in such a short span of time. Again, I was told that if I fell into a crevasse while working on top of the glacier, my body would emerge several thousand years later. (What a comforting thought, knowing I wouldn't be trapped for all eternity.)

Due to location restrictions, time schedules, and weather, several close-up shots of John were continually postponed. As time flew by we never got his close-up on location. It was the last day of filming and we were back in the city on a warm, sunny day. Our problem: We needed a snowy background to complete John's tight shots. The solution: Truck into town from the mountains a couple tons of snow, enough to fill a parking lot. I prepared John in makeup as I had been doing for the past several months. For the shot John laid his head down onto the imported snow and the camera captured a few feet of film. The director yelled "Cut!" and we moved on. Suddenly I felt a chill creep up my spine; something was wrong. I pulled a Polaroid picture out of my pocket and glanced at the previous work that this new close-up had to match. There in my hand was the iceman's image with a large blood streak down the side of his face. I'd forgotten the blood. Would anybody notice? My second thought was, "Of course they would!" I had just created a great movie blooper.

I approached our director and admitted my error. Without blinking he requested the camera be brought back to reshoot the scene with the blood. I breathed a little easier until our outspoken hairstylist said, "If that was a Canadian who'd made that mistake, you would be all over their ass." Fred calmly turned to me and said, "Michael, f**k you," then turned back to the hairstylist and said, "Happy? Next shot."

Everyone has seen pictures of the Northern Lights that hang in the Canadian night skies, but few have personally experienced their wonder. While in Churchill, Manitoba, we were told by the locals that the shimmering lights might appear, as the weather conditions were perfect. I told the clerk at the lobby desk to call me if it was occurring.

The next morning she greeted me with "They appeared last night!" I said, "Why didn't you call me?" She responded, "I didn't want to wake you; it was after midnight."

"Call me anytime" was my reply. That night my phone rang about one a.m., and the voice said, "They're on." I quickly dressed in my arctic gear and stepped out into a freezing winter wonderland. Overhead, suspended in space, hung what looked like an undulating theatrical curtain lit in pastel colors, concealing a stage that was miles in length. Although the air was deathly still and no real sounds were audible, this was a great performance, accompanied in my mind with classical music. This is one of those natural wonders that you have to see yourself to truly grasp its magnificence.

Final makeup test for John Lone. *Universal Studios*

It's one thing to fall into a glacier, but I never thought going to dinner in Churchill was dangerous. Every night after returning from filming we would remove our arctic gear, clean up, and proceed to dinner. There were no restaurants on the hotel premises, so that meant dining at one of the local eateries down the street. By dinnertime the sun had set and the air temperatures were quickly dropping into the minuses. With the extreme cold setting in, it meant running, not walking, to dinner. None of us wanted to get back into our arctic gear. We all thought we were back in Southern California. As we made a mad dash several hundred yards downhill, you could feel the cold start to enter your body. The first person to reach the restaurant held the door open so the stampede could run through. Out of curiosity I asked the proprietor what would happen if by chance the restaurant was closed. His reply: "With the wind-chill factor, you probably wouldn't make it back up to the hotel." Great! I could see the headlines of the newspapers: "Movie Crew Found Frozen to Death in the Streets of Churchill, Manitoba."

During several of the frosty scenes in the film, the script called for the actors to have their faces, beards, eyebrows, and eyelashes laden down with crusty snow. They had to appear as if they'd been outside, exposed to a blizzard. The solution to this makeup trick was simple, as long as you could find the proper tools. I needed a hot plate, double boiler, a block of wax from the canning section of a supermarket, and an old-fashioned pump sprayer used to kill insects. The sprayer was almost impossible to find, but a local hardware store had two tucked away in the back room and were glad to get rid of them. I cut the wax in small chunks and inserted them into the canister, to be melted in the double boiler on the hot plate. Once the wax had reached its liquid state, the sprayer was ready to go. Holding it about a foot from Tim Hutton's face and pumping the handle, it emitted a mist of fine hot wax that on contact with the skin resembled a coat of frosty snow. At low altitudes, where I had always used this technique, it worked great; but at higher elevations, I received a horrible surprise. I'd set up my gear on top of a mountain. As the wax melted, pressure built in the canister; soon, a geyser shot up into the air, almost emptying the sprayer. At that moment more wax was not available, as Michele had been sent back to camp, and it was in her bag. I thought I was sunk, but with what little was left, I was able to accomplish a few sprays, and that was enough. If you could find one of those sprayers today, it would probably be in the Smithsonian.

As I write these thoughts in retrospect, the events come rushing back with clarity, as if they occurred just a short time ago.

Iceman received an Academy Award consideration, but the film *2010* was nominated in its place.

MASK, 1984

In 1983, twenty years into my career, I received a call from Universal, asking if I would be interested in discussing a project that was to be directed by Peter Bogdanovich. It was a film about a boy who's the victim of an extremely rare disorder known as *lionitis* in the vernacular, and medically, as *craniodiaphyseal dysplasia*. It causes calcium that is normally distributed throughout the body to be deposited in the skull, enlarging and distorting it, and placing an increasing amount of lethal pressure on the brain and other parts of the cranium. The film was the true story of Roy Lee "Rocky" Dennis, who had miraculously survived the condition to the age of sixteen.

The movie was to be called *Mask*, and I learned that Cher had been cast as the boy's mother, a hard-living member of a motorcycle gang who against the odds, including her own addiction, tried to make Rocky's life as fulfilling as possible.

While I was waiting to see Peter Bogdanovich at Universal, a fellow makeup artist emerged, looking a bit surprised to see me. We exchanged a few pleasantries and realized that we were part of a makeup artists' "cattle call."

Peter and I met for about an hour. He asked me a lot of questions, looked at my scrapbook, and then showed me a number of photographs of Rocky Dennis. I studied them for a moment and confidently said, "I can do it." I gave him a preliminary report on how I would go about achieving his likeness, and said, "When do we start?" I was given the job during that meeting, even though several other "cattle" were in line to be inspected. Thinking back on it now, I realized that had I not been selected, I would have missed one of the greatest rides of my life.

At the time I was still working on the set of *2010* at MGM Studios. A phone kept ringing on a far distant wall. A voice yelled out, "Hey, Westmore, phone!" I rushed across the stage and picked up the dangling phone. The voice on the other end said, "Hello, Michael? This is Frank Price." Mr. Price was the president of Universal Studios. He wanted to know if I could re-create with makeup the image of the disfigured boy known as Rocky Dennis for a new movie project titled *Mask*, and if so, could it be filmed in color? My answer: Yes, and Yes! That was all Universal Studios had to hear, and the film made history.

I was offered the use of Rocky's skull, which his mother had donated to Stanford University's medical school, but had plenty to go on with the collection of photographs I had been given (and still have). The first thing I had to do was to have a replica

Clay sculpting the detailed makeup forms under a magnifying glass for the Eric Stoltz role in *Mask*. *Universal Studios*

of Rocky's head sculpted and cast in wax. It was lifelike, with glass eyes and a red curly wig. This was the look we wanted to achieve. We began testing the makeup before any actor was hired, and my ever-patient son, Michael Jr., sat in as the test subject.

Rocky's appearance was typical of this affliction. He had a significantly enlarged skull with bone growth distorting his features. His eyes were three and a half inches apart.

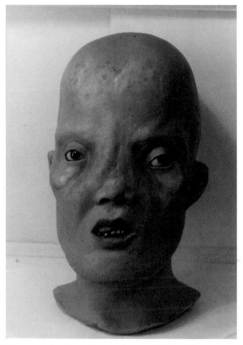

Prototype head sculpture of the real Rocky Dennis.
This was used as a reference guide for measurements.
Universal Studios

Eric Stoltz, the talented young actor who had been cast to play Rocky, had a narrow face and close-set eyes that were less than an inch apart, an added problem to be solved.

Cher was committed to the role of Rocky's mother. She was "The Money," and the studio would not have gone forward without the audience she would guarantee. When we were testing the makeup with my son, Cher was often present. To keep everything secret, the early film tests were conducted at my house in the hills above Studio City. An entire film crew would show up so Cher and the latest model head could be viewed together on camera. In the course of more than two months, we created eight separate versions of Rocky's makeup.

Early on, the face appliance was not as pliable as I wanted it to be, due to the nature of the foam latex that was the standard material at the time for such work. To allow more flexibility and stretch, I carved hollow pockets on the inside. What this actually did was to weaken the material, allowing for more movement.

The research and development period of *Mask* was as exciting and frustrating a film makeup project as I'd ever been involved in. With each of the eight makeovers, a new problem or two would arise that had to be solved. The head had to fit comfortably. The face had to be flexible and move with the actor's own expressions, without the use of outside cables or electronics. Among other remedies, the lower jaw was lined with a plastic plate that forced the jaw to open and close without a distorted stretch. I designed into the appliance a bridge that was one and three-quarters inches wide. It gave the illusion of greater width to the eyes; anything wider would have cut off Eric's vision.

The director exercised his authority, requesting that changes be made for one reason or another . . . taller, wider, longer, and so forth. One of the final problems was a wrinkle that appeared around his mouth and chin. One night I awoke in the dark, visualizing the solution. The next day I made a small patch about the size of a silver dollar and applied this over the wrinkle. In later years, my little trick became known as a "blender," something all special-effects makeup artists are familiar with today.

One detail plagued me, and I wanted desperately to solve it. The real Rocky Dennis's eyelids had a small droop to them that could not be achieved with just makeup. To test my possible solution, I glued down a strip of gauze directly under the middle of each of Michael's eyes and pulled the strip down, thus pulling Michael's lower lids down, and then fastened the lower end of the gauze to the

front of Michael's cheeks. This was a miniature version of the "facelift" I had applied to Shelley Winters's face two decades earlier. I had no worry about the gauze showing, since it would all be underneath the appliance. The effect was just what I had hoped for: a perfect match to Rocky's photographs. But ultimately, it was a failure; Michael was unable to blink enough to lubricate his eyes, and during filming, there wouldn't be enough time to administer eyedrops. Some tricks work and some don't. This one was abandoned.

With the eighth head we had accomplished all we could. When filming began, it would take three and a half hours to get Eric into makeup. The final touch of realism was the time-consuming application of freckles and acne blemishes.

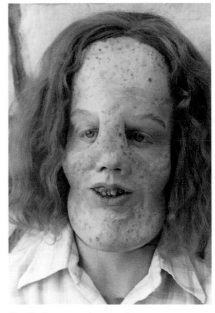

Eric Stoltz in completed makeup. *Universal Studios*

I was joined on this project by a dear friend and colleague, Zoltan Elek, another makeup artist with whom I had worked on the television special *The Day After*. His assignment was to make up Eric every morning and attend to him throughout the day.

Eric did his best to turn into Rocky. On set and off, he insisted on being called Rocky. He would even slip on a used appliance to enter and leave the studio every day.

Some of the filming was done in Rocky's old neighborhood. One day a local couple came up to Eric/Rocky and asked him where he'd been all this time. This was music to a makeup artist's ears.

One of Rocky's passions had been to write. When the filming came to an end, we each received a plaque with Rocky's favorite poem:

These things are good:
Ice cream and cake,
A ride on a Harley,
Seeing monkeys in the trees,
And the sun shining on my face.
These things are a drag:
Dust in my hair,
Holes in my shoes,
No money in my pocket,
And the sun shining on my face.

Mask received the 1985 Academy Award for makeup, the film's only nomination. I was saddened that Cher had not at least been nominated for best actress. She did, however, win the Golden Globe for Best Actress.

MY ACADEMY INITIATION, 1985

To be nominated for an Academy Award, candidates (in my case) have to run a gauntlet that begins with presentations to a Makeup Committee, comprised of a large group of entertainment professionals, mostly makeup artists. To this committee, scrapbooks and references are submitted for consideration. There is no limit on the number of submissions, but after numerous committee hearings, only a few are selected. In some instances, contenders will discuss various unique techniques and even proprietary methods they used to convey what it is that makes a particular makeup worthy of a nomination. On behalf of *Mask*, I explained all my pitfalls and solutions. Finally comes what is called the Bake-Off, when the committee eliminates all but three contenders up for consideration. The Academy sends out a ballot containing the nominees in all the award categories to the approximately (in 1985) 5,500 voting members. A luncheon was held at the Beverly Wilshire Hotel, and after that, it's nail-biting time until the night of the awards.

This was the fourth year the award for makeup was presented. Until 1981 there had been no such category. On a few occasions special makeup awards had been given. My uncle Ern won a special award for the film *Cimarron* in 1931, and Jack Pierce won in 1932 for *The Mummy*. In 1964, a special Oscar went to William Tuttle for *The Seven Faces of Dr. Lao*, and three years later, John Chambers garnered one for *Planet of the Apes*. In 1980, there was still no individual category. I was presented to the Board of Governors of the Academy, this for my work in creating all the makeup and special effects in *Raging Bull*. John Chambers wrote a letter to Fay Kanin, president of the Academy at that time, saying that Mr. Westmore had done one of the most outstanding jobs of research, creation, and application of a difficult makeup in his memory, and that each of De Niro's four faces were virtually undetectable as a makeup—the highest compliment an audience can bestow on a member of my profession. But even with Chambers's accolade, the effort was doomed.

Raging Bull was honored with two Academy Awards. When Robert De Niro was presented with Best Actor, he thanked me during his acceptance speech. That moment was very special for me, as it was years earlier when Paul Muni had thanked my uncle Perc when accepting his Oscar.

Not long after the awards that year, my phone rang late one afternoon. I answered it, and a voice said, "Hi, Michael, this is Fay Kanin. How would you like to become a member of the Academy?" Until Fay had become president of the Academy in 1979, there hadn't been much enthusiasm to establish an annual makeup award. In fact, an old, half-serious objection began to circulate again. Why should the Academy give an award every year for makeup, seeing as a Westmore would probably win it? Fay Kanin was an accomplished screenwriter, playwright, and producer. She was aware of all the press requesting a special award be given for the *Raging Bull* makeup. Even Stallone was pushing for my makeup as a special category award. In any event, when Fay asked me on the phone if I would like to be a member, I asked, "What do I have to do?" She said, "Send me a check for the annual dues, and I'll send you your membership card."

So far as I know, no one else has become a member of the Academy without passing the ritual application process and voting test. I am still Number 6235, and every year I get to make my personal selections for Best in Show in each category.

A NIGHT AT THE OSCARS, 1985

Have you ever imagined how it would feel to attend the Academy Awards?

About three p.m. on that day in 1985, a long, black stretch limousine pulled up to our house with a cold bottle of champagne in an ice bucket. After a short ride, the limousine arrived at the Shrine Auditorium, and Marion and I stepped out on what is surely the most famous red carpet on the planet. Row after row of movie fans line the red carpet each year, hoping for a glimpse at the who's who of Hollywood. In front of us were countless celebrities. I noticed that many of the men, when asked who they were wearing, had to open their jackets and read the label.

Of course there are degrees of celebrity. There are two noticeable groupings: those above the line, and those below it. Producers, directors, and performers are all above the line; everyone else is below. We below-the-line nominees for such things as makeup slip behind the celebrity interviews and keep moving. One often hears a not-so-sotto-voce question: "Who's that?" And the answer: "That's nobody." Owing to my daughter McKenzie's success on television and my eighteen years designing the characters on *Star Trek*, I occasionally hear someone say, "Hi, Mr. Westmore." But for the most part, we below-the-liners enter the star-studded building unmolested, and go on the hunt for our assigned seats.

Seats are assigned for very good reasons. Once a person has won, the cameraman has to be able to find the winner instantaneously. Also, you don't want a winner to have to hike from the rear of the vast theater (or worse, from the balcony) to the stage. That would waste time and make for pretty boring TV. Marion and I have attended the Academy Awards five times when I've been among the nominees, and in each case we were allotted seats about a third of the way back from the front row—not up front, but not so far back as to waste time were we to win. I don't mean to sound negative, but that's just how the game is played.

I reflected on the two other nominees for Makeup. The first was the ever-popular Oprah Winfrey film, *The Color Purple*, which had amassed eleven nominations. The second was *Remo Williams: The Adventure Begins*, which contained a masterful Asian makeup created by Carl Fullerton. I would not have felt defeated losing to him, only disappointed.

Once we'd found our seats, we sat silently in the crowded auditorium, trying to look cool. In fact, most nominees are close to hyperventilating until their category is announced. Your heart begins to pound so loudly you imagine it might be audible, and breathing is practically nonexistent. As the three nominees in my category were announced, I developed a mighty urge to make a run to the men's room, but it was too late. Our presenter Teri Garr opened the envelope and announced, "And the award for best makeup goes to Michael Westmore and Zoltan Elek, for *Mask*."

There was a pause of disbelief before I realized that it was really my name Ms. Garr had announced. Zoltan and I had won! I planted a big kiss on Marion and the two of us

Oscar photo with Teri Garr, Zolton, and myself. *Academy of Motion Pictures Arts and Sciences, reprinted with permission*

looked at each other in amazement. She dug her fingernails into my thigh and I stood up. Moving down the aisle, I trod on many shoes with few apologies. Zoltan and I ran up the stairs and we received our awards. Zoltan did not wish to speak, so that task fell to me.

Your thank-yous are just a fleeting moment. You are ushered backstage to meet the press and the photographers, and answer such profound questions as "What does it feel like to win?"

The entire event, from the announcement of your name to the return to your seat, is a highlight of anyone's life, no matter how many times you have been nominated or won.

At this point you begin to realize that the Oscar itself, which you have been swinging around, is not an insubstantial thing. It weighs eight pounds. It can be a problem to find your way back to your seat. You realize you are passing by figures lurking in the shadows along the aisles, men in tuxedos and women in evening gowns. They have been hired by the Academy to fill any seats that have been abandoned. It would not be proper for the television cameras to pick up any empty seats. But after an award has been announced, the just-nice-to-be-nominated folk often leave their seats and proceed down the stairs to the bar. There lies consolation in the form of toasts and expletives.

Following the night's ceremony is the official Oscar dinner that few stars attend for any length of time. Marion and I have always found this to be most rewarding, as we meet new people and are treated to gourmet dining. I confess to hoping for a no-show or two at our table, as that means an extra dessert—another form of celebration.

When it was over that night, we got back in the limo. Once inside, we settled into the plush black leather seats with our new golden houseguest. The passing streetlights glistened off our prize as we began to realize the awesome fact that he was ours. We'd won!

Full realization wouldn't occur until the next morning, when no one came to take him away. He now stands in our living room, a proud symbol of a lot of hard work and of my family heritage. For all time, the Motion Picture Academy records will read "1985 Best Makeup: *Mask*."

The next day I gave an interview from my home. I spoke about how thrilling it was to be recognized this way. I realized that I was the first Westmore to be officially recognized by the Academy. In my heart I felt I had accepted the Oscar on behalf of all the Westmores whose talents had graced the silver screen for so many decades, well before there was a makeup category. I was suddenly overcome with my family's history of excellence, including *Gone with the Wind*. I had to stop the interview when I broke down, crying.

ELIZABETH TAYLOR

One afternoon, I received a phone call inquiring whether I was available and interested in interviewing with Elizabeth to be her makeup artist. When my heart stopped pounding in my chest, I casually agreed.

I arrived at her house early and had time to wander through the living room, viewing the works of art adorning the walls. With a degree in art history, my eyes were bulging. These were not simple decorations but serious works of art. The only other private residence I had seen like this was Greer Garson's penthouse.

When Elizabeth came out to greet me, we chatted about art and the Westmores. The next thing I knew, I had the position. Over the next two years, I followed her to all of her engagements. Most of the time she preferred to get ready at her house rather than drive to the location first.

What was so refreshing about Elizabeth was that when you were with her, you really felt like a part of her family. On the set her trailer was always open, and there was a constant stream of visiting celebrities. I saw a wide range of guests coming out of her trailer, including the always-exuberant Sammy Davis Jr., the shy Bob Dylan, the suave Roddy McDowall, the ever-so-humorous George Hamilton, and an Indian guru. Her list of famous friends was endless. She had a genuine love for everyone, and anyone who has ever been in her presence loves her.

One morning at work, she asked me, "What do you want for lunch?" Earlier we had been talking about chili, since my wife and I had competed in several sanctioned chili competitions for the International Chili Society. Elizabeth decided we must have Chasen's chili. Chasen's was one of Hollywood's most prestigious restaurants, and its chili was often ordered by the rich and famous. They would deliver all over the world.

Elizabeth and me. *Courtesy of the author*

When the chili arrived, Elizabeth had also ordered a fresh Maui onion, which she personally chopped into little pieces. We devoured a whole quart of this famous chili in no time. If you want to join in my memory, here is the recipe as told to me.

Elizabeth Taylor's Chasen's Chili

½ pound dried pinto beans
5 cups canned tomatoes, in juice
1 large green bell pepper, chopped
1½ tablespoon vegetable oil
3 cups onion, chopped
2 cloves crushed garlic
½ cup chopped parsley
½ cup butter
2½ pounds beef chuck (chili grind)
1 pound pork shoulder, ground
$1/3$ cup chili powder
1 tablespoon salt
1½ teaspoon black pepper
1½ teaspoon ground cumin
corn flour (masa), optional

1. Prepare the dried pinto beans, following the directions printed on the package. Do this in a Dutch oven. When they are tender, drain off any liquid and set aside.
2. Stir the tomatoes with their juice into the beans and simmer for five minutes. In a large heated frying pan, add the oil and green pepper; sauté for five to six minutes. Add the onion and cook until translucent; continue to stir. Then add the garlic and parsley, blending this mixture for several minutes. Add the vegetable mixture into the beans.
3. Using the same large pan, melt the butter. Then add the beef and pork, cooking until brown and crumbly. Drain off any liquid. Combine the meat with the bean mixture, including the salt, pepper, cumin, and chili powder. Note: I prefer to add the spices to the butter when it is melting; watch it so it doesn't burn.
4. Bring to a boil, cover the pot, and reduce to a simmer, for at least one hour. Remove the cover and continue to simmer for thirty minutes or more. Skim the fat from the top before serving. To thicken the chili, add a couple of tablespoons of corn flour (masa) mixed with warm water; stir into mixture.
5. Serve with shredded cheese, tortillas, and chopped onion, especially when it's prepared by Elizabeth.

This is the stuff of which Hollywood legends are made. Rumor has it that back when Elizabeth was filming *Cleopatra* in Rome, she craved the chili made at Chasen's so much that she was willing to pay $100 just to have the order shipped to her. For years the recipe remained a closely guarded secret. It seemed the owner David Chasen came to the restaurant every Sunday to privately cook up a batch, which he would freeze for the week, believing that the chili was best when reheated.

Elizabeth was a lady of surprises. She loved to receive gifts and she also enjoyed giving them. Thanks to the 1994 Northridge earthquake, I only have one lone survivor of a dozen Baccarat crystal glasses, a Christmas gift from Elizabeth that we treasured.

How would you like to receive a gift a day? One of the TV movies that I accompanied Elizabeth on, she received a gift a day. Either it was in her contract, or the producer was just intimidated by her; whatever the reason, a nice gift arrived every morning, including pieces of jewelry. Some were deemed "okay," while others received a comment like "Isn't that nice!" It's important to note that Elizabeth owned some of the most magnificent jewelry in the world; even the Queen of England might have been envious. Her collection included a thirty-three-carat diamond, a royal diamond brooch, and a set of brilliant emeralds. From Richard Burton she received a famous pearl and a sixty-nine-carat diamond.

I was in her trailer touching her up one day when a package arrived. It was from an East Indian admirer. She was excited to receive a gift from such an exotic location. Inside was a matching set of gold jewelry set with precious stones, including a necklace, bracelets, and rings. The style of the jewelry reminded me of something that would have come from a mystical Far East temple. There was enough precious gold and stones to weigh a person down when adorned with its brilliance. When I first saw it, it didn't seem real, as it was too beautiful to comprehend. Of course, she had to model all of it before placing it back into the box before we left for the stage, happy, and late as usual. (The Queen of the Nile couldn't be hurried, especially if the phone rang and she wanted to talk.)

Elizabeth and Richard Burton had purchased a house in Puerto Vallarta while they were filming *Night of the Iguana*. Out of the blue, she said to me, "Please take Marion and go vacation in my house in Mexico. Everything is there!" This was the real deal, and I regret never taking her up on her offer!

In Elizabeth's house, her makeup and dressing room was right next to her bedroom, in which she had a large cockatoo perched on a stand. When we were getting Elizabeth ready, George Hamilton came to visit and the bird appeared out of nowhere. He was traveling from person to person until he landed on my shoulder. Little did I know, he liked earlobes, and mine became his appetizer of the day as he sank his beak into it. How many times have you said "It's okay—it doesn't hurt," as you muffle your screams and tears of pain run down your cheeks!

George was a humorous and frequent friend of hers. Being a good storyteller, he told me that in his early days, while working in a restaurant, he had a need for a turkey. So upon leaving for the night, he stuffed a frozen one down his pants. Before he could get out the door, he was called back. The next time you see him, have him tell you the rest of the story, with all of the facial expressions and body language only a defrosting turkey can inflict.

Elizabeth always knew what she wanted, and that included how she wanted her lighting to be handled. When I accompanied her on filmed interviews, she would always tell the lighting director exactly how she wanted to be lit, to ensure the most natural appearance. She taught me the placement of the seating and the height and position of the lights. Later, I taught this method to Stallone, and on a publicity junket to New York he sent me ahead to change the lighting that a photographer had spent days setting up. I could never quite hear what the lighting director was saying about my suggestions, as they snarled the new directions in hushed tones and foreign languages.

Just after the new year of 1992 I received an invitation in the mail to attend Elizabeth's sixtieth birthday bash, to be held at Disneyland, California, on February 27 at eight p.m. Marion and I didn't hesitate to affirmatively respond. Andy Warhol was a friend of hers, and did a painting of colored boxes that alternated between Mickey Mouse and Elizabeth's famous image. The picture adorned the invitation, the program, and our party gifts. Only the napkins imprinted with her name came in one signature color, violet. On the wall behind her makeup and hair vanity hung an original Warhol. It had to have been a daily reminder to her of his artistic genius. The names of the invitees read like a who's who of Hollywood. The invitation also said: "Dress for fun—jeans, très casual. Adult children only, please."

At the time of the party I was on assignment to *Star Trek* at Paramount Studios. As usual I didn't get away from work as early as I had anticipated. I rushed down the Hollywood freeway to our home in Studio City to pick up Marion. We headed south during rush-hour traffic to make it to the Happiest Place on Earth. On a good day it takes at least an hour to drive the one-way trip. As we parked the car at the park and hurriedly jumped out, I heard a familiar voice calling, "Hello, Michael!" It was Roddy McDowall, a longtime friend of the Westmore family.

As we entered Disneyland we were greeted by a sea of celebrity faces. It looked like the Academy Awards. The program announced: "Welcome to the Happiest Birthday on Earth! Tonight is a night of fantasy. Step through Sleeping Beauty Castle and join us for an enchanting evening of entertainment, fine food, spirits, and magical adventures. Here, no one is grumpy and everyone is happy. We're celebrating Elizabeth's 60th birthday!" The program went on to say, "All of our buffets have character. There is Mickey's All-American Barbecue, King Louie's Feast, Ariel's Gourmet Grotto, and Pinocchio's Pasta Villa. Eat as much as you like as you wander the attractions in Fantasyland and visit the enchanting shops and boutiques."

While taking in all the sights, we came across a former acquaintance, David Bowie, and his wife Iman, between the spinning carousel and "Mr. Toad's Wild Ride." In front of "It's a Small World," the familiar face of Shirley MacLaine came into focus, and we shared memories. What was so amazing that night was that we all shared a common thread between us, and that was our love for and the life of Elizabeth, who I think knew everyone on earth.

The Storybook Finale was scheduled for 10:45 p.m. The program said "Join us at Sleeping Beauty Castle forecourt for birthday cake, a champagne toast, magical surprises, and a fireworks spectacular." It all happened. Everything I could carry away from that night is safely stored away. It includes two Warhol sweatshirts that Marion and I wore the next day. We had to answer a lot of questions, because the event had been highly publicized. Also stored are the invitations, the program, and a bottle of Elizabeth's perfume. The best souvenir of all is a piece of Elizabeth's chocolate birthday cake with a violet flower on top. The next day I took it to a plastic impression shop and had them suspend it inside of a clear plastic block. The man did warn me that he couldn't guarantee perfection, and he was right. From the pressure of the process my cake is one inch thick and the flower is blue. I even kept several of the violet napkins with her name printed in the corner. These are all treasures.

The application that impresses me the most about Elizabeth's makeup were her eyebrows. They were styled in the perfect classical eyebrow shape my uncle Perc created in the 1940s, which makeup artists are still using today because it is the most natural and timeless style.

Uncle Perc, who was at Warner Bros. for more than thirty years, used to say, "Your eyes are the windows to your soul." Therefore a woman's eye makeup, including eyebrows, tells something about the inner person.

If you would like to re-create this famous style, the secret steps that were passed down through the family are revealed on the next page.

It has always been reported that Elizabeth had very unique violet eyes, and she never refuted this. One day when I was applying her eye makeup, not wanting to stare too deeply, I mentioned the violet eyes. I stopped my makeup when she exclaimed, "Mike,

SHAPING AND COLORING THE EYEBROWS

The shaping of the eyebrow is extremely important because in their very shape and contour, eyebrows dramatically express emotions. A raised brow denotes surprise, while a drooping brow expresses sadness. From these examples, it's easy to understand why a natural brow style is most effective.

I recommend that people of all complexions, when in doubt as to which color to use, start with a soft gray pencil. To begin, lightly use it to mark out the basic shape. Then go over this with fine hairline strokes, using a color that matches the natural hair. If the natural hair color is very light, the gray pencil will suffice.

The following is a general pattern which may be used as a guide for creating a natural brow.

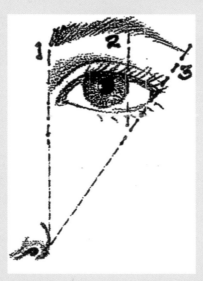

1. Always brush and draw the eyebrows in the direction of the natural growth of hair.
2. Begin the eyebrow by envisioning an imaginary line along the outside of the nose and the inside of the eye. This is point 1. It should also be the widest part of the brow.
3. Look straight ahead and envision an imaginary line up from the outside edge of the iris. This is where the arch will be. Be sure to taper the brow all the way from point 1 to point 2.
4. Envision another imaginary line from the corner of the nose beyond the outside corner of the eye. At an angle of 45 degrees, down from point 2, is point 3. This is where the brow should end in a very fine, soft taper.

Note: If your eyebrow pencils are too soft, place them in the freezer or dip them in a glass of ice water for a few minutes.

look into my eyes." From six inches away I focused deep and long for several seconds, and then she said, "What color are they?"

Makeup Man Appears On-Camera

Malice in Wonderland was a book and a television movie based on the real lives of powerful Hollywood gossip columnists Hedda Hopper and Louella Parsons. They were once great friends and later great rivals. Elizabeth Taylor was cast to play Louella, and Jane Alexander, Hedda.

In 1985 Elizabeth asked me to be her personal makeup artist on this film about the war of the columnists. It seemed strange to be with Elizabeth and not Jane, as I'd been her makeup artist on *Eleanor and Franklin*.

The historical period for the film was the 1930s and '40s. Before production commenced, I was reading the script and noticed a small part for a makeup artist. The scene called for the artist to be making up Louella when Hedda storms into the room and accuses the artist of jumping ship, and Louella, of stealing her dressing room. He had been her personal makeup artist before Louella pulled some tricks. That's what it felt like to me in reality.

I asked Elizabeth if I could be considered for this nonspeaking part. The scene called for the actor to react to Jane with a sheepish grin.

My father Monte had been a makeup artist during this period, so I brought in a picture of him. Wardrobe dressed me in a similar fashion. He and I both wore caps, an argyle sweater, knee-high pants, and long stockings. I even had makeup applied and my hair styled. I played my part brilliantly, with my "I've been caught" expression. The scene was complete except for a close-up of me. Gloria Swanson said to DeMille in *Sunset Boulevard*, "I'm ready for my close-up, Mr. DeMille." I was greeted with, "We can't do your close-up because we are out of time." Out of time! That might have been my moment of discovery! Dreams are what make Hollywood and my job exciting.

Malice in Wonderland was not without tragedy. For Elizabeth, love, loyalty, and generosity were her life's passion. A dear friend in need, a member of the Rat Pack and a relative of President Kennedy, Peter Lawford, needed an emotional pick-me-up. Elizabeth arranged for Peter to come in as an actor for a few days to feel the warm lights and to stand in front of the camera. I was told to take care of him. He arrived early Friday morning. I noticed his skin and eyes had a strange yellow pallor. I sat him in my makeup chair and proceeded to warm the color of his skin with concealers and foundation. After makeup, hair, and wardrobe, Peter was called to set to rehearse the scene.

Following the rehearsal the director called me over. "What can you do about Peter's eyes?" he asked me. Upon closer examination, I saw that the whites of his eyes and pupils were bright yellow. If I'd had time, contact lenses could have been made to correct the situation. Adding to our color problem was the fact that Peter was having trouble remembering his lines. I have seen this situation before; the more the performer tries to remember, it only gets worse as frustration sets in. It was so noticeable that Peter's performance couldn't even be pieced together in the editing room. Elizabeth stood by him all day with words of encouragement. At the end of Friday's work everyone knew he was not going to be able to complete the few days' work for which he was needed. Elizabeth told me she was personally going to call him over the weekend.

When we arrived at work on Monday, there was no Peter. He had passed away over the weekend, on December 24, 1984. No one knew how close he'd been to his final day on earth. The film crew and Elizabeth mourned the loss of another friend and Hollywood icon.

On March 23, 2011, while listening to the many news reports profiling Elizabeth's death, one thought kept recurring. Yes, she was a leader in the fight against HIV, and yes, Rock Hudson was her dear friend and fellow thespian in health and sickness. But one name was never mentioned, and I feel he was a very early inspiration that led to her devotion to personally fighting the cause for the disease. When I first started to travel with Elizabeth, she had an incredible assistant and friend named Roger who was always by her side; wherever we went, he was always there. During one photo shoot they had been expecting an army of forty to accompany her. Instead, it was only Elizabeth, Roger, and me. Roger was the first person I personally knew who passed away with HIV, and I am sure his death inspired Elizabeth to use her reputation and inspiration to honor Roger's memory.

Elizabeth commanded so much respect in life as well as death that no one who knew her personally would think of referring to her as "Liz." *Elizabeth* is her trademark, and to say her name meant the one and only. As I was writing my autobiographical notes years ago, I found that even when my pen touched paper, I couldn't bring myself to abbreviate her name. I had to write out "Elizabeth" every time. She will always be Dame Elizabeth to me.

THE CLAN OF THE CAVE BEAR, 1986

The Clan of the Cave Bear started out as a sixteen-hour miniseries for television and ended up as a feature film. I had been involved with this project since its inception.

When it became a feature film, Michael Chapman, director of photography on *Raging Bull*, had been assigned as director. We knew each other well, understanding each other's thought processes, so it made communication between us easy. While the hundreds of pages that fill the novel intertwine plots and subplots, ours was simple: A young Cro-Magnon woman is raised by a group of Neanderthals.

To ensure that my makeup was as authentic as possible, I visited with the curator of the Los Angeles County Museum. When I told him about my project, he invited me into the back room where most everything is carefully stored. I asked to see a real Neanderthal skull; he pulled out several deep drawers and there before me was a whole tribe, men, women, and children. I was then able to hold and feel the difference between modern man, Neanderthal, and Cro-Magnon. I could see that the forehead protruded, the skull was elongated, the jaw was powerful, and the large teeth were used for tearing and grinding. My next step was to duplicate this in rubber and make a wig.

Neanderthal makeup. *Warner Brothers*

A very expensive test wig was constructed using yak hair. The test was great for authenticity but had the reality of a budget. They couldn't afford wigs that cost $3,000 each. A less-expensive version was made in Canada for $300. When possible the actors were asked to grow their own facial hair. If not, I had false beards and mustaches ready to go.

There were many latex foreheads, noses, and plastic teeth to prepare, so my little lab in Los Angeles went to work. It was felt by the powers that be that the actual Neanderthal brow ridge protruded too much and would hide the eyes of the actors. While fabricating, I significantly reduced this area, along with historical reality. For all the speaking performers I hand-crafted dirty and chipped false teeth they could pop in or out of their mouths during the day. For some strange reason these performers broke more false teeth than any other performers had done on previous projects I'd worked on. At the close of each day, one, two, or ten of my Neanderthals would approach me with a clenched fist to say "Sorry," opening a dirty palm to reveal their false teeth in pieces. As the sun went down each day I would pray for just a few broken sets, as I couldn't go to dinner until all had been repaired for the next day.

Daryl Hannah played Ayla, the Cro-Magnon woman. She is as kind and sweet as she appears. Film crews bond for life, and Daryl and I are still friends today. Years later when she was attending film school in New York, she called me for a favor. She was producing a short film and needed a prop arm to go into a refrigerator. My reply: Right or left? It was in the mail shortly thereafter. What was my payment? She knew my weakness: a tin of chocolate chip cookies.

James Remar played the part of Creb, the wise old one that had one eye gouged out by a bear. James was my daily makeup responsibility. Actors must suffer for their art; along with only one eye to maneuver, we also fitted one of his legs into a fiberglass cast, holding it in a contorted position when he walked. This was worn all day, six days a week. James is a trooper.

Zug, "the storyteller," was portrayed by Tony Montanaro. He was a professional

mime, had a school on the East Coast, and personally knew Marcel Marceau. His ability to convey a story with his hands and voice was amazing. His main performance in the film was to tell stories at tribal gatherings by the use of his hands. Tony was a great teacher; he taught me how to walk my hands across an imaginary pane of glass, and that is how we would greet each other every day, along with a laugh. Zug's

Neanderthal Zoug wearing a latex bald cap.
Warner Brothers

bald latex head was my one and only chance to re-create the actual Neanderthal skull as we know it. Tony was meticulous, and didn't break his teeth (very often)!

There is a scene where a brave warrior is killed by a bear, so the shamans cut off the top of his head and eat his brains. Just another day at the office. To prepare for this, a copy of his head made of wax was sent to my Vancouver apartment. I propped it up in front of my large kitchen window where the light was best. I proceeded to cut off the top of the head and paint it. On the stove I cooked up edible gelatin brains. Looking out my window, I realized that I had drawn quite an audience from the apartments across the street. What is one to do but wait for the police? I guess no one seemed to care even if I was actually cutting someone apart, as the police didn't show up.

Another of our locations was on an island. The scene consisted of many Neanderthal clans gathering to pay homage to the bear, and many makeup artists and hairstylists had to be transported to the island. We would leave the docks every morning at three a.m., along with the actors. It was still dark out, the sky and water pitch black, and we

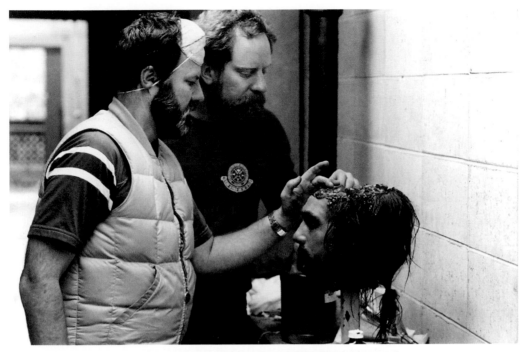

Prepping a wax head of a dead Neanderthal for *Clan of the Cave Bear*. *Warner Brothers*

had to cross the Strait of Juan de Fuca against the current. Since Canada is a logging country, huge tree trunks were continually crossing our path. The captain kept a steady eye and a light on the water. I inquired, "What would happen if we hit one of those bobbing rams?" He shouted over the engine noise, "We'd sink." Oh great! I can see it now: "Movie Crew Sinks Off British Columbia—No Survivors." With the speed of the current, we would end up in San Diego. (Boy, would Marion be mad if I went to San Diego without her.)

This was the only movie where I rode to work almost every day in a helicopter, twenty minutes to and from our base camp. The exterior cave scenes were filmed high in the mountains of British Columbia. The cast and crew enjoyed quite a ride to our beautiful and desolate location. Every day after completing our makeup applications, we

The wax head close up. *Warner Brothers*

would pack up the supplies we needed on the mountain and climb into the whirling machine as if going to war. The engines were so loud that once inside, everyone had to wear ear protection that looked like giant earmuffs. Our ride to the mountain was like the "Soarin' Around the World" ride at Disneyland. We passed over natural wonders, rushing rivers, bright blue lakes, crystal glaciers, craggy mountain peaks covered in snow, and lush green valleys. If we wanted to enjoy these beautiful sights, our flight captain would quickly bring us back to reality with a warning: "Never approach the tail of the helicopter with its rotating blades." A mistake like this can cost you your head, which is what happened to Boris Sagal, a famous director who was not paying attention.

At another location a campsite was set up at the foot of a glacier, with all the amenities of home. Again the entire cast and crew were flown in and dropped off in the middle of nowhere. The campsite was located next to a rushing stream that emanated from the foot of the melting glacier. At night we would be lulled to sleep by the sound of cascading water as it poured down the mountain. We ate like kings, gourmet food for breakfast, lunch, and dinner, and watched the most recent videos for evening entertainment. A loaded rifle was always at the ready behind the kitchen, as a Kodiak bear or mountain lion could at any time invite itself in for a meal.

Talk about bathroom humor; I laugh about it now, and we laughed about it then. Our sanitary facilities consisted of about six cloth-covered outhouses, the kind you find at large sporting events. As the days progressed it became impossible to sit in your enclosed tent, as the odor became unbearable. The only way to survive the chamber of death after you sat down was to poke your head out of the front flap. So this was the picture: Six heads, men and women, all chatting away while taking their morning constitutional. All personal modesty was lost after the second day. One might ask, "Why didn't anyone hike into the woods for privacy?" Well, remember the old saying, "Does a bear shit in the woods?" The answer is yes!

In our glacier camp we slept four to a tent; Michele Burke, Todd McIntosh, Maurice Parkhurst, and I called this home. It was like living in a refrigerator with the door closed. We all slept in thermal underwear, tucked nicely into toasty, fluffy sleeping bags. Once in, you never wanted to get out. Early morning always seemed to arrive too soon, and someone had to start up our heater and lantern. The job of "lamp lighter" became my responsibility. The others were afraid of burning our tent down.

Saving the ecology of Canada was practiced there long before Al Gore. All around our exterior cave entrance was untouched tundra, and Canada wanted to keep it that way. With so many of us walking back and forth, it wouldn't have taken long to trample nature into the ground. To solve the problem, existing natural pathways had to be traveled, even if it was the long way around. Wooden walkways were constructed and suspended over the delicate tundra. The rule: We had to leave it like we found it, and the park service was there to enforce it.

An audience viewing the movie would accept this make-believe Hollywood representation as a genuine depiction of primitive grunts and movement. Behind the scenes, the producers and the director wanted the characters to be as authentic as possible, so experts were hired to teach our actors the art of being a living, breathing Neanderthal. From studying past skeletal remains and primitive cultures of today, our experts were able to infuse into our actors what was once our living past.

Peter Elliot was hired to teach body movement. He had a reputation as one of the best in the business when it came to choreographing proper animal motion. Peter taught the actors how a real Neanderthal might have physically moved as they swayed in a bow-legged fashion. Lou Fant, an expert fluent in primitive sign language, developed the hand gestures of The Clan. The other experts were vocal coaches Maggie Damon, Deborah LaGorce Kramer, and Tony Montanaro. Their assignment was to make sure every performer was on the same page for tonality and audible expressions, including grunts.

Many months later a few shots were planned to be filmed in Los Angeles. A large, stinky, and distressed buffalo hide to be worn by one of the characters was sent from Canada to the United States. US Customs believed the buffalo had been treated inhumanely and killed recently, despite its obvious appearance as an old moth-eaten piece of rank junk. Believe it or not, it took a while to convince Customs of the latter, and they insisted the hide be returned to its point of origin when we were finished. Thank God!

After all was said and done, in 1987 I received my third Oscar nomination for this film, along with Michele Burke.

PSYCHO III, 1986

Norman Bates is still running the motel and Mother is still rocking in her favorite chair. This time, Norman falls in love with a mentally unstable nun. Mother orders her son Norman back into being his old serial-killer self.

Anthony Perkins was to wear two hats in this film: He was to be the star as well as the director. To pay homage to the original *Psycho* and *Psycho II*, Tony and Universal Studios tried to put together as much of the original film crew as possible. By 1986 everyone still living and available to work the grueling hours had scattered to the four corners of the earth. I worked under the shadow of the old *Psycho* house that stood ominously on top of the hill. My uncle Bud had supervised the original makeup, and my mother was involved as a hairstylist. I was the next Westmore to represent the family in Norman's world.

I met with Tony so we could discuss all his scripted needs. They included a whole new "Mother," a woman who slits her wrists and bleeds out in a bathtub, an arm in an ice machine, and a woman with a bloated face, floating in the water.

At the end of the film Tony wanted to take Mother's sawdust-stuffed head and place it on the kitchen table. He would than take up a large French carving knife and destroy it violently, until it was shredded. Sawdust filled the air like a dust storm. I only made two heads, so I was glad when he was happy with his performance on head number one. The skin on the heads was made with silicone, so the head disintegrated just like Tony wanted.

The bathtub scene was a once-in-a-lifetime challenge. I had to attach mini hand-made metal sprinklers to the inside of the actress's wrists. Connected to the sprinklers were long lengths of clear plastic tubing through which I could pump fake blood. To disguise all this on her arm, it was covered with a latex skin. During the scene the actress is sitting in the tub and she lowers her wrists below the water. She makes a motion with a dull razor blade to slit her wrists. I asked Tony how much blood he wanted, and he said, "Spurting!" I pumped so hard on my blood source that the blood shot out of the holes high enough to cover the bathroom walls, and especially me. There must have been a misconception in semantics. Tony said, "Not a fountain; more like a pulsating flow." To do what Tony requested I needed to make the holes in the two sprinklers larger. My son Michael took our actress back to the makeup trailer for "metal surgery." I held her wrist steady on the arm of the makeup chair and Michael took a micro drill and widened the holes. One slip with the drill and with the force behind it, it would have buried itself into her arm. It did slip on the first try, but my reactions were so fast that I actually caught it before it touched her skin. Michael's and my eyes met but we didn't say a word. The second time was perfect. By now the bathroom set had been cleaned up. Our girl got back into the tub and the blood began to flow.

In another scene, after a young woman is murdered she is stuffed into an outdoor ice machine. Tony's first thought was to place the real girl into the ice. Goose bumps, shivering, and hypothermia were not an option. My advice was to make a silicone arm that resembled hers, and that's what I did. When it was time to film I shoved the arm down into the ice. Our silicone arm had no physical reaction to either the cold or union rules.

My underwater bloated girl was more difficult, as we didn't have all the waterproof glues, paints, and materials that are available today. I constructed her fake face with foam latex, glued it onto her skin with spirit gum, and sealed it all over with a liquid plastic—all of which does not remain intact after a long soaking. As our actress remained submerged for a period of time, her face began to grow as it absorbed water like a sponge sitting in the kitchen sink. Its swelling was to my advantage, but I was more thrilled at the end of the day when I wrung out what appeared to be a pint of water.

It is never too late to learn new tricks, and Tony Perkins showed me a technique for bringing a healthy glow into a man's face. On the first day when I had finished his makeup, he said, "Let me show you a little makeup trick." He took the dry suntone blusher and a wide blusher brush. He whisked the brush across the makeup and applied it lightly to his frontal bone above his eyebrows, the tip of his nose, and the point of his chin. These are areas where blush is not regularly applied to women, but on a man it brings color and life to the skin. From that day on whenever I was applying makeup to a man, I always invoked the Anthony Perkins technique.

I will always remember standing on the backlot of Universal Studios on a moonlit night, watching Mother rock back and forth in her mechanical chair in the upper window of the Bates home. I thought of the original *Psycho* film crew, including my mother, that had been doing this same thing in 1960. In 1986 the motel was still open for business.

ROXANNE, 1986

In 1986 Fred Schepisi asked me to design and create test noses for Steve Martin's newly written whimsical comedy entitled *Roxanne*. The story is lightly based on the original love-triangle theme of *Cyrano de Bergerac*, with the imposing legendary proboscis. Steve's comedic version is nestled in a quaint little town that resembles a Norman Rockwell painting. Martin is the fire chief with the sensitive nose, and our heroine is Daryl Hannah, an astronomer.

Many people are under the impression that comedians are always switched on, like a refrigerator light when the door is opened. When I was around Jonathan Winters and Robin Williams, they were always ready with a joke (or twelve). I found that in person, Steve was just the opposite. He was quiet, delivered intelligent input as to his character in *Roxanne*—no wisecracks, no jokes—business with a smile.

Every step of the process had to be approved, so sculpting a clay nose for Steve's "show-and-tell" day was not as easy as it may sound. The sculpture had to be straight, not too thick or too thin, not too large or too small, and it had to physically balance with his face. Every surface of the clay had to be perfect. I knew what I had to do, but no one could decide on how far the latex nose should extend. I created six different versions. On individual plaster casts of Steve's nose there was one sculpture that was a quarter of an inch long, another, a half-inch long, another, three-quarters of an inch long, one that was one inch long, the next, one and a quarter inches long, and finally, one and a half inches long. A decision was not immediately forthcoming, so I molded and tested each one on his face: three-quarters of an inch long was the winner. The final choice literally sloped and tapered right off of Steve's own nose. Not too long, not too short. At different angles and lighting, the viewer can't tell he's wearing anything unless he turns into profile. The latex noses themselves had such delicate edges that they were used only once, then destroyed in the evening removal. This meant I had to manufacture more than one hundred noses (exactly the same size) for testing and filming.

Aside from our everyday needs, the script called for two stunt noses. With one Steve had to put his nose down into a glass of wine and almost drain the glass. The second one had to be firmer, so a canary could perch on it. With one finger Steve removed the bird from its cage and gently placed it on his nose, its little talons gripping the latex. (Glad to report, no birdy accidents.)

Steve became very friendly with his nose, saying in an interview: "I took it out to dinner; we relaxed and talked." *Roxanne* is one of my many films that have been submitted to the Motion Picture Academy for Best Achievement in Makeup; needless to say, I lost by a nose.

STRIPPED TO KILL, 1986

For those who have seen *Psycho III*, you might remember an ice machine next to a gas station. Upon opening the lid you saw a frozen hand and arm protruding upward out of the ice. No, there wasn't a real person under the ice. In the film it was the arm of a lady victim that Norman Bates was keeping on ice. The real name of that girl prior to her movie demise was Katt Shea. Later she called me because now she was also a writer and a director. She had written a low-budget thriller called *Stripped to Kill*, and Roger Corman was the executive producer.

The main premise of the film was to make the viewing audience believe the killer was a female. Katt asked me to create a thin latex frontal torso that extended from the throat to the waist, and it had to have voluptuous breasts that would jiggle. This entire female frontal piece would have to be glued onto the chest of a male actor. What really would sell this disguise would be the attitude of the performer. Katt hired a professional female impersonator who had all the right moves and body language.

To start the project I made a plaster cast of the actor's chest. Katt gave me some pictures for research, saying, "I want the breasts to look just like this." They were pretty amazing! The breasts were duplicated in clay onto the cast. My friend Jim Kagel was given the task of transforming the pictures into clay. Believe it or not, this was not an easy sculpture; most female breasts are not equal in size and shape, but for the movie, they had to be perfect. It took Jim several days, adding and removing and rounding the clay, until everyone was satisfied. I made another plaster mold on top of the clay sculpture, just as I'd done on actress Claudia Cardinale years ago (but hers weren't clay). Inside the plaster molds I formed my latex bust. To achieve a little more bounce for the buck, I hollowed out an area behind the breasts and inserted small baggies filled with a gel-like substance, much like the plastic surgery procedure women endure today.

I was now ready to test my work to see how realistic it actually was. One evening when I was working on another project, my makeup artist friend Todd McIntosh and all concerned parties met at my makeup trailer. The latex chest was attached and made up to match the actor's natural skin tone. Our performer applied his drop-dead Diana Ross makeup and wig from his show. A little more pink on the nipples, and we were ready for our own reality show.

His wardrobe consisted of high heels, a pair of extra-tight jeans, long eyelashes, and a sheer blouse. With swaying hips, a luscious mouth, and alluring eyes, he stepped out of the trailer and floated among the film crew. I decided we made our point that night. My disguise worked for Katt, and every member of the crew fell in love. At the end of *Stripped to Kill* there is a big reveal (hence, the title). I guess I just ruined the story for you.

MASTERS OF THE UNIVERSE (MOTU), 1987

From the beginning of my career I had longed to create the special makeup and makeup effects for a good sci-fi fantasy film. Then the story was laid in my lap. It had it all: creatures galore, fighting a war between good and evil in a struggle to save the universe. That's a lot to ask for in 106 minutes of celluloid. It all started with a phone call from the coproducer, Elliot Schick, who requested that we meet. I was excited. It took my breath away. When I arrived at the studio office I discovered that eight other makeup artists had been approached before me, and they'd all submitted competitive budgets. Elliott asked me to do one too. I took a pessimistic outlook and decided I wouldn't bother to fight the competition. Elliot kept calling me, wondering where my budget was. After thinking over the situation and not wanting to waste my time, I finally said, "Show me the existing budgets and let's see if I can bring down the costs." He agreed. I scanned through multiple pages of financial figures covering how much it would cost to sculpt, make plaster molds, and create the appliances, and how long it would take to paint and glue them on. This is known as labor and materials.

I found so much overhead in all of them that it was a cinch to develop a reasonable budget that would be instantly accepted. By the time I signed on to start my preproduction process, Bill Stout, a brilliant artist and production designer, had drawn and painted the character designs. They had all been approved by the production office and Mattel Toys. Mattel was the original creator of all the action figures, and I'd been selected to bring them to life. I was told later that this movie was Mattel's hope to resurrect the Masters of the Universe franchise.

There were seven major fantasy characters to create. It started with me making a plaster mold of each actor's head on which to sculpt their character. I hired James Kagel, one of Hollywood's finest sculptors, to re-create each of the characters from Bill's drawings.

Gwildor (good), the main character, was played by the famous Billy Barty. He was buried under a lot of appliance latex and dyed red yak hair. Gwildor had long pointed ears that were hand-controlled to twist around and wiggle. There wasn't enough room on the top of his head to mount radio-controlled motors, so the ears were moved by twenty feet of connected cable that ran down his back and out his pants, and were then attached to a board holding two joysticks. My son Michael was very adept at following director Gary Goddard's hand signals and maneuvering the joysticks to bring the ears to life. To achieve Bill Stout's lip design for Gwildor, Jim had to sculpt the upper and lower lips quite thick. These lips applied to Billy for the first test didn't give him much movement. To solve my situation, I used a wax burner to burn three small holes from the back of the lips to almost the outside surface. Into each hole was slipped a small round piece of a wooden toothpick coated in clear silicone. On the next test, when the corrected latex lips were applied, any pressure outward from his natural lips while speaking registered a natural movement on my latex lips. Conclusion: "He's alive."

Beastman (bad) was a cross between a *Star Trek* Klingon and a werewolf. The makeup for Tony Carroll, the actor, included a set of long lower fangs that were so big

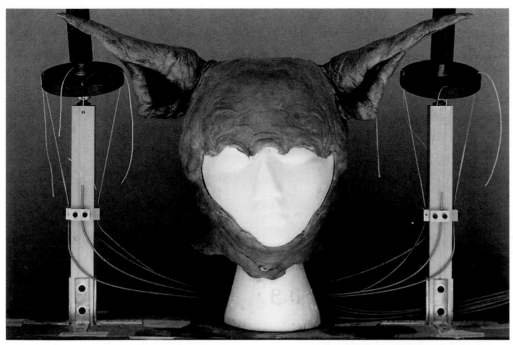

Cable-driven Guildor ears. This apparatus was worn under the wig and hand powered with joysticks. *Cannon Films*

Guildor, played by Billy Barty, in makeup. *Cannon Films*

he couldn't shut his mouth. His eyes were covered with full, handpainted scleral contact lenses, not very comfortable to wear. At that time scleral lenses did not allow the eye to breathe, so they could only be worn for a short period of time before a lens technician had to remove them. Everyone knew when they were overdue to be removed, as the whites of the eyes would turn blue due to lack of oxygen. During one scene it was requested that smoke appear to be emitting from Beastman. I used a particular liquid that is no longer available due to its toxicity. When the liquid is exposed to the air it creates a white stream of dense white smoke. I had used this material before, but outdoors. This time we were indoors, and in very close proximity. When I unleashed my genie

The alien lizard creature Saurod with contact lenses.
Cannon Films

from the bottle it consumed all the oxygen around Tony and me. We got the shot, but it took us a while to catch our breath afterward.

Saurod (bad), played by Pons Maar, was a two-legged lizard that didn't get much exposure on film when the script was rewritten. Under his scaly throat appliance I constructed a latex bladder, much like a balloon, that could be expanded and contracted by Pons blowing through a connecting tube that was hidden under his appliance. This was very effective in animating his character. He also wore contact lenses that were as irritating as Beastman's. Unique to Saurod's character was a four-foot-long mechanical tail that was strapped around his stomach and attached over his buttocks. With a flip of a switch and a wiggle of the thumb on the radio control, his tail would swish back and forth. I was told this was all the movement I could achieve, but thankfully my son Michael added two more servo motors inside the tail that allowed it to also move up and down.

Karg (bad), played by Robert Towers, and Mata Shei (bad), the alien name of a national contest winner, both had to endure full appliances, hands, acrylic teeth, and contact lenses. They were bad guys, and bad guys are supposed to suffer.

Christina Pickles embodied the Sorceress (good), who through an evil spell has to progressively age over a period of time. It was a wonderful old-age makeup design, except she hated the thought of it from the start, like many female actresses do. They don't want to know what's coming. When we reached the final makeup stage, it was applied once, and that was enough for Christina; she refused to have it applied a second time.

The other good characters were all up-and-coming actors. Dolph Lundgren as He-Man brought all his muscles and a semi-truck loaded with gym equipment so at a moment's notice he could pump some iron. Chelsea Field was Teela. Her costume was so tight, Wardrobe could have saved the cost of materials by spraying it on. Our young leads were played by Courteney Cox of *Friends* fame and Robert Duncan McNeil (*Star Trek*). I worked with both of them again, years later. There always has to be a bad, sexy female, so Meg Foster was selected to be the beautiful Evil-Lyn.

The pièce de résistance was Skeletor, our main villain, played by Frank Langella. To assume his character he wanted to understand and have input every step of the way, including wardrobe, makeup, and props. Frank was interested in the height and design of his boots and the length and flow of his cape. With me it was a question of his skull mask; should the false teeth be positioned on the outside of the mask, or should he wear dentures to make his teeth visible? Both designs were constructed, painted, and tested. Frank decided he liked the idea of teeth on the inside, so I created a character set of large dentures that would snap over his own teeth. This was the first time I know of that a skeleton had lips.

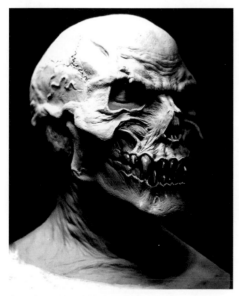

First clay sculpt of Skeletor by James Kagel for *Masters of the Universe*. *Cannon Films*

Latex Skeletor mask and dentures as seen in the film. *Cannon Films*

All this and more had to be ready for the first day of filming. Along with all the fantasy creatures, battle scars, and laser wounds, I would also have to fill the screen with burns, scars, and splats of blood.

All of this would not have been possible without my amazing crew, consisting of Todd McIntosh as department head; makeup artists Gerry Quist, June Westmore, and Robin Beauchesne; hairstylists Lori Benson and Zandra Platzek; and body makeup artist Lauren Hartigan.

By 1987 a makeup category had been established by the Academy. I submitted *Masters of the Universe* for consideration, and it was selected as one of seven films that would be screened. Part of the acceptance process is to edit together the best ten minutes of footage that displays the contribution of makeup to the total film. These ten-minute clips are then viewed by a panel of judges that select the three films to be placed on the final Academy ballot. Since Cannon Films was going bankrupt, all they could offer me was a copy of the movie with no sound. Try watching ten minutes of any film with no sound. It becomes an eternity in hell. My film didn't make it onto the final ballot, but I still feel it was a great contender, with exceptional makeup artistry.

At the conclusion of the film, Skeletor's head rises up from the bottom of the screen and says, "I'll be back." I'm still waiting.

Working in my lab preparing the makeup for the film. *Cannon Films*

BLOOD OF HEROES, 1989

In 1988 producer Charles Roven had approached me to design the makeup for an apocalyptic *Mad Max*–style world, called, at that time, *Night of the Jugger*. It emphasized brutality, barbarism, and buckets of blood. Two different roving teams out of many would challenge each other in a football type of entertainment. Instead of a Roman Coliseum it was a dirt field. Instead of swords or a football, it was a dog's skull. The purpose was to attempt to impale the skull on the end of a sharp pole which stood at each end of the playing field. As the teams maneuvered down the field, each player was exposed to bashing, breaking bones, and having their bodies torn apart. The losing team would go and lick their wounds. To win brought glory, and a celebration with wine, women, and bandages.

Each performer was known as a "Jugger," and started the film fairly unscathed. As the contests are played, the bodily injuries, deformities, and suturing would increase.

Most of the actors and main production people lived in Los Angeles. This is where the creative work would begin. Much had to prepared in LA before everyone would be transported to location in Australia. I had to take a facial cast of Rutger Hauer and sculpt all the principal character designs that would be needed Down Under. When I finished, I had to ship hundreds of pounds of plaster molds from Los Angeles to Sydney, Australia.

The next thing I knew, I, too, was on an airplane headed south. My first stop was Hawaii, where we refueled and continued on to New Zealand. I was off the plane long enough to stretch my legs and then back on for a short hop into Sydney. As soon as I sat back down I was asleep. I do remember the airline hostess trying to wake me up to enjoy a broiled lobster breakfast. I was beyond any interest in food. I opened my eyes long enough to view the famous Opera House from the air, and then we were on the ground. When the plane doors opened I decided to forget about jet lag and went right to the studio.

In Sydney, Bob McCarron, my co-artist, and his team of makeup artists would take my molds and manufacture the foam latex pieces that were necessary for the daily applications. Before I arrived Bob's team had been preparing an assortment of scars and bruises, and stitched and wrinkled skins. This was an enormous undertaking, as each character had his or her own personalized facial designs.

Between preparing and testing, Bob gave me a lesson in Australian reptiles. I had seen many in cages at the Sydney Zoo, but these were loose all over the countryside. As we traveled the dusty highways that seemed to have no end in sight, Bob would come to a screeching halt and say, "Look over there." We would leap out of the car onto the burning ground and he would show me a new and exotic reptile that was plodding across our path. My first question always seemed to be, "Is it poisonous?"

After all the makeup applications were tested and approved, it was time to fly to our first location. Leaving Sydney we passed through Alice Springs. It was like riding on a roller coaster due to the up-and-down drafts. We finally arrived in the middle of nowhere. This was a flat, dry, extremely hot, dusty little Outback town called Coober Pedy, known around the world as a primary source for some of the most brilliant precious stones, fire opals. As we circled the desert floor over the town, one couldn't help but notice the thousands of holes in the ground, with adjoining mounds of earth. These mining holes were vertical shafts about one hundred feet deep and five to six feet in diameter, dug by the international miners who'd made a living searching the dry earthen walls and digging for the precious stones. We were told in no uncertain terms not to wander into these fields, as a misstep would be our last one. There was no way you could survive the drop—and even if you did, no one would ever hear your cries for help. As a curious American, I did have to go see for myself.

The heat was so intense during the day that when not working, we actually lived in a very comfortable windowless hotel that had been carved into the side of a mountain. It even included a spacious restaurant and an exclusive gift shop that sold, what else: opals.

After a short time I had to return to the United States to start preparing for *Johnny Handsome*. Chuck Roven flew me out in a single-engine, two-seater plane that usually carried the mail in and the previous day's film out. We flew so low to the ground that I could count the bushes. For miles and miles there was not a person or kangaroo to be seen, only bushes. To visit the Australian Outback is like visiting another planet in space, something I would do many times when designing *Star Trek* for the next eighteen years.

JOHNNY HANDSOME, 1989

When I was in Australia preparing for *The Blood of Heroes* with my friend Bob McCarron, producer Charles Roven wanted me to return to America and start preparing for his next film, entitled *Johnny Handsome*. It was about a facially deformed man whose occupation was petty thief. During a robbery he was double-crossed and sent to prison. After rehabilitation, extensive plastic surgery, and parole, Johnny, with his new face, is obsessed with payback.

Rutger Hauer makeup test for *Blood of Heroes*.
Newline Cinema

Delroy Lindo. *Newline Cinema*

Anna Katarina. *Newline Cinema*

Justin Monjo. *Newline Cinema*

Vincent D'Onofrio. *Newline Cinema*

Our lead character was to suffer from a cocktail of several facial deformities. I actually worked and researched the project with medical specialists at the UCLA Medical Center. They showed me pictures of former patients who'd had the same deformities Johnny would live with in the movie, until his surgery.

Al Pacino had been cast to play the part. I had to get home to take a plaster cast of his face and sculpt the deformed face. The final script had not been completed or approved by Al, and his committed time period had elapsed, so he was out of the project.

Next up was Richard Gere. Had he accepted the role, we were ready to use Al's appliances to film his test, but Richard dropped out. Mel Gibson was the next candidate, but he was obligated to another project called *The Man Without a Face.* In this film part of his face is mutilated. He didn't want to do another story with a facial problem. I can only guess that he didn't want the reputation of being the King of Quasimodos.

Mickey Rourke accepted the role, so I cast his face and followed the new, approved sketches that were given to me by the producer. I have taken hundreds, maybe thousands, of facial casts, but Mickey was one of the few who were claustrophobic. I can relate to this, because I'm also claustrophobic. During the casting he wanted me to leave his right eye open so he could control his emotions. At the same time his good friend and personal makeup artist Ken Diaz was there for support. Ken would remind Mickey at times that he was all right by giving him a solid punch on the arm. It was critical I get a good face cast, so we talked Mickey into letting me close up the right peephole for one minute. That was the longest minute in history as I counted the seconds: one . . . two . . . three . . . I stretched sixty seconds into four minutes.

Mickey survived and I got a great casting. At the time my lab was still in my garage, so I sent Mickey up to the house to clean up and wash off in our little front bathroom. After he left, Marion called me to come and witness the aftermath. Water was dripping from the ceiling and down the walls. All I can think was that he took a shower, except there was no shower in that bathroom.

I wasn't on the set once the makeup tests were completed, but I heard that Mickey's wearing of the makeup day after day was a struggle for him and the makeup artists. This type of makeup takes hours to apply and, after a long working day, an hour to remove, making cleanup very taxing on everyone.

Had Pacino or Gere accepted the role, I might have won another Academy Award. The film didn't receive a lot of recognition, although the story, direction, and Mickey were great. My makeup was very unique, but at Oscar time I was edged off the ballot by *Driving Miss Daisy.* It was rumored that Jessica Tandy didn't wear any old-age makeup appliances; at that stage in the movie, she was basically playing herself. This

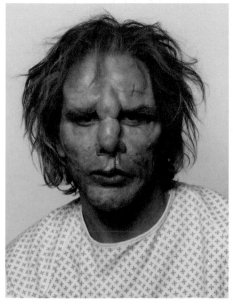

Mickey Rourke makeup test for Johnny Handsome.
Tri-Star Pictures

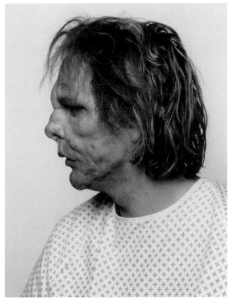

Mickey in makeup profile. *Tri-Star Pictures*

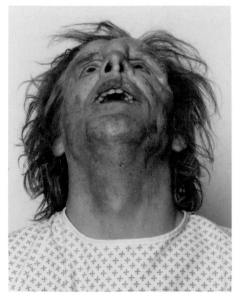

Mickey from underneath looking into his mouth. I constructed a cleft palate that fit on the roof of his mouth for an operating scene. *Tri-Star Pictures*

was a clever reversal of techniques, as the makeup challenge came when she had to appear younger. It was fun to get as far as I did in the competition.

In later years it was great to see Mickey resurface and to see him receive recognition for his talent.

I hope that most people are fortunate enough to have at least one successful and enjoyable career in their lifetime. Errol Flynn once said, "I have done everything twice," and he meant *everything*. I met him when I was a youngster at Warner Bros. Studio, and I saw him again at Columbia Studios, six months before he passed away. The one thing we had in common was that I've been able to experience two successful and enjoyable careers.

After living and working in Hollywood for years and traveling around the world, doing the work I loved, a new door was about to open for me in the 1990s.

Star Trek: The Next Generation and the Nineties

My *Star Trek* Introduction

In the spring of 1987 I kept receiving phone calls from makeup artist friends, inquiring about my availability to create and supply them with Vulcan ears, Klingon foreheads, and special alien makeup for the rebirth of a new *Star Trek* series called *The Next Generation*. David Livingston, the line producer of this new venture, told me later that since so many interviewed artists had referenced me to assist them, he decided to contact me directly.

I agreed to meet on a Thursday morning at Paramount Studios in Hollywood with the powers that be. I showed up at my scheduled time with my scrapbook under my arm. That book contained my life's work, including photographs of all my accomplishments and a list of awards I'd received to date. David ushered me into a room where a group of men had been assembled. David introduced me to these unknown faces. First was Robert (Bob) Justman, supervising producer; Rick Berman, executive producer; and Gene Roddenberry, *Star Trek*'s executive producer, creator, and guru. Each one flipped through my picture book and made note of my biography. Having won an Oscar and a half-dozen Emmys didn't hurt my chances of landing this plum assignment. I excused myself and told them I had an appointment to meet up with Whoopi Goldberg, to deliver her false gums. She was performing in a one-woman show portraying toothless comedian Jackie "Moms" Mabley. I would be home later in the day if they wished to contact me. By the time I arrived home in the late afternoon there was a message on our answering machine from David: "If you are interested in the assignment, it's yours!"

Working on *Star Trek* sounded intriguing. The Westmore family's initial interest started in 1966, with the original series, when my aunt Patricia was the show's creative hairstylist. At that time we were spending most of our nights at home because Marion was pregnant with our son, Michael. Every Thursday night Captain Kirk and the *Enterprise* gang was a must on our entertainment schedule.

Taking on this new job meant a momentary end to my world travels for the motion picture industry. I was going to be doing stay-at-home television. Marion and I both thought, "What the heck; it probably won't last more than a year or two, or three," because that was about the longevity of the original *Star Trek* series from the 1960s. So I called David the next morning and said I was interested, but I would like to think about it. David responded that I had to think fast because this was Friday, and they wanted to start makeup tests early the following week. With a positive nod from my better half I accepted the challenge. Besides, this meant I'd be able to be home for a while and watch our kids grow up. I might even be able to sign up for season tickets to some live theater performances or sporting events.

As a carryover from the original series and early movies, our new Starfleet officers wore what became known as "pointy sideburns." All the makeup artists and hairstylists that we hired had barbering and hair-layering skills. Just to make sure, I drew up a diagram explaining all the proper lengths and angles. The paper diagram was duplicated and hung everywhere so there would be no excuse for mistakes. If an actor showed up and didn't have any sideburns, the same diagram pattern could be used to create the look; all the makeup artist needed was glue, scissors, and a handful of matching, artificial hair. Like the prophets of old, this diagram became the law with no deviation. It became known as "The Bible"; now there was Matthew, Mark, Luke, John, and Mike! Every so often if a sideburn wasn't correct, I would hear someone say to another, "Look at the Bible." So ended my basic preparation, with Gene's blessing.

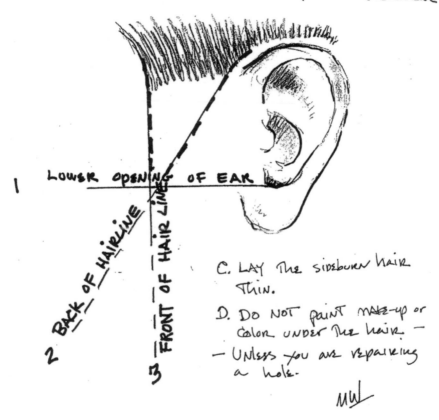

SIDE BURN BIBLE

A. HAIR (crepe wool) must match Natural Hair color

      BLENDED HAIR is Always better than Single-Color.

B. LAY HAIR (wool) iN Direction of Natural Growth

LOWER OPENING OF EAR

1

BACK OF HAIRLINE

2

FRONT OF HAIR LINE

3

C. LAY The sideburn hair Thin.

D. DO NOT paint make-up or color under The hair.

— UNless you are repairing a hole.

The Next Generation Begins

Star Trek: The Next Generation (TNG), a reprised science-fiction television series, began filming in 1987, following the adventures of the starship *Enterprise*. The plot is set in the year AD 2364, one hundred years after the original 1960s series. Its mission: to explore the regions around the Milky Way galaxy, and at the helm is Captain Jean Luc Picard (Sir Patrick Stewart). Each week at the beginning of every episode Captain Picard proclaims the familiar words: "Space—the final frontier. These are the voyages of the starship *Enterprise*. Its continuing mission: to explore strange new worlds, to seek out new life and new civilizations, to boldly go where no man has gone before." For all of my eighteen creative years in the service of *Star Trek*, those words could be my mantra too. Along the flight crew's journey, and mine, we encountered many new aliens, humanoids, and robots. I had to construct and fill this new world of outer space with some bad guys, like the Ferengi, Cardassians, and Borgs, and the familiar nasty Klingons and Romulans. Finally, it was my responsibility to cosmetically bring them all to life in their new extraterrestrial forms.

First Aliens

In the beginning I was under the impression that I could create and manufacture any and all of the special makeup effects or aliens in my California lab, located in Studio City. The distance from my home to Paramount Studios was fifteen miles, and on a good day, with no traffic, it took at least twenty-five minutes one way. My dream of driving back and forth during the day quickly faded. It was just wishful thinking as the creative requirements grew. I had to move my lab onto the studio lot, so they gave me a small makeup room with a sink on Stage 10. This was one of the rooms where all of the makeup for the series *Mission Impossible* was created. When my need for space grew and took over 20 percent of the stage, they decided to move me to larger quarters.

My first day on the job, I was sent to visit with senior illustrator Andy Probert to look at three color renderings that Gene had approved. The first sketch was of a large, bald-headed alien called the Ferengi. In the rendering they had extremely large pointed ears that connected to their brow ridge, a long chin, a bulbous nose, and pointed teeth. While this was all doable, I had some concerns. The points on the large ears had to go, or people might think they were related to the legendary Vulcans or Romulans. I also wanted to eliminate the long chin, as it was just another latex piece that could come loose during the long days of filming, which meant time and money for repair. My suggestions were accepted. Andy's illustration also showed sharp teeth sticking out between its lips. I designed an upper pair of practical, snap-on piranha-like teeth for each of our first three Ferengi. Gene was stuck on the color, which he referred to as "pumpkin" (looked orange to me!). I added a few more wrinkles to the bridge of the nose. Not realizing what I was creating in the clay sculpture, the back of the head formed two large balls with a furrow that ran down between them. Once the heads were made into workable latex and painted "pumpkin," they looked exactly like someone bending over, exposing their bare bottom. Hence, the Ferengi had to be known forever as "The Buttheads." In the very first episode where the three appeared, no one knew exactly how they should perform, so they came across as the "butt-headed" Marx Brothers, laughing, scratching, and cracking whips.

The next designs were of two large, well-known Earth creatures, a dog and a snake. One race was called the Anticans, aka, "the dogs," and the other, Selays, aka, "the snakes." The Anticans were mainly bald with a long canine snout. They did sport some hair, but mainly to cover up obvious seam lines. A mechanism twisted out of a wire coat hanger was mounted into the latex mouth so that when the actor bit down on it, it would open the mouth, then release. At least it gave the immobile head a little mouth movement so the viewer would know it was alive. One day I realized that the actor, while wearing the head, could stick his tongue out through the wire apparatus. It photographed well in close-ups, so that is how the Antican got his tongue.

The dogs were such a time-consuming ordeal to complete that I had to farm out the manufacturing of the snakes. Something got lost in translation, so the heads arrived not soft and pliable as I'd expected, but rigid. There was no time to make more, so when wearing them, the actors had to turn from their shoulders as opposed to twisting their necks. Again, there was not much mouth movement, so I made a six-inch snake tongue, with the fork on one end and a little cup on the other. Ideally the cup would slip over the actor's tongue like a glove. I hoped it would all stay in his mouth while pushing his real tongue in and out. In theory it works well, but in reality, when saliva built up, the cup inside would get lubricated and six inches of forked tongue would come shooting out. The only major event that happened with the Selays, aside from tongue spitting, was on a day when the actor wearing the costume didn't feel well and we were not able to get the head off in time. Needless to say, he filled it with vomit, and that was the end of one snake head.

The Traveler

My first humanoid was christened "The Traveler." The part was played by Eric Menyuk, who'd read for the part of Data. Like most contests, there is a first runner-up, and that is where Eric placed. It must have been a close race, because the producers brought him and his new character back to be in the series again. He was a member of an advanced race, and appeared in the fifth episode as a highly intelligent dimension-hopping humanoid. The Traveler's makeup consisted of a latex forehead that went back as far as his receding hairline and extended down to the tip of his nose. A pronounced ridge extended horizontally across the forehead that looked like a bird in flight. I brought more attention to his eyes by covering his natural eyebrows (it always looks good to have no eyebrows in space). His most obvious addition was a large pair of slip-on hands with three fingers (that's one less than Mickey Mouse). Each finger sported a large fingernail constructed with acrylic, the same material used in everyday nail salons. Why three fingers, you ask? It seemed like a good idea at the moment. Maybe a superior race of humans doesn't need as many digits any-more, because all they have to do is sit around and push buttons or press keys—and that is exactly what The Traveler did.

Since there are no beaches in outer space and The Traveler was a control-panel type of guy, I decided to give his skin an inner glow. After painting Eric with a pale grease makeup, I packed his face and hands with an opalescent powder and slicked back his hair. An ethereal fellow is what I wanted to achieve. Although I was quite pleased with my first humanoid, there would be thousands more to come during the next eighteen years.

Face on the Box

My first hands-on special effect was in episode number eleven, "Haven," when Armin Shimerman was cast to play the talking face on the top of a box. In the scene, Lwaxana Troi (played by Majel Barrett-Roddenberry, Gene Roddenberry's wife) beams onto the transporter pad within the starship *Enterprise*. Sitting on the ground next to her is a painted box, and on the lid there is the semblance of a human face with its eyes closed. At a point in the scene the eyes open and it speaks.

The box stood twelve to eighteen inches high, and I had to make an entire person disappear except for his face. Like the construction of illusions for a magic show, a hole was cut out in the transporter floor allowing Armin to physically drop into it. In the makeup room, with Armin cradling the entire box in his arms, the front of his face was glued and painted through a hole in the middle of the latex lid. When Armin climbed down into the floor opening, he took the entire box with him, face glued in place. He then set its legs onto the transporter floor and pulled his arms in too. All one could see at this point was the box, and on the lid, the front half of his face peering upward.

As an artist I had a bright idea to improve this original concept, only to find out I didn't have the final word. Just to have a human face on the lid seemed sort of blah to me. Having been an art major in college, I had other concepts of how it should look. My brain settled on the images of a Modigliani painting, famous for his elongated faces. In my clay sculpture prior to making the box, I extended Armin's plaster forehead and

AN ACTOR'S VIEW: ARMIN SHIMERMAN'S ACCOUNT OF BECOMING THE FACE ON THE BOX

When I was hired to perform the role, I was then recurring on another sci-fi show, *Beauty and the Beast*, with Ron Perlman as the Beast, who was encased in several hours' worth of makeup. When the agent told me the date that I was needed on *TNG*, he made it quite clear that I was also scheduled to appear on *B&B* on that same day, and heartily recommended that I pass on the *TNG* offer and not jeopardize my relationship with *B&B*. However, I was such a rabid fan of the original *Star Trek* that I decided to overrule my agent's sage advice (not without a lengthy "debate") and take the one-day offer on *TNG*. As this appearance led to so many wonderful things on the *Star Trek* franchise, it is without question the wisest (and luckiest) business decision I ever made.

On the day of the shoot, after I was escorted to the *TNG* makeup trailer, I met the incomparable Michael Westmore. I had no idea he was makeup department head, nor did I have any indication just how entwined our lives would become over the years. Mike was ably assisted by Werner Kepler. Both men were warm and comforting, which I have come to learn is a necessary trait for makeup artists applying prosthetics. Indeed, Mike Westmore has an unusually gracious warmth that he never seems to lose, even when he is under immense stress. I have no idea how he does it, but it is a quality that he impresses on all his crew, and they were some of the nicest people I've ever worked with. Anyway, the two men explained what they were going to do to me and set about the four-hour process that transformed me into a talking prop. Werner did most of the applying, although Michael helped with an extra set of hands when needed, as well as general guidance. As the hours passed, both men were constantly asking about my comfort and state of mind. The appliances left me unable to smile (or perhaps I could have—I just didn't want to disturb the glue).

When we finished I was thrilled at the transformation, although unable to look down or see my feet. This led to needing several people to guide me as I stepped down from the trailer, walked to the set, and stepped up and then sat down in the transporter. My total time on-set seemed like ten or fifteen minutes, including rehearsal and one or two takes. I suppose it might have taken longer, but time passes quickly when you are ecstatically enjoying yourself. The juxtaposition of the time taken for the application (and the later removal) of my makeup compared to the actual time needed to film the scene was not lost on me. Still, it was heaven! I was being beamed aboard the *Enterprise*. Can you imagine what that was like for a *Star Trek* geek like me?!

throat to make him appear more stretched and decorative than his normal human image. I was so proud of this brilliance that I called Robert Justman for his approval. At first glance he responded that he didn't like my artistic extensions of throat and forehead; turns out he'd hired Armin for his humorous face. Sadly I removed the clay, restoring Armin's face to normal. This was my first creative rejection, but not my last over the coming years. This wasn't an in and out for Armin, as he played one of the original guest Ferengis on *TNG*, and returned in the *Star Trek* series *Deep Space Nine* to reprise a new Ferengi "Quark" as a regular cast member.

Data the Android

Brent Spiner playing Data the android was my personal charge from the first day of his makeup testing until we turned off the lights for good. Gene Roddenberry had created this character in 1974 for another pilot for a TV show called *The Questor Tapes*. Although Data's personality is devoid of emotion, he was always seeking to understand humans and their emotions. Gene's favorite colors for Data's skin were bubble-gum pink or battleship gray, but I won the palette contest with pale gold. Although Data had human features, his skin always appeared to have a metallic, pale gold shine unless he was standing next to another reflective colored source.

A small toy figurine of Data was delivered to me for approval, and its skin was painted pink. Apparently, in the photograph that had been delivered to the toy company for reference, Data was standing next to a red blinking light, thus reflecting red off his skin. The doll was sent back to the manufacturer with a gold paint swatch for correction. Every bit of visible skin on Data's face and hands had to be painted with gold, including his ears, neck, palms, and fingernails. A pair of very yellow contact lenses disguised the natural color of his eyes. To complete his mechanical look, using a black eyebrow pencil I filled in his entire frontal hairline so it would appear artificially dense. As time went on and we filmed the movies, I used up a little more pencil to bring his hairline forward. The makeup colors and the application process never changed throughout the TV series and the films. What did constantly change over the years was the removal, on camera, of different body limbs and body parts. Also changing were the types and sizes of electronics that would be exposed beneath his artificial flesh. This all enhanced the illusion that Data was a real android.

Over Data's "lifetime," I never thought I could find so many unique ways to display his inner electronic workings. I called upon my electronic expert, Michael Jr., every time the script called for a new exposure of circuitry. Michael had the ability to program the inner lights to blink, flash, run in sequence, sputter, or rise and diminish in intensity. The very first exposure in 1987 was a small area on Data's left forehead, where his skin had been rolled back due to a scripted kick in the story. Michael programmed a string of mini green lights that ran in sequence as if blood was pulsing through his veins, but with Data, it was pulsating electricity.

Over time we opened each side of his head, the top and back, his neck, forearms, wrists, hands, feet, a thumbnail, and even his entire head. This became a true combination of special makeup and technology. Michael was able to create and program all the circuitry needed to display the scriptwriters' most vivid imagination. As the exposure of electronics became more popular, the construction of the makeup and light programs became increasingly complex. Michael, desperate to keep up, designed a universal controller with a microprocessor. By just tapping a button he could program any light patterns that were requested. Of all the items that were stolen from our lab one time, this was the most precious.

Brent Spiner as Data. *CBS Consumer Products*

Brent was a trooper whenever anything had to be made or applied, including the time I needed a plaster copy of his chest to create an effect. I didn't use enough Vaseline to grease down his chest hair before applying my molding material. (I never admitted to Brent that I only had a smidge left in the jar.)

Brent was in good company for getting trapped into a mold by his hair, as my uncle Bud and I were once involved in momentarily trapping Rock Hudson's entire head. Bud had another story of the time he trapped actress Loretta Young in plaster leg molds many years ago. Remembering Bud "Scissorhands's" solution, I retrieved a pair of long-handled surgical scissors from my tools and slowly separated the plaster mold away from Brent's chest by snipping each entwined hair. Every pull was answered with an *Ouch!* (Ms. Young's rescue was just as painful, but it was a little lower. A protective covering had slipped off when the wet plaster was applied to her lower body, from her feet to her hips. After drying she was trapped in the hardened plaster mold from the waist down, until the rarely used scissors became a necessity for snipping removal.)

Through all the years of applying his makeup, gluing down appliances, and cleaning up afterward, Brent has remained one of my favorites with whom to share stories, laugh, and torture (not on purpose).

I've been fascinated to learn that many of the talented performers I've worked with over the years didn't start out their careers by saying, "I want to be a television or film star." Performers come from all walks of life, but one particular moment in time changed their original direction or interest, and Hollywood turned out to be the place where they could best fulfill their dreams.

Brent had performing in his blood. Along with his acting ability, he was also blessed with a beautiful voice. His talents led him to many Broadway and off-Broadway stages. Many times off-camera, Brent would break into a song. Why not Data, too? He could do everything. Brent knew Data personally. He knew his android's personality and mechanics. When a director would request that he perform an action or recite a line that was not in Data's personality, Brent would say, "That's not in Data's program," or "Data wouldn't do that!," and he wouldn't.

Brent will always be connected to Data like all the rest of the *Star Trek* cast members are to their characters, showcased when they appear at *Star Trek* conventions around the world. Data's bright yellow contact lenses inspired Brent to produce an album titled *Ol' Yellow Eyes Is Back*, where he croons in his melodic voice the classic songs of the 1940s. It's always ready to play in my car, conjuring up the good times with Data, which could fill volumes.

From the beginning of *The Next Generation* series, Data was a work in progress, with more of his powers and capabilities displayed over the years. He was created by Dr. Soong, who was also played by Brent. His positronic brain allowed him to perform computational wonders. In the beginning Data was unable to feel emotions, until he was implanted with an emotional computer chip. I believe this happened in a scene where a panel opened in the side of his neck and a handheld tool inserted the chip. For this scene I had to construct a latex head in the likeness of Data, with hair and makeup.

Data was stronger and more intelligent than any human or alien. He was wiser and more sensitive and curious than any other being. Curiosity led him into romantic encounters, as he was fully functional and wanted to try out all his mechanisms, whether he could feel them or not. His first romantic encounter was with chief of security, Tasha Yar; I believe her resounding response was *Yeah, baby*. The saga of Data with all his capabilities and Brent Spiner's in-depth understanding of his complex character cannot be totally explained in a few paragraphs. The life of Data existed from his introduction in the first episode of *TNG* to the off-screen speaking part in the series finale of *Star Trek: Enterprise*, eighteen years later.

LeVar Burton / Lieutenant Geordi La Forge

LeVar didn't have to wear appliances very often, but he was confronted with an uncomfortable physical routine that he had to endure part of the time. Whenever the script called for him to remove his visor on camera and expose his eyes, they appeared milky white as if he was totally blind. This was accomplished with the insertion of over-sized opaque contact lenses. When the contacts were in place LeVar *was* almost totally blind. There was no way for him to find his way to the stage on his own. He could feel his way out of the makeup trailer, where the lenses were inserted, and I would meet him outside at the bottom of the trailer steps. I would stand with my back to him. He would place his hands on my hips or shoulders. Then, like soldiers marching in step, right, left, right, left, I would guide him into the stage and onto the set where his scene was to be filmed. Whenever he wore his futuristic visor his eyes were concealed enough that he didn't have to insert the white contacts.

LeVar Burton as Lt. Geordi La Forge.
CBS Consumer Products

Of course, to complete his on-screen look with the visor removed is when the famous "blinkies" were also adhered to his temples.

We decided the visor removal needed more dazzle. Something needed to be added to LeVar's temples so it would appear the visor made contact with his skin. My son found two small metal pieces that looked like the starship *Enterprise*. Michael mounted red-blinking LEDs into the center of each one. A thin copper wire was soldered onto each miniature *Enterprise*. The two wires were concealed in LeVar's hair and glued to the back of his neck. They continued down his upper back and connected to a nine-volt battery that was hung under his left armpit. LeVar could control the on/off mode with the push of a button. These quickly became known as LeVar's "blinkies," the first of many genius electronic appliances Michael would devise.

After many years LeVar thought that it would be swell if Geordi could see without the use of the magic visor. A plan was devised to create a contact lens that appeared to look like computer circuitry. My son Michael designed several graphic options that I took to producer Rick Berman for approval.

The selected design was sent to an ocular lab to be black-screened (printed) onto a pair of white contact lenses. These lenses allowed for his normal vision through a centered pupil. At the appropriate time the episode's storyline explains that Geordi has had a high-tech operation on his eyes, allowing him to see without the visor. From that point on the visor, more commonly known as "the banana clip," was retired to the prop room.

Of all the aliens over the eighteen years, LeVar's transforming alien was the one that took the longest to prepare and apply. In an episode called "Identity Crisis," he had to mutate through several stages to become a strange lizard, with two arms and two legs. When we reached the final stage of the mutation, LeVar had to wear a latex head, full face, bicycle pants that went from mid-thigh to above his navel, and alien hands and feet. After all the appliances were in place he was finished in black body makeup from head to toe. His eyes were transformed with glowing, yellow, reptilian-like contact lenses (here we go with lenses again).

The first stage of the mutation started with a few subtle blue veins appearing on his body. As the stages progressed, more veins started to show, until the patterns connected. It took six hours and six makeup artists to complete his alien character. Every single vein had to be individually glued to his body and then colored with an ultraviolet blue paint. It was a very long and trying experience for everyone. LeVar let everyone know that they were going to have to film everything that day, because he was not going to go through the torturous process again. I seconded that motion, and we proceeded to film late into the night.

Along with his patience, LeVar is one of the smartest people I have ever known. While sitting in the makeup chair he would eat his bowl of morning cereal out of a coconut shell while at the same time memorizing all his lines for the next scene. What is more amazing is that he hadn't looked at the script before that moment.

The Next Generation Women

Each one of the women on *The Next Generation* was very different in both looks and personality.

Gates McFadden (Dr. Beverly Crusher) was our redhead. She was not keen on wearing unflattering makeup or latex appliances. Whenever a script called for an unattractive cosmetic change to her appearance, Gates would start to wipe it off as fast as I would apply it. Her theory was that very subtle was always better. To her credit she is also a great dancer and choreographer. Brent Spiner (Data) could also cut a rug; in one of the episodes Gates choreographed a dance number for the two of them, and it was magic. She was given the opportunity in 1994 to direct, and it's one of my favorite episodes. Called "Genesis," in the story a number of the crew personnel morph into an array of prehistoric humans, reptiles, insects, and animals. Gates was so far ahead in her creative directorial mind that she came up with ideas beyond the writers' conceptions. Although the producing office rejected most of her suggestions, she was a step ahead, and her thinking was way outside the box.

Marina Sirtis (Counselor Deanna Troi) was our brunette. Throughout the seven years of the series and in the feature films, she had to wear oversized black contact lenses, indicative of her humanoid race, called Betazoids. (Her eyes are actually a shade of brown.) Every additional Betazoid performer that graced our show had to wear them, including Majel Barrett-Roddenberry. Marina also appeared on the original series as a human crew member. She had to wear latex appliances several times, and she sat patiently as they were applied. In Gates's directorial episode, Marina's face, hands, fingertips, and coloring began morphing. As she turned into a frog, she sought refuge in a tub of water. Another time when she had to wear an old-age makeup, her response to me was, "Mr. Westmore, I hate you" (although I'm sure those words were spoken with love).

Majel Barrett-Roddenberry (Lwaxana Troi) was also a Betazoid, and played Marina's "Auntie Mame" type mother. Every time Majel was ready to go on camera she would struggle to get the lenses into her eyes. She would preface each and every time with "Oh boy, here we go," and we did, tears of her struggle streaming down her freshly made-up cheeks.

Denise Crosby (Lieutenant Tasha Yar) was our blonde. She also could have been known as the floor show, seeing as she would stretch and exercise in her spandex suit while the crew was setting up the next scene. Due to these kinds of distractions, sometimes it took a little longer to get everything prepared. I didn't know until 2012 that she had played Carole Lombard in a 1985 TV movie called *Malice in Wonderland* (I was attending to Elizabeth Taylor at the time). Denise and I didn't remember our paths having crossed several years earlier. She has a joyous personality and is always laughing. About twenty-three episodes into the first season she wanted out of her contract to pursue a career in feature films. She had been offered a part in *Pet Sematary* (1989). I'm sure Gene Roddenberry and Paramount Studios were not thrilled with her request, but to our amazement the two powers agreed to let her out of her contract but with a price. The episode "Skin of Evil" was about a vicious, powerful mass of black sludge that rises out of what looks like a tar pit and confronts the crew, killing Tasha Yar. This is how Denise got out of her contract. Years later she made it back to *Star Trek* several times as a hologram or a half-breed Vulcan—whatever it took to resurrect her.

Vulcans

Hollywood is a place where six degrees of separation is reduced to three or four. For example, in 1961 my future wife Marion Bergeson was an Inglewood, California, beauty. She was competing in the Miss Los Angeles Pageant, affiliated with the Miss California Pageant and culminating in Miss America. Every contestant had to display some kind of talent, and Marion had decided on a Shakespearean reading of *Macbeth*. It was a short drive to her acting coach's house where she would practice on the stage he'd set up in his garage. This kind and lovely acting coach was none other than Leonard Nimoy.

Gene Roddenberry's first description of the Vulcan that was to grace the *Enterprise* bridge was much different than the one we saw in 1965. Gene wanted to give him a satanic appearance based on his eyebrows, a reddish complexion, and semi-pointed ears. As all *Star Trek* fans know, Leonard's skin tone became a light yellow so he would appear more human, but his ears were more than semi-pointed. His hairstyle—with the straight bangs and pointed sideburns—was also a part of his classic look. Mr. Spock, the science officer, was the only actor to appear in every episode of the original *Star Trek* series.

When I took over *The Next Generation* series in 1987, Spock remained the ultimate Vulcan. My wigs, lace eyebrows, and pointed latex ears all kept the image alive. This image was so important to me that I stuck on the wall of every makeup room two hand-drawn diagrams I called "The Vulcan Bibles." Not one makeup artist was to deviate from these sacred Roddenberry designs. One of the sheets displayed the proper placement of the latex ears, with the point straight up. The second sheet was for the upward-angled placement of the classic Vulcan eyebrows. And don't let me see any Vulcans coming out of a makeup room looking different. One day, and only one, an artist actually applied the ears backward, which made the actor look like the god Mercury, or an elf.

In *TNG*, principal Vulcans weren't seen immediately, but background ones could be seen passing in the corridors or mingling in crowds. The powers that be wanted the viewers to be reminded that the Vulcans still existed in the *Star Trek* universe. By the second season there was a female Vulcan medical officer played by Suzie Plakson, who became a favorite performer. By now their light yellow coloring was so established that Max Factor Cosmetics had even named a foundation color after Leonard. It was known by everyone as "LN-1," and its main purpose was to reduce any natural redness in the skin.

To make a Vulcan ear I would first take a mold of the actor's ears and cast them in plaster; this is known as the positive side. On the positive mold the Vulcan ear is modeled in clay. Then more plaster is poured over the clay. When dry, this is known as the negative side. When both sides are very dry and hard, they are separated and the clay is removed. Whipped foam latex is then poured into the negative and the two halves are pressed together. About twenty minutes later the foam latex gels and the mold can be placed into a two-hundred-degree oven for two hours. The heat vulcanizes and firms the latex, just like a rubber tire. After the time allotment, the mold is removed from the oven, cooled, and separated. The latex ear is peeled out and ready to go to work.

After several principal Vulcans had been hired, custom ears were created for each one. I accumulated a backlog of large, medium, and small sizes of pointed ears. With this variety pack I could fit pointed ears on almost anyone. There was one actor whose ears were so large that nothing fit; it meant a custom pair just for him. I designed and created every pointed ear so they would not appear obtrusive.

In the early days of Spock, Leonard's own ears with the latex ones applied would stick out so far that Fred Phillips would have to glue them back to the side of his head. In a *TNG* episode that took place in the spaceship schoolroom, the class was filled with several human children. The director said to me, "Can you make one of those children into an alien?" The quickest alien would be a Vulcan, and it just so happened that my daughter McKenzie was one of those children. I grabbed her by the hand and we ran to the makeup trailer where I applied a pair of Vulcan ears, penciled some Vulcan sweep to her eyebrows, and returned to filming.

As the Vulcan world entered the *Star Trek: Enterprise* series (2001–2005), several experiments were attempted to make a black man yellow. It didn't work; they turned gray. Actor Tim Russ became the first black Vulcan, Tuvok, as well as the first Vulcan since Spock to grace the *Enterprise* bridge as a principal cast member. Also in *Enterprise*, Jolene Blalock became the first Vulcan with naturally arched human eyebrows. In my estimation (which apparently didn't count), it didn't visually work. I never liked changing the signature brow, but I was there as a crew member, not as a decision maker. In the following seasons I had Jolene's makeup artist slowly start to raise the ends of her eyebrows. If we had filmed all seven years of the *Enterprise* series, instead of four, I might have gotten them up to Spock's level.

Romulans

Related to the Vulcans was an alien race called the Romulans. Theirs was a warlike culture that became more menacing, yet they retained a look similar to the Vulcans'.

Susanna Thompson as a Romulan.
CBS Consumer Products

Vulcans were passive and wise; Romulans were aggressive and untrustworthy. Their eyebrows were the same, their ears were the same, and their skin color was very similar, except sometimes they were a little more yellow. For a built-in mean look I added to our nasty pointed-ear race a latex forehead that would give them a constant "V" frown and sunken temples. I eventually designed into my Romulans a bang with a center wedge that followed the "V" in the forehead. It was a nice addition to their overall Romulan look. Several times, unknowingly, a hairstylist would trim off my wedge-shaped bang, thinking the wigs were too long in the center. Want to see me go crazy?! This was one of the very few instances that would fry my butt. The hairstyling department head was constantly purchasing more wigs to be trimmed and styled with the widow's peak. I always had an overabundance of straight-banged Vulcan wigs to add to our growing collection.

How do we know that Vulcans and Romulans descended from the same race? Not because they look very similar, but because they both bleed green blood, squirted out of the same squeeze bottle.

Klingons

Undoubtedly, the most popular aliens in the chronology of *Star Trek* history are those of the Klingon race. The evolution of these hostile, warlike humanoids started in the original series. They were a swarthy group with dark skin, bushy eyebrows, false mustache, and a goatee. I am sure it drove the director of photography crazy because their skin was very shiny, and photographers always want everyone in front of the camera powdered. Two of the original Klingons were played by Michael Ansara and John Colicos. Both of them returned during my tenure to reprise their Klingon heritage but looked completely different in my makeup and long wigs. Following the original series the early feature films reprised the warrior race, but added latex foreheads designed with subtle bumps and ridges.

Michael Dorn as Worf. *CBS Consumer Products*

My first Klingon creation began with Michael Dorn as Worf. Production was hoping to speed up Michael's makeup time, so he agreed to shave his head and let me glue a latex ridge onto his forehead, over his head and down the back of his neck. I saved Michael from appearing bald for the next seven or more years by creating a latex forehead which included all the bony forehead ridges we needed. The rest of his head was covered by a wig. The wearing of just an alien forehead didn't work for me, so I suggested we add a very hawk-like ridged nose and some gnarly snap-on teeth. My two additions became the standard Klingon look for the next eighteen years.

From Worf on, I wanted every member of the race to have their own individuality. Skin tones varied from a warm Malibu tan to a very dark brown. As I crafted each pair of teeth I made sure no two were exactly alike in style and coloring. I stored every set in a small plastic jar with the actor's name printed on the lid. I never knew when a particular set would be back. Each latex forehead was crafted with its own character. In all, there were more than fifty individual designs in large, medium, and small. Before driving myself crazy I found a common denominator that I referred to throughout my eighteen years. At the beginning of each season I would go to the local bookstore and peruse the shelves for new books on animals, reptiles, birds, fish, fantasy, dinosaurs, robots, and horror—oh my! In one beautifully illustrated dinosaur book I found a cross section of all the different bony vertebra, and used this as a guideline for all of my future forehead designs.

Even though Klingon facial hair, including Worf's, had always featured a chin beard and mustache, I couldn't glue the same repetitious style on all of them. In my library of books I discovered one that featured the different styles of beards and mustaches throughout history. I selected one time period on purpose: The faces of my gnarly-headed warriors would be complemented by the elegance of the Elizabethan era.

As the seasons wore on we added more men, women, and children of all sizes and ages. Family groupings were designed with similar foreheads, like the Duras family, to display their DNA connection. There was a large storage room that contained wigs with varied lengths of hair and colors that ranged from gray to dark brown to black. In another room, pinned to the wall, were mustaches and beards of every Shakespearean design.

Most everyone in the *Star Trek* world is aware of William Shatner's philanthropic work and the special Hollywood Charity Horse Show event that has been held for years at the Los Angeles Equestrian Center in Burbank, California. One particular year my daughter McKenzie was invited as a special celebrity guest, representing her current soap opera at the time, *Passions*. McKenzie invited Marion and me to come along as her guests. The main show in the arena was performed for all the guests and the kids he was supporting. In honor of Captain Kirk there were a number of Trekkies that attended in Klingon costume and makeup, like they do at the yearly *Star Trek* conventions.

Following the gala performance, everyone was invited to attend a banquet dinner. During the evening Shatner made the rounds of the tables to say hello, and I was introduced to him for about the twelfth time (literally). I had first met him in the 1960s at Universal Studios. He was very cordial and "pleased to meet me," again. During the dinner I felt about four dozen sets of alien eyes upon me (that's two per humanoid). I asked Marion, "Do you think they know who I am? Maybe I should walk over and introduce myself as the makeup director of *Star Trek*?" I slowly rose from my chair and made my way around several large party tables. The two tables I was heading for were filled with *Star Trek* Klingon fans in full regalia and makeup. Their eyes grew wide as I approached. When I was about to speak they all stood up with clenched fists, and in unison they pounded their chests, women too, and shouted "Father!" This was one of those shit-in-your-pants moments. I felt very proud that I had been recognized for redesigning and advancing Gene's Klingon world.

After a space battle, the bridge of a Klingon ship called for several dead lying around. I inquired if I could make one noticeably deceased by imbedding a small piece of metal into his forehead. The answer was "Yes," so I proceeded to make out of plastic a two-inch circle with angry cutting edges that looked like a Ninja throwing star. I implanted it into our Klingon's forehead and dressed it all up with dripping Klingon blood. The next day I got a little note from Production that said I had taken television death to a new level.

One day I had a very early call at the studio because there were going to be fifteen makeup artists and twenty-five actors arriving at 4:00 a.m. The night before I couldn't get to sleep because I kept running through my mind all the coordinating that had to be done to ready them for 7:30 a.m. filming. To help me get a good night's rest, Marion had decided to give me a swig of her very potent cough medicine. It knocked me out and I enjoyed a very peaceful sleep. It was so potent and peaceful that I had a difficult time waking up at 3:00 a.m.

I stumbled out the door and made it to a twenty-four-hour Starbucks in Hollywood near the studio. The coffee didn't really work its magic, so I drowsily drove into my parking place and proceeded to the makeup labs, where I made sure that every artist had a latex Klingon forehead and nose to apply to their actors. There was one special request by the director: He wanted a dead, bloody Klingon slumped over a console following another rocking-and-rolling Klingon battle in space. He wanted the death to be by a flying, jagged metal object to the forehead. I'd already done this, of course, but decided to take it to another level by using a piece of mirrored plastic. If the camera was at just the right angle, the mirror would reflect double damage.

Now, I'd been in a cough-syrup stupor all morning. Out in the makeup trailer where all the principals were being prepared, I instructed makeup artist Jill Rockow to embed my chunk of mirrored plastic into the head of her Klingon. Later, when the clouds parted and awareness returned, I learned that Jill's actor had insisted that he wasn't supposed to be dead.

About seven a.m., the time everyone was just finishing their makeup and gluing on beards and mustaches, Marion's potent elixir had finally started to wear off. That's when I came face-to-face with a bloody, dead Klingon that was supposed to be alive and a live Klingon that was supposed to be dead. I told myself, "Self, stay calm and regroup." Quickly, the mirrored object of death was removed from the skull of one, the hole it left turned into a dueling scar, and then the object and blood was embedded into the forehead of the other. It was all accomplished so fast that they were both ready before the morning cameras rolled. The next day there were no little notes from Production.

Whenever we had Klingons, there always seemed to be a lot of guttural growls, an unknown language spoken, and much gnashing of—and some spitting due to—their nasty false teeth. Death usually occurred from the swing of a bat'leth (a Klingon sword for dicing and slicing, but not in the kitchen).

One spectacular fight to the death occurred in the *Enterprise*'s engine room among the flashing lights of the central core. Now, to be in the presence of the engine room when it was powered up was awe-inspiring. It was like a monolith—a large, round room with a huge, tall central column that pulsated lights in sequence whenever the ship was under power and flying through space. The floors of the walkways around the room were made of clear Plexiglas, so it was easy to look up from the ground for several flights. During this particular fighting engagement the second-story walkway shatters and the Klingon stuntman makes a death-defying plunge onto the first-level walkway. What made this scene so unique was the mounting of the camera. It was not off to the side or overhead; instead, it was mounted just under the first level. It caught all the action of the stuntman, in Klingon makeup, falling directly into the camera lens along with all the shards of broken movie glass. The creativity behind the designing of such scenes was another unique strength of *Star Trek*.

Bolians

The blue-skinned Bolians can be seen in all four of the television series and several feature films. It was an easy but very visually effective makeup to apply. The first Bolian appeared in *The Next Generation* series. At that time we hadn't yet reintroduced the Andorians of classic *Star Trek*, so the Bolian skin was much the same color blue. In other physical matters, Bolians were differentiated from Andorians by being totally hairless, and they also wore a split ridged latex appliance starting at the back of the neck, extending over the top of their bald scalp, down the front of the face, nose, lips, chin, and throat. The split made the face appear as if it had separate right and left sides. The inner color of the split was emphasized not as a scar but as a physical characteristic, with a darker shade of blue. Horizontally across the top and back of the head was painted a dark blue pattern or stripe that extended from ear to ear. As time progressed the stripes became more like a pattern on a watermelon. Another exclusive feature was lengthening their earlobes, with the bottom of the hole curving backward.

The first speaking Bolian was played by Michael Berryman as Captain Rixx, in an episode called "Conspiracy." Michael was bald, so his own physiognomy was the inspiration for this new humanoid alien in 1988. Over the years most Bolian actors, both men and women, agreed to be bald when they arrived at the makeup lab. For one reason or another several of the speaking Bolians legitimately couldn't shave their heads, so a plastic cap was applied over their own hair before applying the appliances, ears, and blue makeup. This always added additional time to the makeup application. I would hear stories from out-of-work extras, like, "You're not going to shave my head; I have an audition for another role next week," or "I'm working on a movie." Blah, blah, blah! I had heard all the excuses, but was understanding.

Over the years the shade of blue makeup varied from the original powder blue to turquoise. Some speculated that the different shades of blue denoted different climate areas or regions on their alien planet; others said they denoted different skin tones, just like humans. I liked the speculations, but the truth is, the blue makeup was hand-mixed and tinted as needed. Sometimes the human technician would drop into the white base too much or too little blue color, or just the wrong shade altogether.

The four latex pieces of ridged appliance extended for two and a half feet. That means, including both sides, five feet of edges had to be glued down, plus the earlobes. If a performer's head was too small or too large, the main appliance could be shortened by removing a chunk to shrink it, or lengthened by inserting an additional wedge. With the snip of the scissors one size would fit all. It could be adjusted to fit a small Bolian lady as well as the portly Mr. Mott, the recurring Bolian barber on the *Enterprise*. To complete their hairless appearance, the performer's eyebrows were covered over with a thin, latex patch. Everyone in sci-fi knows that aliens and humanoids don't have eyebrows.

Borgs

Of all the alien life-forms that were created for the reprise of *Star Trek*, the most memorable in the eighteen years of the new series was the Borg. Their appearance has deeply influenced the designs used in other science-fiction projects. It has not been uncommon to hear when viewing a different sci-fi show, with characters that contain mechanical parts, "Oh, that looks like a Borg!" They were so popular that the writers reprised them over and over in the television series and featured them in the movie *First Contact*. From the original concept in "Q Who" (1989), their design continually evolved, with more menace and terror. The Borg is a fundamentally emotionless creature that exists only to assimilate others, living in a collective atmosphere, all of one mind—not unlike a hive of bees.

It all started with a sketch given to me by our costume designer at the time, Durinda Rice Wood. The sketch was of a man wearing a dark spandex-like suit with molded, metallic, urethane pieces covering specific areas. Several of the parts resembled electronic circuitry, and wrapped around all of this was yards of black automotive tubing. This is very descriptive for a sketch, but most of the top designers attach swatches of materials to the drawings so a viewer can imagine what a completed costume will look like.

Here, I am surrounded by Borgs. *CBS Consumer Products*

My responsibility was to coordinate the head and hand appliances to blend with the approved coloring and fitting of the completed suits. I designed a totally enclosed helmet and different eyepieces. Every Borg would wear a helmet and eye that would have some random electronic part adhered to it. At first I borrowed small urethane castings from the wardrobe department; then Michael Jr. and I found it more interesting to actually cut up sections of his old electronic circuit boards and glue them on the helmets for a high-tech look. In makeup they had to appear zombie-like, with a near-death (or dead) appearance. The actor's exposed facial skin was painted with ivory/white grease and airbrushed with a smoky color to create skull-like shadows. I discovered very quickly that using an airbrush to shadow would diminish the shading time from ten minutes to two minutes. Time is precious, but most important, they all looked alike, which was perfect for their supposed collective consciousness.

Every helmet was alike, but every eyepiece was different in its original molding and final dressing. Dressing consisted of individual castings from parts of binoculars, pieces from model kits, crystals, diodes, and rhinestones. To connect the suits with the helmets, the black tubing was attached from one to the other, or to an area of exposed skin. There is nothing creepier than having a tube sprouting out of a face or arm.

When the Borg returned for "The Best of Both Worlds" (1990), I redesigned the helmets to have an opening in the back of the head, top, front, and both sides. Any of these openings could be closed up with a form-fitting patch or left open so it would appear as if the viewer could see the Borg's bald head inside. I wanted to make the new Borgs more exciting, and I wanted to sell the idea that there was something electronic happening inside them. Marion and I scoured gift and hobby stores for anything that would illuminate, bleep, or flash with the flip of its attached switch. One of our best discoveries was a store that sold circular and square holograms that fit perfectly into my eyepieces.

We then hit another television milestone. It was the first time a mini laser was used for a practical effect. Captain Picard was kidnapped and Borgified. The laser was mounted to the right side of his head so it would follow with its red stream of light any of his movements. What we didn't know was what would happen if he looked directly into the camera lens while filming. The moment of truth arrived; without any testing, Patrick as Borg "Locutus" stared directly into the center of the camera lens with his laser. The next day after the studio had watched our previous day's "dailies" (as they are known), I received an excited call from producer Rick Berman. I don't think I ever heard him more excited in our eighteen years together. He told me the effect was fantastic. On screen it made the picture look like the lens of the camera had shattered into a million red shards of glass. This was not a costly visual effect. It was accomplished with a tiny laser that cost around $200.00.

Just when I thought the Borgs were as good as they could ever get, Paramount would make another *Next Generation* movie titled *First Contact* (1996). It is my favorite of all the *Star Trek* movies. Rick and the studio wanted the Borgs to be lean, mean, fighting machines, more terrifying than ever, and they would be led by a queen, the ruler of the hive. *First Contact* would change the look of the Borg forever. In the beginning it took five hours (each) to apply the makeup, get them into costume, and hook up all the electronics. The suits had all been redesigned by Robert Blackman, and the helmets had been eliminated in favor of totally bald heads decorated with random chunks of large and small circuitry. The bald heads would appear as if all the attached accessories and tubing were embedded into their skulls.

Alice Krieg as the Borg Queen. *CBS Consumer Products*

Jake Garber was the makeup artist/sculptor who created most of the geometric Borg pieces used on their heads. When Jake got bored he inserted a little humor into his sculpting that was not detected unless pointed out. Even I was not aware of it right away. On one side piece it said "Westmore's House of BBQ." Hidden among other Borg pieces were all the names of the makeup artists that were working on the show. It was so subtle I never caught it; I was only made aware of it after the fact. Every Borg was a billboard.

The most enterprising effort came again from my son, Michael Jr. The old Borg eyes were retired and new, more-detailed, and sharper ones were sculpted by Jake and Barry Koper. A total of thirty-two new ones were needed for the movie. Michael hand-wired each one with its individual sequences of blinking LED lights in an array of colors. Each one was powered by a new and improved battery pack concealed in the circuitry of the Borg's new suits. Michael must have talked with Jake, because he installed his own brand of humor by making every eye blink someone's name in Morse code, including that of his dog, Bonnie.

First Contact was the first time a female Borg really looked like a recognizable woman, even wearing an extended bald head that I had designed. Actress Alice Krieg suffered the torture of Borg Queen makeup for many days in the tight-fitting costume, multiple layers of makeup applied by Scott Wheeler, and her scratchy metallic contact lenses. Alice was a real trooper to the end. She was not the last of our female Borgs; several others were reprised for *Voyager*, including Seven of Nine.

Jeri Ryan was cast as Seven of Nine on *Voyager*. In the beginning she portrayed a total Borg with a bald head, eyepiece, and circuitry implants. As she was introduced a quick de-Borgification took place, until she was finally left with a few inactive attachments that our futuristic scientists couldn't figure out how to remove. Jeri's character makeup included a Borgified piece around her left eye and a section of a small, lethal-looking wheel in front of her right ear. I wanted to attach something on each side of her face so the audience would never forget where she'd come from. She also wore a partial webbed glove on her left hand. The gloves were a pain in the butt to make because they were so thin and delicate.

When Jeri returned to human form she also changed from her Borg suit to a skin-tight silver suit that displayed all her features. She wore the body-hugging, high-heeled outfit in only a few episodes. I talked about it with Robert Blackman, but he was never told why she was quickly changed into a less-conspicuous outfit. (I can only speculate that *Voyager* would have become *The Seven of Nine Show* had she remained in the silver suit.)

Life never got boring with the Borg world, as each one was unique and yet similar. Once there was a baby just a few months old, and I constructed a mini Borg helmet on a doll's head that would fit him, lights and all. I remember while we were filming, as he was lying in his incubator, he kept grabbing and teething on the plastic tubing that connected his helmet to a light taped to his chest.

One episode featured a twenty-ninth-century Borg whose suit was bluer than most, with fewer tubes and smoother implants. Instead of the regular eyepieces with LEDs, Michael Jr. wired in a small two-inch-long neon light.

Patrick Stewart wasn't the only cast member to be Borgified. In an episode of *Voyager* Captain Janeway, B'Elanna Torres, and Tuvok were all captured and started the process. To show the Borg's range of space travel, in another episode, I had Klingon Borgs, Vulcan Borgs, and Bolian Borgs.

As is quoted in Borgdom, "Resistance is futile"; that is an applicable quote for every day when working on *Star Trek*.

MEMORABLE EPISODES

"Conspiracy," *TNG* (Season 1, Episode 25, 1988)

In 1988 a first-draft script with a plain red cover was delivered by courier to my office on the Paramount Studio lot. The sun was shining brightly and there was a bustle of studio workers on the street below. I peeled back the cover page and started to read. It was about a conspiracy of Starfleet officers on the *Enterprise* that had become possessed by parasites who were planning an invasion. I became very excited, as this storyline was going where no *Star Trek* plot had gone before. This was going to give me a great opportunity to work my special-effects makeup magic. As I came to the final pages, I read that when a recognizable crew member's body is invaded by small alien creatures, his head explodes and the alien mother from hell pokes her head out. Now it was my job to make all of these descriptions come to life.

I accomplished the first task—a baby parasite enters the officer's mouth and it starts to bulge—by using air bladders attached to the actor's neck. Over the bladder was glued an appliance. Extending from the balloon down his back and coming out from under the chair where he was seated was a ten-foot length of rubber tubing. To create the practical visual effect of "Hey, what's happening in there?," air had to be passed through the open-ended tubing at breath-like intervals. Since I'd created this nightmare, I acted as the personal air compressor. I hid on the floor behind the actor's chair, out of sight of the camera, and waited for the director to instruct me when to puff in and out. What I didn't factor in was just how long it would take to film this scene, as there was take after take (as some directors like Martin Scorsese like to say, "One more time").

As time progressed and my lungs were getting a workout, I slowly turned from a light shade of pink to a darker one, and then red. As the latex throat expanded and contracted, director Cliff Boles called out, "Mickey, are you all right?" Cliff and I had known each other for a long time, having gone to grammar school together. (Who else would call me Mickey?) I needed a moment to lie there on the carpeted floor to recover from my near hyperventilation. I refused to relinquish my blow job to anyone. We had established that this Starfleet officer has been swallowing something that is not agreeing with his digestive system. Could it be the baby bugs crawling around inside him?

Next, it was time for the alien mom to make an appearance. The real actor sitting in the chair was replaced by a duplicate dummy. As the head of the dummy explodes from a phaser blast, alien mom, a hand puppet, makes her appearance. She was quite ugly and upset. Later I learned my son-in-law Patrick Talopoulos sculpted alien mom. To make the fake head I didn't have time to take a cast of the actor's, so I used a copy of Paul Newman's head that I had from another project. How did that false head look so real as it exploded? A little raw meat and studio blood works just fine. The general opinion of the powers that be was that it was too graphic of a barbecue for *Star Trek*. It was glorious and exciting, however—so exciting that I guess the studio received many complaints regarding our on-screen gore. This wasn't *Spartacus*. This was never done again to such a degree of human destruction. If it was even hinted at in future scripts, it was rewritten into an effective but watered-down version by the time we filmed.

Because of its visual content, "Conspiracy" was initially banned from viewing in the United Kingdom, and Canada required a warning before viewing. Although it may not be considered one of the top ten episodes, it is certainly one of the most memorable. It won three awards at the 40th Emmy ceremony, and one of those was for Best Makeup. Cliff and Mickey, those two kids from Lankershim Grammar School, did okay.

"Pen Pals," *TNG* (Season 2, Episode 15, 1989)

The fifteenth episode of the second season was based on a very young humanoid girl who is in danger on her exploding volcanic planet. Data ignores the prime directive, and has been secretly in communication with her. He must intervene to save her life, and she is eventually transported up to the *Enterprise*. In the conclusion, her adventures with Data are erased from her mind and she is returned to her now-saved planet.

One of the main problems working with child performers is the amount of time they are legally allowed to perform in front of the camera. This means the producers didn't want Nikki Cox (Sarjenka) to spend too much time in the makeup chair. The quickest and most effective makeup I could create was a latex piece that included a high receding forehead, cheeks, and a wig. Finger extensions were made to fit over her fingertips. They were translucent, so any nearby light would shine through them. The forehead was pre-constructed and pre-painted orange. Orange was my color of the week, as it hadn't been used recently except for the Ferengis.

The false forehead was high enough to cover her real hair, and any edges were concealed by the spiky, red-orange wig. While I was applying her forehead and cheeks, another artist was adhering her fingertips. When all was securely in place, a heavy coat of orange makeup concealed any exposed skin on her face and hands. I had her special skin makeup custom-made so it would match any pre-painting on the latex. I was under pressure to complete her transformation in less than thirty minutes. To finish her alien appearance, gold glitter was applied to her colored skin and wig to give the appearance of a star-like metallic sparkle.

From her first day on the job, Nikki complained of a slight burning sensation on her skin. I had never had a performer experience this before. After a few more days of listening to this whining child, I had one of my artists apply the same orange makeup onto my face. Just as I expected, at first I felt nothing; then it was like I had applied a muscle-ache remedy cream. My face started to warm up, and finally I was experiencing a burning sensation. Damn, the whiner wasn't a whiner! Nikki was right. We made it through Sarjenka's trial by fire by slathering her face down each night with aloe vera after her makeup was removed. The manufacturer never did discover what was causing this reaction, but any leftover orange makeup was destroyed. Now I can say, "Sorry, Nikki."

Aside from my major concern for her skin, a problem also arose with her fingertips. On the first day of filming she raised her hands while extending and spreading her fingers. There was a bright light behind her, so her transparent fingertips glowed just like E.T.'s. I had actually planned for this, but had forgotten to tell anyone. Marvin Rush the cinematographer was horrified, and called for me to come and apply more makeup to her fingers because he could see light streaming through them. I quietly told him that it was planned, and his response was "Oh, okay," and we went on with the show. It was a great effect, inexpensive, and quick to apply. You might say it was childproof.

Unfortunately the fingertip effect was never really focused on; this was not the first or last time that our creativity was for naught. When I'd first conceived Sarjenka's makeup, I had included a pair of short antennae high on her forehead, but my sketch was returned with the comment "I love the makeup, but lose the antennae." I still believe in those extra protrusions. They would have enhanced the aura of "alien" and would have had no resemblance to the Andorians.

"The Offspring," *TNG* (Season 3, Episode 16, 1990)

Spanning my entire career as a makeup artist, this was one of my most favorite makeup applications to create and apply. Lal was an android created by Data. It was my assignment to re-create the scriptwriter's vision of how this being would be visually expressed. The script called for it to have an androgynous, sexless, nude appearance. Later in the episode, our android would select an alien or human form in which to transform itself.

My first thought was, "What actor is going to allow me to put them through so much extra time and makeup torture?" The actor/dancer Leonard Crofoot was cast to play the part, and he agreed to endure a lot of discomfort. Only Leonard's attitude allowed me to design such a complex makeup. In the end it took four hours to apply,

twelve hours or more in front of the camera, and another two hours to remove everything. The makeup consisted of an entire latex head-piece that covered everything except his eyes. Even at that, he only had partial vision, as his sight was obscured by having to wear silvered metallic contact lenses. The head contained no ear holes for him to hear, so the director had to shout instructions and Leonard would nod his head if he heard them. There were no nostrils in the design, as androids don't have to breathe. He would breathe through his mouth between filming. This was only a small problem, as the latex mouth opening was sculpted down in the middle of his chin. Claustrophobia didn't even begin to cover it, as all of his senses were severely impaired.

To lose the human contour of his chest, I created a chest that squared off his pectorals and covered his nipples. The greatest discomfort came from the full latex body pants. They extended from over his belly button, covering his crotch and continuing down to mid-thigh, like a pair of bicycle pants with tapered edges. After everything was glued in place his entire body was coated with an adhesive-based bronze makeup and rubbed down with a bronze powder to keep him from sticking to everything. Standing in the perfect position he resembled an "Oscar" statue. One prob-

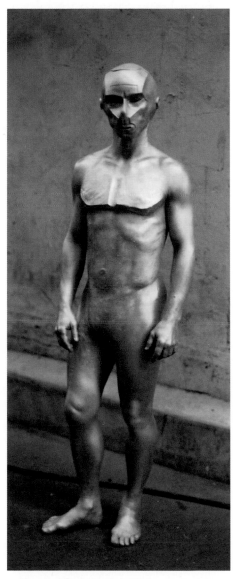

Leonard Crofoot as Lal. *CBS Consumer Products*

lem creates another. There was no way that Leonard could relieve himself for at least fourteen hours. During this time he avoided all food and water.

One day he stood on one leg for a long period of time without wavering. The other leg he held up behind his back so the camera couldn't see it. In his hands he held a false leg to match his real one. The false leg appeared as if it could be removed, and it was. While all this was happening he was running a mechanism to control a series of lights that were attached to the removed leg. This was the wonder of Leonard Crofoot.

At the end of a long, sixteen-hour day Doug Drexler and I would remove all of the appliances and makeup as fast as we could so Leonard could at least pee. Doug feverishly worked in the back as I worked in the front, removing his latex pants. Doug and I were peering between his legs at each other when the latex crotch came loose and his testicles dropped into view, blocking our eye line of each other. We both laughed hysterically, and still do to this day when recounting the incident. To complete our cleanup Doug would get into the shower with Leonard and scrub his skin down with my wife's borrowed loofah sponge. The bronze makeup was difficult to remove. I'm not sure Marion was pleased when I told her that her sponge had gone to a good cause, but in any case, she didn't want it back.

As I mentioned, Lal was given the opportunity to become another being, and it chose a human female. Hallie Todd was cast to be the innocent android, aka, Data's daughter. She played most of her part looking like Snow White, but that all changed when in a special scene, the top of her head pops open and her positronic brain is revealed. The surface structure of her skull lights up like the Great White Way in New York City. Michael Jr. had constructed and wired a multitude of bright, blinking lights to her fiberglass skull cap that amazed even the film crew.

Only one in a thousand performers would endure what Leonard did. His look and performance was amazing on-screen, and this is one of my most memorable creations.

MOMENTS TO REMEMBER

Gene's Philosophy When It Came to His Aliens

Full-headed alien creatures like the early Anticans (dogs) and Selays (snakes) didn't return on-screen very often, as Gene Roddenberry had an edict: The eyes and mouth are the communicative openings to our life-form's soul. If it was not possible to look into a character's eyes and mouth and see living movement, it was only a mask. We were never trying to compete with a *Star Wars* bar; we were following Gene's vision of the future.

A Moment in Time I Have Never Forgotten

One day I was walking down a very narrow alley between Stage 9 and the plaster shop (I was told cars and trucks were much narrower in the early cinematic days). In a small electric golf cart, Gene came whizzing down the passageway. I jumped to the side, pressing myself against the wall, wholly expecting to give my life to *Star Trek*. Gene screeched to a halt, smoke rising from the wheels, and motioned me over. I didn't think he would have a clue as to who I was, and then he spoke. "I want you to know, I really like the work you're doing." I stood there in shock. Gene's foot hit the pedal and he disappeared around the corner of the stage.

General Colin Powell

One morning while working in my lab there came a soft knock at the door, and as it opened a crack I saw the face of A. C. Lyles. A. C. was the most famous dignitary on the Paramount lot. He said he had some *Star Trek* fans with him; might he bring them in? I didn't say no, but I had mixed feelings. My lab was a messy place, where all the sculpting and plaster-mold making took place. The walls were surrounded with makeup tables and banks of bright lights. Above were rows of shelves that contained the remnants of alien masks. I welcomed him and his *Star Trek* guests into my inner sanctum. Much to my surprise—I tried to tell myself to stay calm—it was General

With General and Mrs. Colin Powell. *Courtesy of the author*

Colin Powell and his wife, Alma. We chatted for quite a while as I pulled down all sorts of show-and-tell items. General Powell was especially fascinated with the Klingon warrior foreheads. After some time one of his aides came in and said, "Sir, we have to go; there is more to see." Reluctantly General Powell and his wife left with A. C. to see more of the *Star Trek* puzzle. But, before he got too far out of sight, we had our picture taken together, and A. C. made sure I received a copy. Unbeknownst to all of us, at the time he and I were talking *Star Trek*, he was also preparing for the Gulf War. I always knew he was a good guy, because he liked to repair Volvos (Marion and I drove one).

President Reagan

A. C. Lyles was always popping onto the set with one famous personality or another. I think he knew everyone in Hollywood and Washington, DC. This particular day it was retired President Reagan sans Nancy. All filming came to a roaring halt, and the film crew surrounded him like bees to honey. We all knew the president was having memory problems. In the past he'd been known as a great storyteller, and with A. C.'s prompting, he was still able to entertain the crew. A. C. never left his side. While the president was not able to sign autographs, he carried a pad of white paper and a stamp with the presidential seal. Lining up, we all received a treasured memento. A. C. and President Reagan's relationship went back many years, as A. C. is credited with introducing Ronny to Nancy and being best man at their wedding. A. C. also had a seat of honor at the president's funeral.

Mr. Gerry Quist

In one of our Holiday Inn–themed episodes, from the planet "R&R," our costume designer Robert Blackman wanted to try a new concept for *Star Trek*. He designed a clear, see-through jacket for the spa hostess. Seeing bare breasts was okay, but exposed nipples were a no-no. Bob asked me to take a cast of our actress's breasts and construct for him a pair of nipple covers. When the young lady showed up at my lab door she appeared to be very nervous. (There are a thousand young women in Hollywood who will disrobe faster than you can blink, and the casting agent had sent us one with principles.) I explained the casting procedure: Her nipples would only be exposed for less than thirty seconds as we applied the molding material, and the entire procedure would take only fifteen minutes.

She decided to dictate the rules, and we respected her wishes. She wanted to select one person to complete the casting procedure. With four of us standing there, three were in committed relationships. She selected the one youthful bachelor who had steam coming from his ears. My purpose was to have several assistants there so we could get her in and out as fast as possible, because there was a lot of work to be finished on other projects. To solve the problem I sent Mr. Quist, along with the casting materials, into a small, outside trailer.

We continued our work in the lab. An hour later a production assistant arrived with two perfect little nipple molds that looked like clamshells, with a note from Mr. Quist that said, "I don't think these turned out well, so I'm doing them again." Another hour passed before a smiling Mr. Quist arrived with a second set of molds that appeared to be just as good as his first attempt.

Star Trek: Deep Space Nine

STAR TREK: DEEP SPACE NINE, 1993–1999 (176 EPISODES)

The *Deep Space Nine* plot takes place in the Milky Way between the years of AD 2369 and AD 2375. Unlike the previous *Star Trek* series with a central spaceship, this one centers around the huge floating Space Station DS9. Directing operations here is Captain Sisko (Mr. Avery Brooks). I always referred to him as Mr. Brooks because he always called me Mr. Westmore. In the beginning of the series the Station is relocated near the entrance of a "wormhole." This is a black hole in space that allows our characters to travel through and into unexplored space known as the Gamma Quadrant, setting the stage for DS9 to become a center for exploration, trade, and conflict.

Unlike a constantly moving starship, this stationary space station allowed for more recurrence and interaction of humans, humanoids, and aliens. The interior of the station was designed with circular corridors that were lined with specialty shops and a popular hangout known as Quark's Bar.

Rick Berman allowed me to let the creative side of my mind run wild. Background alien characters strolled the corridors, ranging from tall giraffe-like aliens to little people with bulbous aquatic heads. In between the tall and the small, there was every alien creature imaginable, including exotic humanoid females.

On a weekly basis my challenges never ended, as I had to create new looks as well as reprise several of the *Next Generation* characters. Now the aliens came in groups and families, which included women, children, and the elderly. The humanoid race most expanded from *The Next Generation* was the Bajorans, as the Space Station was located near the planet and culture of Bajor. Again we crossed paths with Ferengis, Cardassians, and Klingons. I always enjoyed crossing earthly species to create a new alien look. When there wasn't the hustle and bustle of an earthly promenade going on inside the Station, during quiet moments I would gaze out the windows. It looked like a million twinkling stars were filling up the depths of the universe.

Bajorans

The Bajorans are a humanoid race that was first introduced by a character called Ensign Ro Laren (Michelle Forbes, 1991) in *The Next Generation*. I was told to keep Michelle attractive, with a slight touch of alien. The concept I used was to create an ever so slight multi-rigged latex nose. The design was simple and small enough that a makeup artist could apply and paint it very quickly. In the following *Star Trek* series *Deep Space Nine* the Bajoran race was expanded to include men, more women, and children. Featured in the roles were Kira Nerys (Nana Visitor) and Winn Adami, played by none other than Louise Fletcher. The application and cleanup was so simple that now I could have multitudes of Bajorans all working on camera the same day. The only problem that arose was that one size did not fit all. As the need grew, more sizes and ridge styles were added to the makeup lab's collection. The numbers of horizontal ridges across the bridge of the nose varied so as to give variety and individuality to each Bajoran character. Eventually I had such a variety I could fit anyone in the universe.

Quark, the Ferengi

The nasty little pumpkin-colored aliens with wrinkled noses and sharp teeth were established in *The Next Generation*. At that time their oversized, hairless heads had very large ears and they wore in their mouth an upper set of pointed false teeth. Go forward seven years to a new series called *Deep Space Nine*. Like most large cities with massive populations, there are areas for rest and relaxation, and DS9 was no exception. Established among its circling mall passageways were exotic shops, a colorful bar, and a casino that would become famous in the annals of *Star Trek* lore. Even Las Vegas duplicated one that survived for ten years.

How or why a Ferengi was selected to be the proprietor of a bar in *Deep Space Nine*, I don't remember, but it worked. Who better to oversee this establishment of intrigue and hologram rooms than an alien Ferengi called "Quark." When you first entered the odd-shaped circle doors, you were mesmerized by the design, dimensions, illuminated bar, and brightly colored lights. To the right of the door was the angled bar where the nonspeaking alien Morn would sit for the next seven years, drowning his sorrows. My purpose for laying the background information is more to introduce proprietor Quark, played by actor Armin Shimerman, a truly genteel man who for seven years would endure the early hours of glue and makeup. In *The Next Generation*, one size head would fit all, but in the new show, Rick wanted our Ferengi to be more prominent.

Armin Shimerman as Quark. *CBS Consumer Products*

Armin's head was cast in plaster and a new oversized alien head was molded that was much larger than our original ones. It even allowed him some more ear room, which the previous ones didn't have. Armin understood the makeup process because he had been there before. The pointed upper teeth were not that comfortable to wear all day. I added lower teeth, because straight pearly whites ruined the illusion. It was a real challenge with the upper and lower teeth worn together, as they had to intermesh and he had to be able to talk intelligently. Instead of just a ridged latex nose and a separate pair of cheeks, I connected the three together. This was called a "Quark wrap," because it wrapped around the front of his face and blended off in front of his large latex ears.

Armin was going to be more prominent and thus needed more attention to detail, which included his raccoon-like maroon eye shadow, applied daily by Karen Westerfield. What was nice about reprising an established species was that over the years of *Star Trek*, whenever they returned I would have more time to improve the design, coloring, and detailing of the species like I did with the Klingons, Vulcans, Borgs, Andorians, and especially the Ferengis.

To complete the makeup, Quark's hands were painted orange to match his head and his fingernails were painted with the traditional blue nail polish that was established years ago. The early Ferengis had the same sly personality as Quark, but they were more militaristic and money-grubbing, so their symbolic rank was stenciled in green

TO BE QUARK
BY ARMIN SHIMERMAN

Without question Quark is and will always be the high point of my career. The gods blessed me with a butt-headed, comical, complex, enigmatic, charismatic, self-serving, generous, ugly, beauty of a role. Despite the ears, the teeth, the overhanging brow, and the orange skin, Quark is the most human of *Star Trek* characters—with the possible exception of Dr. McCoy. To my mind most of Starfleet is way too self-sacrificing to be a mirror for current humanity. Rather, they are role models that viewers hope to aspire to and emulate. This is, after all, the function of all mythological characters. But Quark is an amalgam of the worst and best in mankind. We all try to overcome the baser parts of our natures, and, on rare occasions we succeed—but only rarely.

My first agenda for Quark when I was cast was to try to remaster the Ferengi race on *Star Trek*. After all, it was my miserable portrayal of Letek on *TNG: Last Outpost* that stamped the race as buffoons rather than the original concept of ruthless competitors. Up till that time, I'd lived with the shame that I had "failed miserably." Moreover, I always saw Quark as a dramatic role with comedic possibilities. All actors know that successful comedy comes out of dramatically playing for high stakes. I never played for laughs; I played for objectives and then heightened the need.

But this is a book by Michael Westmore, so let's talk about the makeup. Originally, the Ferengi makeup on *TNG* had consisted of five prosthetic pieces. On *DS9*, Michael got it down to two: a helmet and a face. When I took the job, I made it a stipulation that there had to be more room for my own rather oversized ears. On *TNG*, there were no cavities for them, and the pain that came from having them folded back upon themselves after ten hours of imprisonment was excruciating. Michael, who is always sympathetic to his actors' discomfort, made no bones about re-sculpting the entire mask. In doing so, he finally created and included a neck, which had been left out of the original *TNG* sculpture. The result was more ear room, but it led to the unfortunate loss of fresh air in the head cavity, which Max Grodenchik (Ron) and Aron Eisenberg (Nog) enjoyed with their veiled and unglued necks. This resulted in puddles of sweat accumulating in my head and the feeling after eight to nine hours of being overheated, suffering a lack of focus, dehydration, and short attention span. It felt very much like having a bad head cold. I remind you that my average day on *DS9* was fifteen to seventeen hours.

Despite all of his responsibilities, Michael was invariably there in the wee hours of the morning, making sure all his artists had all their materials and marching orders.

If it was a Dax day, he applied the makeup himself—always numbering his finished work like the Picasso that he is. Michael's presence in the trailer was always one of conviviality and bonhomie. We looked forward to it for all sorts of reasons. He was the eye of calm in our tempestuous preparations. I never failed to be dazzled by Michael's concern and comforting approach toward new actors in the makeup trailer. He made sure that any latent fears were put to rest, and that they knew they would be well taken care of. In other words, the same generosity of spirit to a nervous first-timer that got me through "the face in the box" never slackened one iota in the decade that followed. This to me is more impressive than the nine or so Emmys Michael has won for his extraordinary work.

One last thing about being Quark that I have only shared with Ethan Phillips, who played Neelix: Quark was an international celebrity. In the 1990s, I was a slightly familiar character actor. The disconnect was both desirable and disheartening. It was desirable because I got to keep my privacy in public places that is often denied actors like Jonathan Frakes or Avery Brooks. But the lack of visibility was also disheartening. There have been many occasions when I have been applauded by one group of people for my work on *Star Trek* and then immediately thought of as a nonentity by another. It can be very disorienting.

The best example of this was a day when I had to go to SONY Studios to audition for a film role. The office I was looking for was situated a long way from the parking lot. As I walked the lot, many people waved and saluted me as Quark, including a tour guide with a tram-full of people. I felt on top of the world. However, when I got to the audition, the director asked, "Who are you, and why don't I know your work?" To him, I didn't exist. Despite three *TV Guide* covers, I have often felt like the most anonymous celebrity in television. There are worse things in life, but it does give one's ego whiplash.

I'd like to relate an incident that happened just before our show first aired. It sort of ties all I've said together. Paramount did a lot of publicity prior to our debut to generate excitement. A newspaper in Wisconsin ran a picture of Quark and Sisko together on the bridge. A lady rang the newspaper and informed them that it was inappropriate to use a picture of such a disfigured person as Quark to promote a TV show. The paper responded, "Madam, he's wearing makeup." The lady rather superiorly countered, "Well, it didn't help, did it?" Ladies and gentlemen, that's how good Mike Westmore's designs, molding, and applications are. They make you believe.

on their right forehead lobe. Consistent with their attitude, it symbolized the quote "Dog eat dog." (Rummaging around my *Star Trek* mementos recently, I found that little stencil, still smeared with green makeup.)

During the Ferengis' yearly appearances in *Deep Space Nine* I had a vast variety of male, female, and youthful ones. Some had smaller heads and ears, and another, the Grand Nagus called "Zek" (played by Wally Shawn), had ears larger than his latex head. His face, head, and ears had more wrinkles and crevasses than an old prune. Over the years no Ferengi ever lost his or her famous nickname; whether one of them was the larger-headed Quark or wrinkled Zek, they were all "Buttheads" from the back.

Odo

When I first sat down with the producers, the character Odo was described to me as a shape-shifting entity who could morph into anything he desired, except for the fine details of the human image. They wanted his skin to be smooth like plastic, without texture or pores. René Auberjonois was cast to play this part, and his natural skin was far from baby-bottom smooth. The first thing I did was to take a plaster cast of René's face on which I could mold some small smooth pieces of latex that I hoped would be the solution to his (and my) skin problem. Special makeup always seems to have problems. When the individual pieces were glued on his face, his natural skin texture was still evident around the edges. I sculpted larger individual latex pieces like a chin, cheekbones, and a forehead, then tested them, only to have the same results. What I was trying to avoid was the only solution: I was going to have to sculpt an entire face with openings around each eye, the mouth, and nostrils. Since René's ears were going to be exposed, they too would need

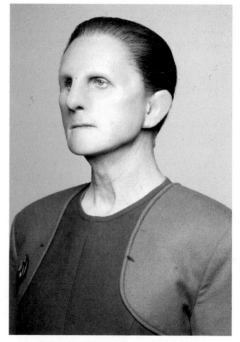

René Auberjonois as Odo. *CBS Consumer Products*

latex pieces to diminish the human contours. When fully applied the mask stretched low under his jawline and chin, back to the front of his ears, and high over his forehead to cover his natural hairline. This design would work for the next seven years.

THOUGHTS ON ALIEN MAKEUP
BY RENÉ AUBERJONOIS

It is hard to imagine *Star Trek* in any of its incarnations without picturing the extraordinary variety of alien characters. Over the years, that amazing roster has defined the show at least as much as its "Captains." It is perhaps ironic that the special makeup employed to create larger-than-life, unreal, and outlandish creatures has most often been used to dramatize the fact that we are all "related," no matter how "alien" we may appear on the surface. An "alien" makeup may not be realistic but, in *Star Trek*, it is always believable and organic. The audience is able to recognize its basic "truth."

The makeup which Michael Westmore designed and created for Odo (the character I portrayed on *Star Trek: Deep Space Nine*) was the single most important aspect of the creation of the character as a whole. The "mask" of Odo influenced the voice and the physical/psychological gestures of the character. To this day, I find it difficult to project the voice of Odo when I'm not in the makeup.

People are always curious as to how long it takes to apply the makeup. In my case it was a mere two hours . . . but, in my opinion, that is irrelevant to the actor. It's the makeup artist who has to stand there for a protracted period of time with intense concentration and endurance. Some actors study their lines while in the makeup trailer (Armin Shimerman). Some actors do crossword puzzles (Michael Dorn has perfected that art). Some actors sleep (no names). Some actors "Zen out." (As long as I don't give myself away by snoring, I claim to be "meditating" on my role—working on my character's inner life.)

It's always strange, that first time you "meet yourself" in the mirror. It's not you . . . it's a stranger, and you have to get to know who that stranger is, staring back at you in the mirror. As a professional, one of the first things I do is check it out on a technical level. Is it applied to my satisfaction? Am I comfortable with the "believability" factor? Next I test the limits of its flexibility, making sure not to damage the makeup artist's painstaking work. Then (usually in the privacy of my dressing room) I really try to get to know my new face. I try to let it tell me who I am.

When acting in an extensive makeup there are certain responsibilities you must fulfill to project "beyond" the latex, so to speak. The same is true when performing opposite an actor who is also working to project through the makeup. Both of you must trust that the makeup can actually magnify rather than obscure the emotions you are trying to project.

It is impossible to overemphasize the importance of Michael Westmore's contribution to the ongoing success of the *Star Trek* "franchise." Whenever I am called upon to take friends or fans on a tour of the studio, I save the best for last. I take them into the "inner sanctum" of the makeup lab. It never fails to astonish and delight the guests, and I never tire of admiring the creativity and seemingly endless imagination of Michael's work. The walls are covered with literally hundreds of characters and creatures who have come to life and entertained audiences for more episodes than seems possible, and they just keep on being "born" from Westmore's tireless and vivid imagination.

All of the latex edges disappeared into his skin except the one across the top of his head, which was concealed with a specially made, wig-like hairpiece which combed into his natural hair. When all slicked back in place, Odo's hair had the same appearance as that of silent-movie star Rudolph Valentino, who my dad had attended to. Every day that René worked wearing makeup, he sat patiently in the makeup chair for two hours as his mask was carefully applied, starting with the bridge of his nose and working outward.

Aside from being able to morph into inanimate objects, the face of Odo, several times, was injured, disintegrated, dehydrated, cracked, flaked, and Klingonized. Each time a change occurred it required a new sculpture and a new mold. Rene once said that he found his time in Klingon makeup "wonderful," because half his face was left free. After a while the show added more shape-shifters, or Changelings, as they were also known. Whenever a new performer, man or woman, was added to this unique world, it meant I had to repeat the molding process all over again, as one size didn't fit all. When René was in full Changeling makeup, his voice would deepen and change. He once said that it was difficult to resurrect his Odo voice and personality when not in his special makeup.

The uniqueness of the Changelings' world was all revealed by the writers as the seasons progressed. They and Odo came from a unique world where they melted their mass and consciousness into a single matrix of metamorphic gelatin, yet at will could walk incognito among the solids in any disguise they desired. Their only requirement, when assuming a solid mass, is to revert back to a gelatinous mass for one hour, once a day. As you see, visual effects played a large part in Odo's life on the screen.

Quark and Odo

In the mid-1980s Armin Shimerman and René Auberjonois performed in a Los Angeles play titled *Petrified Forest*. This was their first meeting, but they had no scenes together; they rarely spoke, and knew each other only slightly. In the early 1990s both of them were cast to play alien characters in *Star Trek: Deep Space Nine*. Armin played Quark, and René was the featureless Changeling who headed up Security at the Space Station. You might think of Odo as the sheriff.

When filming began, both of them arrived at the makeup trailer very early in the morning. As they sat patiently while having their makeup applied, they had the opportunity to share many personal and work-related subjects with each other, thus creating a mutual bonding. Armin told me that as professional stage performers, they prepared for their roles in a very similar fashion. Many shows, especially theater, start with round-table readings so everyone can become familiar with the story and the characters. This didn't happen on *Star Trek*, but the two of them would prepare together either at the studio or on weekends.

The plot of "The Ascent" (1996), episode nine of season five, really exemplified the personal relationship between their characters. It's a telling example of their on-screen love-hate relationship. To start production the entire film crew traveled to a location at the base of Mount Whitney in California. This scenic background was selected so the story could capture the true nature of their trials and tribulations. Armin later told me that his large, oversized head never bothered him at sea level, but the high altitude while filming gave him altitude sickness. To relieve this distress he was given doses of vitamin C, which solved his problem.

The story goes something like this: Odo, chief of Security on *DS9*, has arrested Quark for suspicion of fraternizing with the undesirable and crooked Orion Syndicate. Odo's job is to deliver the accused Quark by shuttlecraft to the Federation penal colony. The two are confined to a small area inside the spacecraft, and it soon becomes obvious they are very annoying to each other, whether they're eating, making noises, or complaining about everything, including the interior temperature. A buzzing sound is the last straw. Upon searching they locate the sound, and it's a bomb about to explode. Odo remarks that it must be the Orion's. BOOM! The shuttlecraft lands on the closest uninhabitable planet. They are without food and water, and they only have one silver survival suit, which they agree to share. Quark repairs the only transmitter that is capable of sending an SOS. For it to work, they must climb to the highest peak on the mountain. From that point they hope to communicate with a rescue ship. The steep path they must climb looks more like an extreme degree of difficulty hiking trail with huge boulders, slippery footing, and fast-cascading streams. As they begin their ascent, they continually banter about each other's shortfalls.

Days pass, and Odo reveals he has always been suspicious of Quark's business dealings, especially with the Orion Syndicate. If you ever saw an Orion, you could understand Odo's concern. The males are very large humanoids with green skin and body piercings; the females are much more appealing. At this time Quark reveals he is not a member but a witness against the Syndicate; hence, the reason for the planted bomb—an attempt to kill him. Quark then says to Odo, "You have been trying to catch a nobody."

Upward they climb over the rough terrain; they mutually admit their hatred for each other, but maintain tolerance for the sake of survival. Odo slips, loses his footing, and rolls down the mountain, breaking his leg. Without the power to repair it, Quark constructs a two-pole litter and pulls Odo behind him as the climb continues. All the way along, insults have become a way of life for both of them. Due to exhaustion, Quark can't pull Odo any further, so he leaves him and begins to climb upward, with only the transmitter in tow. The howling winds and freezing temperatures continue to mount. At this point, I must say, my artists did a great job distressing, smudging, and bruising the makeup on our two performers' faces, along with Odo's hair.

As Quark continues to climb, Odo is slowly expiring, so he decides to leave his last will and testament. He wants to be interred in his little familiar bottle that he always returned to every day. Quark wants to be cremated and have his ashes sold, just like any enterprising, money-grabbing Ferengi.

Odo and Quark are then seen inside a spacecraft, lying in recovery. Quark reached the top of the mountain and was able to send an SOS. Worf and Dax came to their rescue. As the two lay side by side, Quark says, "Remember when I said I hate you?" Odo replies: "Yes." Quark follows with, "I meant it!" And Odo retorts: "So did I!"

So, for seven years, the suspicious Security officer and the devious bar owner continue to coexist and tolerate each other, without a shred of trust. It is truly a love-hate relationship.

One of the most important aspects of filmmaking is the editorial process, as all of the interactions and emotions of the characters are displayed through careful editing. On this particular episode, Michael Jr. was the editor.

Morn

Prior to the start of filming of *Deep Space Nine* I was asked to create ten new alien species that would wander the Space Station's promenade and patronize its shops, along with Quark's Bar. This was to be the giant mall in space and the crossroads to the galaxy, where the good and the bad would cross paths. The ten different aliens ranged from a race over six and a half feet tall with large colorful heads and ears to a little person's race. The tall race towered over everyone as they gracefully weaved their way through the multitudes like giraffe. The heads of the smaller race resembled the body of an octopus, and their faces had an external bony structure. I always found it fascinating to watch my mingling creations passing to and fro.

On the first day of filming in Quark's Bar the director picked out one of the ten aliens and told him to sit at the end of the lighted space bar. This kindly brown alien, named Morn, had a large head and a neck just as wide. He had a little peanut nose and ears, and a large sad mouth with no chin. His head was mostly devoid of hair except for a sparse smattering on top (actually cut from a nylon push broom). One end of the bristle was punched into the head and the other end was curled with a hot iron. The heat from the iron made each hair curl up on the end like a little pig's tail. Mark Shepard, the actor who played Morn, had naturally large dark brown eyes like one sees in whimsical children's illustrations. The only thing visible of the real Mark was his eyes. In his portrayal, Morn appeared to be a very sympathetic character. This bar sitter's name was inspired by Norm, the character who constantly sat at the bar in the television series *Cheers*.

Stoic Mark sat at the end of that bar for seven years, never saying a word. If Morn would have said just a word or two, he would have been compensated with actor's pay. Near the end of the series a script was distributed that included the opportunity for Morn to break out of his mute personality. It actually suggested that Morn might have something to say. Everyone was excited, especially Mark. By the time the final script was approved and rewritten, however, Mark was back to the silent Morn. In the episode called "Who Mourns for Morn," Morn fakes his own death, only to return at the conclusion. Through the approximate forty-two minutes of the show, once again, he never says a word.

Morn's race is known as the Lurians, which I didn't remember or know anything about until I started to write my memoirs, years after the completion of the series. It is also written that Lurians have the reputation of being talkative and excitable. Wow; the writers forgot to include those traits in Morn's TV personality (although maybe this was written post–*Deep Space Nine*).

Jadzia Dax

In *The Next Generation* I had a pantheon of aliens, including a race called the Trills. They were distinguished by their Y-shaped forehead and prehensile pouch, which carried an intelligent symbiont (a life-form that lives inside a humanoid host) that could come and go when needed. This design and concept looked fine on a guy, and the symbiont, which I created by connecting a caterpillar's body to the head of an octopus, was okay too. None of this suited supermodel Terry Farrell, who was cast to play a female version of the Trill species in *Deep Space Nine*. The symbiont was a combination of an insect and an aquatic life-form, and the slimy little guy looked like a male organ attached to a large scrotum. The octopus part of the body was supposed to be its brain, and inside was an air bladder so I could make it pulsate. During Terry's test makeup I tried to keep reducing the size of the forehead, but it just wouldn't work visually. As a child I'd read a book called *How the Leopard Got Its Spots*, and every time I think of Terry I remember that book and think, "How did Dax get her spots?"

The question was finally put to me: "What are you going to do?" Somewhere in my mind, a light switched on. In an early episode of *The Next Generation* in 1992, Famke Janssen of *James Bond* and later *X-Men* fame had been adorned with irregular light brown spots that ringed her forehead and continued down her back. It had worked very well with Famke, framing her natural beauty, so I thought it might work for Terry, too.

To create a similar (yet different) look, I started testing many different patterns, shapes, and colors of tattoo ink on Terry. Two colors were finally approved: a sepia brown highlighted with burnt orange. Unlike Famke's fuller spots, Terry's consisted of interlocking irregular U shapes. With a loose and rotating wrist, in twenty minutes I could apply my dark brown and orange patterns around her hairline and down the sides of her neck. I tried to use a stencil, but it was much faster and more controllable painting them by hand with a small watercolor brush. Each time I completed her facial makeup and spots I would pull her uniform collar away and write the daily number in Roman numerals and sign my initials on her neck. Terry completed her tenure on *Deep Space Nine* with "#538 MW."

A natural question might be, "How did you ever get the spots to match from day to day?" They never did, and I never received a negative note from our producer. There were just too many of them to count.

Several times when Terry had to be scantily clad and more skin was showing than just her head, it meant going to her trailer with two large permanent markers to continue the spot pattern across her shoulders, under her arms, down the sides of her torso, down the outside of her thighs and lower leg, and finishing on the front of her feet. (This was one of those jobs that someone had to do, and I selected myself.)

To ensure consistency with the application of Terry's makeup, I created another Bible. I'd made one for Vulcan ears (points straight up), another for how Starfleet "pointy sideburns" should be applied, and now a third for Terry's spots, if I was not available to apply them.

Over the years when I attended *Star Trek* conventions, I would always meet some Trekkie that was imitating Dax. Invariably I would borrow an eyebrow pencil from someone and on the spot give the Dax lover a lesson in original spotting.

THE CARDASSIANS

Many alien races were introduced in *The Next Generation* and were carried forward as adversaries or compatriots for the next eighteen years. As the years went by I had the opportunity to tweak and improve my original designs, including those I'd created for a race known as the Cardassians.

In the fourth season of *The Next Generation* I was sent a script that called for a serpentine humanoid that was nasty, arrogant, and paranoid, with an untrustworthy reputation. That was about all the information I received. The very first Cardassian, called "Gul Dukat," was played by actor Marc Alaimo. Marc played such a great alien that he was cast to play many more different species over the years. He came to my lab located in a corner of Stage 10. Over several hours I made a plaster copy of Marc's entire head, neck, and shoulders. It looked like a Roman bust one would see in a museum. I studied "plaster Marc" for a while, seeking alien inspiration for a creature with traits from reptiles and mammals. His head was narrow, his face, very chiseled, and his neck, extremely long and thin, with wide and sloping shoulders.

I became inspired to use more than just his face to sculpt my new concept. To follow through with the reptile theme, all the pieces would be segmented bony ridges with scales. I sculpted two ridges about three inches apart that extended down the forehead to the brow ridge, and continued on to encircle the eyes. Double rows of segments extended from the earlobe forward along the jawline. To finish the face I added a nose tip with an attached upper lip and a bony chin. To make good use of Marc's long neck, the sculpture was completed by creating segmented ridges three-quarters of an inch wide that ran from behind the ears to the tip of the shoulders. This was to create the illusion of widening the neck, giving the makeup a hooded, snakelike appearance. A round, sculpted ridge in the middle of the forehead along with the shoulder pieces became the major symbol of their race.

One evening, Marion and I were going to dinner in Studio City and we passed an art gallery that was next door to the restaurant. In the window was a contemporary portrait of a woman with a spoon-like object in the middle of her forehead. It caught my eye, and I exclaimed that someday I would use that concept in an alien makeup. The Cardassian makeup was the perfect opportunity. Between the two segmented ridges that ran down the forehead I sculpted a spoon-like, bony protuberance.

When all the individual pieces became latex and were attached to Marc, they were painted a cold grayish-green. Along with their rough, armored skin the bloodless color lent to the Cardassians a menacing appearance and personality. In retrospect it would have been interesting to have them completely bald, but instead they had shiny, black hair that was slicked back tightly to the head. To adhere all the pieces, paint, wig, and get into their warlike costumes took over three hours.

In *Deep Space Nine* we entered Cardassian Hell; many more were needed to fill up the universe, and it took just as long to get them ready. My biggest fear when we had an upcoming Cardassian episode was that Casting and the producers would hire an actor with a very short neck, which totally ruined the visual concept of their race. It did happen several times, and I was probably the only one that died a little inside.

Eventually there were also women and children, and their makeup was modified with subtler appliances. The ridges were not as pronounced, but there were just as many pieces. Their hair remained black, but with a fuller hairstyle, and longer. A little glamour was artistically applied to the eyes and a touch of purple to the lips. Throughout the seasons I worked very closely with costume designer Robert Blackman, as every so often he would create a costume that would show some alien skin. With many of the Cardassian women he lowered the necklines of their costumes,

Marc Alaimo as Gul Ducat. *CBS Consumer Products*

which meant I had to model a chest appliance that would complement the facial and neck ridges. To differentiate our females instantly, the center of their forehead spoon was colored with a brilliant blue.

Aside from a few stunt Cardassians getting bruised while filming a fight scene, one of the worst accidents happened when Marc transformed himself into a Bajoran. Marc, in his disguise, is in the midst of fisticuffs with Captain Sisko (played by Avery Brooks). As Avery takes a roundhouse swing to Marc's face he was supposed to step back slightly and turn his head away. Instead of rocking backward, however, Marc swayed forward, right into the punch. A sickening crunch was heard over the silence of the stage as Marc slowly dropped down, disappearing from frame. Everyone could hear him groaning, "My nose, my nose." Avery was the first to the rescue. Marc survived, with just some minor swelling.

In my office the next day I received a copy of the accident, on film. I was fascinated by the visual impact, so I viewed it over and over. I cringed every time I knew the crack would break the silence. Marc didn't play by the rules, ignoring the old adage, "Never do your own stunts."

Star Trek: Voyager

STAR TREK: VOYAGER, 1995–2001 (170 EPISODES)

The USS *Voyager* is sent on a mission to locate and round up a group of space rebels known as the Maquis. After the Starfleet crew has encountered, tangled, and aligned with some of the Maquis, they enter a nebula. This nebula is an interstellar cloud of ionized gas which transports them all unwillingly into the far distant corners of the Delta Quadrant. Even if *Voyager* travels back at warp speed, it will still take seventy-five years to return to Federation Space. The time is the twenty-fourth century, around the 2370s. In command is Captain Janeway (Kate Mulgrew), the first female officer to fly a Federation starship on such a mission.

During the seven years of filming, the *Voyager* crew would encounter many new aliens and humanoids, some good and some bad. This was the first time I had so many special makeups to create for the principal performers. They included Neelix (Ethan Phillips), a Talaxian; Kes (Jennifer Lien), an Ocampa; B'Elanna Torres (Roxann Dawson), half human, half Klingon; Tuvok (Tim Russ), a Vulcan security officer; and the popular Seven of Nine (Jeri Ryan), the female Borg. Then, to top it all off, I had to design and apply a partial facial tattoo onto Chakotay's (Robert Beltran) forehead. Chakotay was a former Maquis, now a crew member.

The never-ending bad guys included a species known as the Kazon, whose facial design was based on none other than a Thanksgiving turkey. Other bad guys, the Hirogen, were inspired by the Gila monster lizard. One of my favorites was the

Vidiians, because their bodies and faces were covered with a patchwork of multicolored and textured skin they harvested and grafted from other aliens. Of course there were more Borgs; these resembled the newly designed ones from *First Contact*.

Did the USS *Voyager* beat off the bad guys and return home? You'll have to watch the series to find out.

Chakotay

Actor Robert Beltran was hired to play the part of a special officer. Instead of being an alien with simple prosthetics, he was to have a Native cultural background and appearance, and would be known as Chakotay. Rick Berman decided to try something different, something that would give this character his own individuality. What about a facial tattoo? I had to decide where to place it, so to start, I collected drawings and photos of facial and body tattoos from Native cultures around the world. Each one had its own unique style as to how their tattoos would twist and bend.

On multiple paper sketches of Robert's face I created designs from India, Tahiti, North America, Hawaii, New Zealand, the Philippines, and so forth. The producers selected several designs for me to paint on his face so we could test them all on camera. On our first makeup test I covered his entire face with a tattoo that resembled the Maori from New Zealand. I was very familiar with Maori tattoo application, as I had been involved with the opening of the Polynesian Cultural Center in Hawaii, teaching present-day Maori how to apply their ancestral facial tattoos. For makeup test number two, I reduced the area painted to half of Robert's face, and then for test number three, only a quarter. Number three was the winning design, as it wouldn't be too distracting. The approved tattoo would be applied to the upper left side of Robert's face, encompassing his left forehead and left temple.

In the beginning I thought I might be able to use a stencil to apply it, but found it was much easier and cleaner to apply it freehand with blue tattoo ink and a small brush. Following natural little bumps and freckles on Robert's skin I was able to duplicate his signature tattoo hundreds of times. There are so many fans of *Star Trek*, I just knew someone was going to copy my tattoo, for real. Wouldn't you know it, with a few more curls and swirls, the famous boxer Mike Tyson came pretty close.

My application of Robert's tattoo became such a ritual that I had to follow my movements consistently to create a perfect match from day to day. My applicator was a small #3 watercolor brush with long soft bristles. I had to grasp the handle very lightly and maintain a very loose wrist, so it would act almost like it was on a swivel; that way

I could achieve long continuous strokes. Most important, I always started and finished in the same spot, or else my mind would become confused. The starting spot was directly over Robert's inner left eyebrow, and I would finish with the horizontal temple lines that ran into his natural hairline. Like my numbered spots on Dax from *Deep Space Nine*, I would pull Robert's uniform collar away from his neck and sequentially number and initial each day's application. We ended with "#750 MW."

Neelix and the Gang

The *Voyager* series came hot on the heels of *Deep Space Nine*. In fact, I was trying to finish the final seventh season of *DS9*, which overlapped with my work on *Voyager*. This meant I needed to hire another makeup crew, design new aliens and humanoids, stock a new makeup trailer with supplies, and, for good measure, also run a *Next Generation* movie on the side.

I had an ensemble of principal characters to prepare. Tim Russ was cast to make history as Tuvok, our first black Vulcan. He was also the first regular Vulcan since Spock. Roxann Dawson was to become B'Elanna Torres, a beautiful half-breed Klingon who wore a very soft ridged forehead, so soft that her ridges reminded most every one of three seagulls in flight. I tested her with the normal sharp Klingon nose and nasty teeth, but they were rejected because it made her look like Dr. Jekyll and Mr. Hyde. The youthful Jennifer Lien, the first of her Ocampa race to be seen, wore a different style of subtle ears that extended from her earlobe to her jaw. They needed to be different but not bold enough to distract. Her ears became the model for all the Ocampas that came after her.

Ethan Phillips as Neelix. *CBS Consumer Products*

Once all that designing and molding was out of the way, I had to create a friendly, lovable, trustworthy, Boy Scout of a character by the name of Neelix. Production wanted him to be memorable and merchandisable. Ethan Phillips had the perfect face on which to work my magic. While pondering which way to start, my midnight lightbulb went on (some of my best ideas arrived in the middle of the night). I had just seen the animated Disney feature *The Lion King*, and I was very impressed by the characters and their personalities, most notably the meerkats and the warthog. What if I combined them?

So I did. With the assistance of Scott Wheeler, the lovable Neelix was created and brought to life, with a horizontally ridged head, a slightly bulbous nose with a split in the center, round apple cheeks, and cute ears.

Over all the rubber, Scott painted a warm flesh tone accented with a bright yellow. Over the base paint Neelix got his spots. Every brown spot, in different densities, was individually airbrushed in place. For my warthog design, a Mohawk hairpiece or wig was constructed with very coarse goat hair. It was applied on the top of his head with the ends cascading down the back of his neck. Using a softer hair, mainly for comfort, a pair of curled warthog muttonchops was adhered to Ethan's lower jaw. Not to forget my meerkats, a pair of spiky, stylized floppy eyebrows completed his kindly look. Ethan's eyes were then transformed with yellowish-orange contact lenses. I kept everything on him round and friendly, even his false teeth. Unlike the pointed and sharp scary teeth of other aliens, Neelix's teeth were round on the canines and flat on top of the others, like herbivores. I decided to make Neelix a vegetarian. Everything about his character in the animal world spelled out kindheartedness, and friendliness in the human world—traits also shared by the man with a natural gift for gab, Ethan Phillips.

Star Trek: Enterprise

Enterprise, the earth's first starship capable of traveling at warp-five speeds, was launched at the dawn of interstellar space exploration. As a prequel to the original *Trek*, it takes place one hundred years earlier, during the twenty-second century, around 2151 to 2161. The five-year mission of the *Enterprise NX-01* is centered around areas that are close to the Milky Way. Its technology was not as advanced as the ships and technology that we have seen on *The Next Generation*, *Deep Space Nine*, and *Voyager*. The commander was Captain Jonathan Archer (Scott Bakula), and his mission on this newly designed spacecraft was to go first where no man had gone before — so we did! With the new performing cast there were only two new makeup challenges: One was T'Pol (Jolene Blalock), a female Vulcan sub-commander, and Dr. Phlox (John Billingsley), a Denobulan who possessed many medical talents and alien critters.

It wouldn't be *Star Trek* without some of our old standby aliens like Klingons, Borgs, and Vulcans. With this new show I had the opportunity to resurrect from the original series the blue-skinned Andorians (but now their antennae were electronic); the swine-like Tellarites; and the green-skinned Orions. We had a new bad species, the Sphere Builders, who were smooth and featureless, along with the Suliban and their yellow, pebble-like appearance.

On its maiden voyage the *NX-01* first lands on an ice planet called Rigel-X, which is the crossroads for interstellar traders. When the crew disembarks into the steamy marketplace they walk among never-before-seen aliens conducting their bartering activities and dancing seductively. One humanoid pair of exotic female dancers was body-sprayed with just a thin coat of latex, one blue and the other pink. They could snatch butterflies out of the air with their extremely long computer-generated (CG) tongues. We met many other alien species like the Xindi. There were six variations, all based on familiar earthly forms with similar DNA. My favorites were the Reptiles. Some of the six I created with special makeup, and others were CG. We really didn't get a chance to complete the full mission, because the show was canceled after its fourth season. A fifth season would have brought to the screen new scripts, more new alien species, and more updated creations from the original series. Sigh!

Dr. Phlox

The doctors on the three previous shows were all humans: Gates McFadden as Dr. Beverly Crusher (*TNG*), Alexander Siddig as Dr. Bashir (*DS9*), Robert Picardo as The Doctor, an Emergency Medical Hologram (*Voyager*), and finally, John Billingsley, playing Dr. Phlox as a humanoid in *Enterprise*.

Dr. Phlox puttered in his lab, which contained experiments and alien species. Over the four years of the series I would make small animals and shapes that would inhabit his cages and fish tanks. I feel that *Enterprise* was one of the most interesting of the series in terms of guest aliens. I challenged my artists to up their creative talents. There were both new aliens and ones that had been reprised from the original series. The first episode, "Broken Bow," contained challenging aliens and opticals that continue to amaze me to this day.

This was a four-year roller-coaster ride that I almost missed. When it came time to create Dr. Phlox, the producers were looking for something different, and the Dr. Phlox concept lost a lot in translation. I designed a number of ideas that were all possible, but they were declined. I would continue to sketch only to have my drawings rejected. This was one of those times when no one knew what they wanted, but would "know it when they saw it." I was at my wits' end; I had to come up with a positive direction.

On Friday of that week, I was called into the production office and told that the producers were getting worried; there was a possibility I could be replaced. I was given permission to hire other artists to assist if need be, but something had to be delivered the following ("Black") Monday, one way or another. I called Marion that afternoon with the (not-so-good) news. I told her I was mentally exhausted, since I had not been given any suggestions or directions from my original designs. I told her I was going to resign, to which she replied with an emphatic "No!"

I'd already had other artists working their artistic magic at home, and they'd been faxing me their completed sketches. On Friday night Marion sent me into our upper guest bedroom with my sketchpad and a handful of sharp pencils, telling me I wasn't to come out until she was satisfied. I accomplished ten new drawings. Exhausted, I went to bed, only to be sent back into isolation on Saturday morning. After twenty-five drawings, she said, "More!" By Saturday night I had accumulated fifty. By the end of Sunday night I had a hundred concepts and variations on the concepts, including the faxed sketches from my assisting artists. (Although I didn't really feel there was anything usable from them, I included the sketches anyway; I felt they made my ideas more acceptable, and my portfolio, thicker. I couldn't blame the assisting artists; they didn't fully understand the *Star Trek* / Roddenberry directive, and I didn't have time to teach them all the nuances

John Billingsley as Dr. Phlox. *CBS Consumer Products*

and details at this late date.) I bound everything into a book and presented it to Rick on Monday morning. As he thumbed through the sketches and colored overlays, I would hear him say, "Hmmm." That was a good sign.

After a lot of *hmmm*-ing, he finally selected a forehead from one drawing, a pair of ears from another, and a small chin from a third. I also designed several different colors of contact lenses, skin colorings, size and color of facial and hand spots, and finally, a stylized wig concept. Everything for Dr. Phlox was selected and approved. With a sigh, I was ready to put it all together. After everything I'd gone through that weekend, I finally had the opportunity to sit back and sing to myself the Peggy Lee song, "Is That All There Is?" before calling Marion to thank her for her persistence.

Dr. Phlox sat in Bradley Look's makeup chair for the next four years as he duplicated the application and coloring process day after day. That roller-coaster ride continued for the next four years, with the creation of new aliens and updated old ones. I still had plans to bring more aliens to life, but we reached the top of the hill and quickly descended. Paramount Studios turned off the lights three years too soon.

Suliban

Just the thought of creating a new episodic alien made my teeth tingle. A challenge was thrown into my lap that made me and my assisting artists begin to scratch their heads. It wasn't the design of the alien but its skin texture that created a problem. This new race was going to be hairless, so every square inch of exposed skin had to be covered in texture and color. That included its head, face, ears, lips, eyelids, neck, and hands. Even their contact lenses and teeth had to be taken into consideration. The rest of its body, arms, legs, and feet were covered with a tight-fitting reddish costume. Our producer handed me a computer-generated picture from a scientific magazine. Pictured was the face of a man covered in thousands of little bumps the size of a pimple. My dilemma: How do I duplicate and paint thousands of little bumps, especially when it has to be replicated?

At first we tried to sculpt the bumps in clay, but the process was too slow. *What in our world today looks like this image?* I wondered. What about the skin of a citrus fruit, oranges being the most popular? This textured surface, transferred to a latex pad,

Suliban. *CBS Consumer Products*

has been used many times by sculptors to texturize the surface of a clay sculpture before it is molded into a prosthetic. Somewhere in the darkness a light went on. I had visited hobby stores many times during my career to solve other situations. I knew that model train stores sell plastic molds that are used to duplicate, in miniature, earth textures to be used in model train dioramas.

The next day I couldn't wait to visit the train store in Burbank, California. There, hanging on a rack with other molds, was a semi-flat plastic sheet that could be used to duplicate the small rocks found around the base of the railroad tracks. I purchased several different sizes and took them back to the lab. That same afternoon I tried an experiment: First, the plastic mold was duplicated in fast-setting silicone. When the silicone firmed up, I was able to paint thin layers of melted sculpting clay into that mold. After cooling, a thin sheet of clay could be peeled away that was smooth on one side and pebbly on the other. The clay sheet was so flexible it could be molded and wrapped around any of our plaster body parts. From these enjoined sheets of clay covering the body parts, molds were made, and the clay was replaced with latex. The vulcanized latex skin was then wrapped around and glued to the actor's skin. The mystery of how to duplicate the bumpy-textured skin was solved.

The next challenge was painting this alien's flesh. We couldn't paint each pimple individually, as that would take days, and this was television. The solution made all my artists breathe easier. The entire piece of textured latex, after applying, was colored with dark brown flexible paint and then dried. A mustard-yellow highlight was then lightly brushed over the top of the bumps. This paint scheme created a high-low effect, just like the one in the magazine picture.

For final touches I designed oversized yellow contact lenses that were hand-painted with small brown dots, so all body parts would appear to be textured. A little theatrical "nicotine" tooth stain was applied to reduce the whiteness of the performer's teeth, and then a swipe of yellow makeup across the top of the lower eyelashes. A few drops of caramel-colored food dye reduced the obvious pink tongue and mouth. All of this seems complicated to follow, but once the techniques were learned, it was an easy makeup to apply. I knew there wouldn't be a problem when the makeup artists started having contests to see who could finish first.

In the creation of special makeup, very seldom does an artist get the opportunity to add a new and popular alien to historical space. On *Star Trek* I had several opportunities, and this was one of them.

Andorians

The Andorians were one of the most popular alien species from the original series. The Andorian backstory is quite interesting. The color of their skin is bluish due to the frigid planet they inhabit, and a pair of antennae gave them a heightened degree of sensory perception. Their face was very blue and they sported a pair of static antennae that were mounted to their head. The alien character was completed with an inexpensive white wig and bushy white eyebrows. The original antennaes were sculpted by Fred Phillips, then cast into a rigid material. The tips were widened with the wooden end from a spool of thread, ingenious for its time.

This was the original look I was asked to re-create for a 2000 update, with a note from the producers: "If the antenna don't move, don't do it." Working with Makeup and Effects Laboratories in North Hollywood we devised a fiberglass skull cap that tightly hugged the actor's head. On this shell, cables and a pair of servos were mounted. With the flip of a switch and a simple radio controller in hand, the newly molded, flexible latex antennae could move back and forth and dance in a 360-degree circle. The new and improved expensive white wig and a latex forehead covered the entire mechanical mechanism. I maintained the blue flesh color because I wasn't about to try and change the genius of Gene's original concept. The freshly designed white eyebrows were attached to the forehead, and a touch of blue color was added to the lips. The final update was to have the actors rinse their mouths with blue food coloring to tone down their naturally pink tongue. While they were performing a puppeteer could give the antennaes a life of their own. With a specific wave of his finger, the director would silently signal them and the antennae would respond in like motion. My blue-skinned male and female Andorians had a busy career on *Enterprise* because the antennae worked. The *Enterprise* series became an alien tribute to the classic 1960s.

Tellarites

I feel the second successful alien remake from classic *Trek* to the *Enterprise* series were the Tellarites. The original swinish-looking aliens that appeared in the original series looked hastily constructed, as if they were Halloween masks. The actors' eyes were deeply set behind the eye sockets. On screen the actors always seemed to be looking up their piglike noses because of their partially obscured vision. The use of their hands wasn't much better, as they looked like hairy, pig-like oven mitts. Hair was applied around the face where there was a possibility of an exposed latex seam. Even with all of their makeup faults, they were still classic aliens.

On *Enterprise* I was given the challenge of resurrecting and modifying the pig men based on the original Tellarite design. My thought was never to make it better, but simply more acceptable to the 2004 audience. Having a much larger budget to create with, the new Tellarites were going to see and talk well and be able to use their hands to push buttons.

My upturned snout was a little more alien in its flare of the nostrils, and I added a swine-like lower lip. A set of tusks was designed for the lower teeth so my male Tellarites would resemble wild boars. I raised the hairline to expose more face, and swept the bushy eyebrows upward. Knowing that my swinish group had to be able to push buttons, I opted to dress their hands with a hoofed thumb and a rough, skin-textured pad on the back of the hand that included an obvious dewclaw. Leaving their fingers free allowed them to manipulate a zipper in a moment of need. I maintained the use of wigs and facial hair, but from the early coiffures and undressed beards, my new porcine characters were more coordinated and better dressed. A wig and facial hair for one new Tellarite cost over $4,000, and in one episode there were twelve of them.

REFLECTIONS, 1987–2005

It took eighteen years, using more than one hundred makeup artists, thousands of gallons of liquid latex, and countless adhesives and containers of makeup and makeup remover to accomplish the creation of *The Next Generation*, *Deep Space Nine*, *Voyager*, *Enterprise*, four feature films, and numerous exhibits. My studio was my home away from home. Marion referred to my time at work as "Camp *Star Trek*." Every morning she would send her camper off to work with a kiss good-bye, no matter what the time.

I spent thousands of hours surrounded by the same familiar walls, whether it be filming stages, production offices, makeup trailers, makeup labs, or my office. In the labs, latex alien faces hung in place so long they became crumbling symbols of alien species from long, long ago. Each one became a member of the Camp *Star Trek* family. I can spin you a story about each one—the inspiration, the creative steps from start to finish, the application, and the breathing into life. Each one has its own history.

In a casual chat or when addressing a convention, I sometimes will momentarily lose an alien's origin, but all I have to do is paint a picture, and it will be remembered by many. For example, "It has a light-blue bald head with dark-blue, watermelon-like stripes and elongated earlobes, and an indented ridge runs over the head and down the face." I will hear the reply, in unison: "It's a Bolian!" I never have to worry about the past, because it is remembered by so many fans.

Having recorded so much history, I found it appropriate to chronicle the last six episodes of *Enterprise*, including a final moment on January 5, 2005, after we returned from the holiday break:

> Completed episode with the Klingons. I started to prep the "Orion" episode. There was a production meeting at 11 a.m. Found more time to read the newspaper. Joe (Podner) started to metallize male Orion plant-ons; Earl (Ellis) foamed a bald cap, as we may have to cap the slaves, since they may hire actors who will not shave their heads. Fred Blau has been snowed in at his cabin in Big Bear; he got out today, so I will be able to order more avocado-colored ink—Orion body color. Earl has been

Under attack by my own creations. *Courtesy of the author*

prepping more plastic hooks and small sabers so we can make the male Orion skin appear pierced. We start tomorrow with the first, naked Orion female; arranged all the makeup for Garrett (Immel), including black lipstick, false nails (black polish), eyelashes, and eye shadow. Had to arrange for the spray booth to be used. It has been so cold that additional heaters had to be brought in.

The last day the cameras rolled was March 9, 2005. I wrote: "The Day After—green screen with Jonathan (Frakes) and Marina (Sirtis). I was here in 1987 for Marina and Jonathan's first shot on camera, and at 3:45 p.m., I was here for their last. It is time to boldly go . . ."

THE EMMYS

The rules for joining the Television Academy are different than the Motion Picture Academy; working in the television industry gives credence to almost any individual joining the organization. Thus, there are many thousands of members across the country. Entries for ballot consideration are processed on applications that ask for story outlines and what type of work was accomplished, usually filled out by the supervisor of the project. This is where everybody must toot their own horn. Makeup and hairstyling submissions are compiled on a large master list that is sent out to all peer members in that category. The members then select their favorite choices and return the form to the Academy. The top choices are then made available to be viewed and voted on by a blue-ribbon panel, of which I've been a member many times. These top choices are then invited to the Creative Arts Emmy Awards show, where winners will be announced. Whew! This is the simplest way of explaining it, as the rules have changed many times over the years.

In the early days of the ceremony, when membership was much smaller, it was held as a luncheon in Beverly Hills. It was a swank afternoon for all attendees. As the organization grew, a few of the creative arts categories, like makeup or costumes, were invited to be part of the Big Gala every other year. As more expansion took place, it was broken up into two distinct nights. The Creative Arts Awards, "below the line," one night, and "above the line," another. Above the line are the recognizable personalities like actors, directors, producers, and best shows of the year; in other words, the television extravaganza. Here is where all the winners display, toast, and have dinner with their new winged trophy.

Carole Kabrin's "Tribute" to the characters created for *Star Trek: The Next Generation.* If you look closely at the lower right you can see me holding a sculpting tool. *Courtesy of the author*

The Creative Arts Awards, which is held first, is very social, as friends and family members are included among the attendees. In the past there could be over twenty nominees on a single ballot. If that group won, the winners' circle around the microphone was very crowded. This was an area where the rules had to change, and they did. Now, only the artists most responsible for the project are listed.

There is still the same excitement in winning each time. I have had the pleasure of being nominated forty-two times, and I have won nine times. It used to be that one of the perks of being nominated was that the studio would send a limo to your doorstep.

Everyone had to be at the theater early, so it always seemed strange to dress in a tuxedo or formal gown in the early afternoon. Once we had a limo driver that was not familiar with Los Angeles. I won that year, and Marion and I were very excited and not paying attention on our return ride. Instead of taking us directly back to the Valley, she drove us into a very questionable neighborhood downtown. Imagine this: We were driving down seedy bar-lined streets. On the curbs were men and women drinking out of paper bags, and the sidewalks were covered in prostitutes. We, on the other hand, were dressed in formal clothes riding in the back of a long, black limo. Without speaking a word to each other, Marion and I both had the same thought: *How would we defend ourselves if our driver dared to stop?* Our eyes were focused on the Golden Lady in my lap. Not only is Emmy heavy, but she also sports a pair of long, pointed wings. If we were going to have to fight our way out, our new girlfriend "Emmy" was going to lead the charge. We finally made it home, but our normal half-hour ride had turned into a two-hour nightmare.

On another occasion, instead of attending the awards show Marion and I opted to get away for the weekend. I told my makeup artist associates to buzz me on my cell phone if we won. After a long evening I placed my phone on the nightstand next to our bed and we went into the front room to watch television. Near midnight we started to hear buzzing that sounded like a swarm of bees. I saw my phone jumping up and down and on the screen it displayed "11111." What a nice way to go to sleep!

On another winning evening when I had my crew on stage, Lou Ferrigno (The Hulk) was the presenter. I was standing directly behind him and decided to whisper idle chitchat in his ear as each one received their Emmy. When I returned to my seat I told Marion that Lou had ignored my conversation. Marion turned to me with the strangest glance and a single word: "Really." I'd forgotten that Lou is deaf.

I was out of town on location one year, so Marion decided to take Michael and Michele to the awards ceremony. Prior to the event I had received a letter stating that only the recipients would be allowed to collect their statuettes. When Marion arrived she was told again that only the recipients would be allowed to collect their Emmys, an announcement that was repeated from the stage before the event started.

When it was time for the makeup category to be announced, the presenter said, "Winner of the Best Makeup Award goes to Michael Westmore." There was applause, then silence, as no one stirred. The presenter looked around and was probably about to accept for me, but Marion had primed Michele. She said, "Michele, you only have this one chance to go and get Dad's Emmy." Michele bounded out of her chair and from the back of the room ran through the tables to the front. The presenter commented that she didn't look like Michael Westmore. Michele ran up the stairs to the microphone, collected the Emmy, and said, "Daddy, you deserve this, and we love you!" The room broke into a thunderous applause. The edict should have been, "Only recipients and Michele Westmore are allowed to collect the Emmys."

Snippets

In 1991, I was asked to create makeup for actor Stephen Lang so that he would resemble legendary baseball icon Babe Ruth. Lorimar Productions was recounting his great life in a TV movie called *The Babe Ruth Story*. I met Stephen in my lab and took a cast of his face. I gathered a multitude of research photos of the Babe's face from every angle. For weeks I sculpted on the cast, adding a small amount here and shaving away from there. After several back-and-forth visits with the work in progress, everyone approved my clay portrait.

The next step was to make a series of plaster molds. In these molds I could create all the prosthetics that would be needed for the film. They included a forehead, nose, cheeks, chin, and throat. Stephen had a much smaller face so he needed to be filled out and broadened. Prior to principal photography we did several makeup and wardrobe tests at a baseball field, so the Babe could approach the plate and swing his bat in Ruth-like fashion. Armed with all the individual efforts, including makeup, hairstyling, wardrobe, and the authenticity of the ballpark, Stephen assumed the Babe's body language and famous swing. Everyone left the park delighted, until the following day's phone call. The producer had one comment: "The person I see on-screen looks like Babe Ruth, not my actor Mr. Lang." What a compliment. All the weeks of preparation was reduced to a latex nose. You might say I received my sixteenth Emmy nomination by a nose.

ANIMAL CRACKERS

When you've worked in the film industry for any length of time, you're guaranteed to cross paths with children and animal performers. Here are several of my animal encounters of the third kind.

Poodle #1

Many years ago when I was an apprentice at Universal Studios there was large poodle starring in a film with Tony Curtis. In this movie there were two dogs, one male and one female. It seems that the two working canines didn't care whether a movie crew of seventy-five watched as they demonstrated their affection for each other. Movie studio business is filled with spur-of-the-moment challenges, and this was one of them. "Fix it," came the order from above, and this directive to strap the male dog down wasn't heard from heaven. A four-inch-square patch of fake fur was dyed to match the poodle's own coloring. A string was attached to each corner long enough to reach all the way around his body. The patch was fitted in place over his private parts and the strings were tied snugly on his back. Mr. Hotty was then able to go back to work.

Monkey #1

In the 1940s when my uncle Frank started his makeup apprenticeship at Warner Bros., one of his first assignments was to keep Cheetah the chimpanzee powdered. It seems that Cheetah had a very shiny, hairless, pink butt. Frank's job was to tone it down. So equipped with a sponge and black shoe polish he would apply makeup to the chimp's butt on a daily basis. Instead of this irritating our hairy actor, he would wait for Frank in anticipation. Cheetah was in love, and this was just another Hollywood love story.

Monkey #2

Acton, California, is a desert community where a wild game refuge is located. It houses a variety of trained exotic animals that are used in the motion picture industry. I use the term *trained* to mean "workable," not "friendly." Waiting for me when I arrived was a very large male chimpanzee that was chained and locked to the top of an old picnic table. I needed valuable photo references so I could duplicate this chimp's exact body, head, hands, and feet. I was creating a duplicate out of latex and hair for the film *Project X*. Some animals don't take direction well, so these monkey parts would serve as backup, or, you might say, the chimp's stunt double.

As I walked closer to the chimp, absorbed in my assignment and clicking away on my camera, I heard the trainer behind me, whispering, "Stop . . . Now, slowly, back up." Even though the trainer was tightly gripping and periodically tapping on the ground a good-size baseball bat as a "friendly" reminder to the chimp to be nice, I was too close. Trainers can read in the eyes of their animals what reactions are about to come forth. The trainer told me I was getting into the chimp's space, and he was becoming curious. If he had decided to grab me so we could meet, up close and personal, the trainer couldn't have saved me—at least, not in one piece. This chimp weighed over 150 pounds and sported razor-sharp nails and long fangs. From recent news reports, we know what damage these simian fellows are capable of inflicting.

Tigers

While working with the magician Doug Henning, a master of illusion, I was asked not to lean on the disappearing tiger's cage, or I might disappear, too—and it wouldn't be part of the show.

Poodle #2

On a clear starry night in the middle of the California desert, Marion and I found ourselves standing next to a giant spaceship. I was working on the last scene of a sci-fi movie that costarred a small, white French poodle. Filming had been suspended for some time so that the owner of our canine could have him shorn of his long curly hair in order to play a role in another film. The producer was in a quandary, as this dog would never match all the previous filming. In my bag of tricks was a case filled with assorted colors of curly wool and a lot of spirit gum.

The producer had given me an unofficial "Do it," promising to keep the dog owner busy. I had never heard of this being done in the annals of Hollywood, but it did sound like a challenge. From my bag I pulled out many tufts of imitation white hair. I started by dipping a wide brush into the glue and slathered it on to the hair of our little canine. As the glue became sticky I packed the tufts of wool into his fur. Putting it on was great, but here was the catch: I was not prepared to remove it, as I would have needed a gallon of alcohol.

As the night's filming progressed in this land of scorpions (they were crawling all around us), Marion and I silently stepped over our deadly friends and packed the car. As the sun broke over the horizon, we heard the familiar phrase in moviedom: "It's a wrap." Marion was already in the car with the motor running, and we were the first to hit the highway, back to civilization.

Bullmastiff

Butkus was Sylvester Stallone's personal dog. On the original *Rocky* he traveled with us everywhere, whether in the trailer or on the set. I will never forget that first quiet, cold morning preparing to film in Philadelphia. Sly sounded nervous when he said, "Here we go." The four of us—Sly, his wife Sasha, me, and Butkus—burst from the trailer and entered the world of Rocky Balboa. Butkus was a big dog—I mean, *really* big—but Sly had such perfect control of him that he was allowed to fly in First Class. Sly once apologized to a passenger sitting on the other side of Butkus. The man replied that he'd enjoyed the dog's company, and the flight, because the dog was such a gentle beast. In fact, the man said he preferred Butkus's company to that of human passengers. This was a great love story between man and his best friend.

CHILDREN

At the end of my animal list we can't forget the most uncontrollable ones of all: children. Most animals—whether elephant, horse, chimp, dog, cat, or mouse—come with a trainer or handler, and I have worked with them all. Like the aforementioned creatures, children also come in different sizes, shapes, and personalities. Assigned to every child on a working day there is a trainer and a handler, aka, a responsible adult, as well as a teacher. Each child has an individual purpose or desire to be acting, whether it is their own choice, or, sometimes, that of an adult. Remember, there is a very nice paycheck that goes along with a day's work. It's more than a penny saved is a penny earned; it's more like thousands.

I remember one precocious child who played the part of the young Bobby Darin, back when I was at Universal Studios. To create a more Bobby-like appearance, the child wore a miniature plastic version of Bobby's real nose. Gluing it on was like trying to stick something on a worm. Although this boy seemed to like showbiz, he was just a little wiggler.

Performing on *Land of the Lost*, the child actor who played the monkey boy, Chaka, decided he wasn't cut out for the bright lights, so when his contract expired, he returned to a life of normalcy with family, friends, school, and sports. This was very intuitive for a child.

On *Raging Bull*, a primed little boy, upon entering the set with his mother, marched up to a person in front of everyone and exclaimed loudly, "Good morning, Mr. De Niro; it's nice to meet you." Now, that was polite, and good priming—except it wasn't Robert. It was Martin Scorsese's hand he was pumping. Thanks, Mom!

An unprimed little boy on one of the *Rocky* films kept staring into the lens of the camera when it was rolling—a real no-no for everyone. Calmly, Sly would say "Cut" and take the child aside for personal instructions as to exactly where he should look. The little boy would continue to perform this eye shift each time the director would shout "Action!" Finally, in desperation, Stallone told the child something very scary, like, death would result if he kept looking at the camera—or maybe that he'd never work in this town again if he didn't listen. Whatever it was, Sly's advice worked.

Interestingly enough, I can't remember any stories about little girls on the set, although I'm sure I worked with some up-and-coming divas. On the whole, most children are nice and well-behaved, but at times, animals are easier to direct, and they can work longer hours.

GEORGE BURNS

I once had the opportunity to do a commercial with George. The actor you see on-screen is the same person you get in real life; there is no difference. A "take" is one complete roll of the performer doing their dialogue on film. With George, "take three" sounds just like "take one" and "take two." During our few hours together, I realized that you best love the smell of cigars if you're going to work with him, as he puffed on one constantly. The entire film crew got to share his secondhand smoke. I might say I shared many cigars with George, at least, the smoke from them, and he lived to be how old?

SCREEN GODDESS VIRGINIA MAYO: "THE REST OF THE STORY"

My first movie star crush occurred in the late 1940s when I was about ten years old. I was taken to see a Saturday-afternoon movie starring the legendary screen goddess, Virginia

Mayo. At that age I didn't care about anyone else on the silver screen. I didn't have that same face-flushing, heart-pounding hormonal feeling again until I met my wife Marion.

In 1969 my uncle Perc started a mail-order business at Universal Studios, selling different styles of "flatter wigs" (based on famous celebrity hairstyles). He asked Virginia Mayo, an old friend, to be the celebrity spokesperson. Perc's expertise was as great in designing wigs as it was for applying makeup. He personally designed the prototype of each wig, and enlisted Uncle Bud and I to be part of his new entrepreneurial adventure.

One sunny, Southern California morning we all flew to San Francisco to meet with potential investors and manufacturers. This all sounds pretty normal up to now, but wait . . .

Virginia's husband was actor Michael O'Shea. I had the privilege (or not) of sitting next to him on our flight. As we sat back in our seats he proceeded to tell me a little about himself. He was a successful actor and had been a spy in a sting operation at the famous Friars Club. Michael was interested in police work, so it was easy for the FBI to enlist his help in cracking a ring of card cheaters. He discovered the ring had drilled tiny holes in the ceiling above the card table. From this vantage point the crooked players could be informed of what cards everyone was holding. There were a lot of high-stakes celebrity players at that time, and the Friars Club membership read like a who's who of Hollywood. Michael testified against the card-cheating ring. In retaliation he told me that a contract had been taken out on him.

At this point I was beginning to feel uncomfortable, as we weren't talking about a one-year service contract at a department store. To prove his point, Michael pulled back his jacket to show me a holstered pistol strapped to his waist. Now, I was *really* uncomfortable, because we were trapped in an airplane with nowhere to hide but the lavatory. When we landed I found myself unconsciously putting distance between us as we walked out of the airport terminal, all the while thinking, "Please not today—I have a family!"

Unfortunately, Uncle Perc passed away in 1970, and the Westmore wig business came to a close. And now, the rest of the story: In 2002 I was reading an interview which was given by Virginia to a national magazine. In 1973 she and Michael were performing in a play in Dallas, Texas, called *Forty Carats*. After going to bed she heard some strange noises in the hallway of their apartment that frightened her. When she woke in the morning, to her horror, she found Michael in the bathroom wearing only his shorts. He was dead, lying in the dry bathtub. Cause of death was listed as a fall.

Now I ask you, after several years of watching over his shoulder, was it an accident, or was the contract fulfilled?

MILTON BERLE

Uncle Miltie had a propensity for ingesting spoonfuls of honey for energy. One day when everything was going right, the director wanted me to glue a fake mustache onto Milton's face. Uncle Miltie felt the mustache hair was too long; it was tickling his mouth, and he wanted it trimmed. I took my scissors and proceeded to remove the longer hairs. At this time I didn't know about his habit and his honey-coated lips. All of the little flying hairs adhered to his lips as if he was wearing a few days' growth of beard on his mouth. George Slater, the director/producer, was ready to film. "What the hell?" was a good comment for the situation. At these moments, panic sets in, and being a genius is necessary. I called for my operating tools, which consisted of a cup of hot water and a towel. A little scrubbing and some makeup, and he was back to normal.

BURL IVES

Burl Ives, the singer of "Rudolph, the Red-Nosed Reindeer," was a semiregular on *Alias Smith and Jones*. He had a habit of snorting snuff, and carried a tin of it in his pocket. Occasionally he would take a pinch and snort it up his nose. I didn't mind him enjoying his habit, but when he got in front of the camera with black nostrils that looked like he'd been smelling a lump of coal, it became my concern. Please, Burl, I felt like telling him, send up a red flag when the urge arises!

MS. PEE

In the privacy of her dressing room one actress (who shall remain nameless) liked to pee in Styrofoam coffee cups and leave them on the makeup table. Guess who got to remove them? As the old joke goes, "Don't eat yellow snow," although in this case, I think "Don't drink warm lemonade" is more apt.

TOM HANKS

A production manager friend asked me to save his butt by coming in and taking over a TV series called *Bosom Buddies*. I was between feature films, and it sounded like fun. It was! Everyone was always up. Behind the cameras Tom Hanks and Peter Scolari were always telling jokes and juggling. The girls' ensemble included Wendie Jo Sperber, Donna Dixon, Telma Hopkins, and Holland Taylor. They were always on a roll. When Holland found out I had to leave with Stallone, jokingly she fell to her knees in front of everybody and promised me anything to stay. To this day, every time I see her on the screen I remember her on her knees.

On most shows when you make up a woman, she wears the same eye shadow, blush, and lipstick for the entire day. Not this cast. Whenever there was a costume change—and there were many on every show—I would pull out palettes of eye shadow, dry blush, and shades of lipstick. With the new cosmetic colors at hand I would change the women's makeup to match their wardrobe. On those Friday filming nights the magic makeup changes kept us awake and on our toes, as they had to be quickly accomplished while the cameras were changing sets.

Later, after *Bosom Buddies* had wrapped, Tom called while I was in the mountains of Canada, filming *Clan of the Cave Bear*. An outside pay phone rang and someone yelled to me, "Tom Hanks is on the phone!" I was thousands of miles away, and somehow, he found me. (My wife Marion has that same knack.) Tom asked if I was available to do a film that everyone remembers: *Big*. I wasn't available, and I've always wondered, "What if?"

MICHAEL CAINE

Michael Caine fits the category of "actor and gentleman." His personal biography exemplifies perseverance; he told me one day that he'd gone to more than fifty interviews before landing his first job. His middle name should be "Never give up." I never did his makeup, but I had the privilege of being in his presence on two films, *Gambit* and *Victory*, where I was with Shirley MacLaine and Sylvester Stallone.

KEVIN COSTNER

Before stardom hit, Kevin worked in a movie theater. Prior to going to work he would come by my house/lab in Studio City and visit with his friend, Michael Mills, who at the time was pouring and baking latex Neanderthal foreheads for me while I was in Canada. Kevin and I met when I designed and tested his makeup for a film costarring

Anthony Quinn, titled *Revenge*. My wife remembers very well the day that Kevin came to our house for a facial cast. Upon finishing the molding, Kevin left. Soon after there was a knock at the front door: Kevin had locked his steering wheel in place and needed to call Triple-A. This happened before everybody carried cell phones. We lived on a steep incline, so it was important when parking your car to turn its wheels into the curb to keep from rolling down the hill. Marion is the family mechanic, so she took Kevin back to his new SUV and taught him how to unlock a steering wheel without having to call for assistance.

Madeleine Stowe was cast as the female lead in *Revenge*. Tony Scott, the director, was a great believer in testing and doing your homework extensively before the cameras roll. That is why having his name or his brother Ridley's on a film means quality and entertainment. While I was working with Kevin, Tony had hired a special makeup artist from New York to execute Madeleine's makeup tests. New York is known as the center for fashion makeup, especially for the covers of magazines. The artist, although very talented, was not beyond his Hollywood contemporaries; in any case, it made Tony feel comfortable. The plan was, the New York artist would design the on-screen look (for a lot of money), and then an artist from Hollywood would follow his instructions (for less money).

This is what amazed me: Each day Madeleine and the artist would work creatively on a specific part of her face with a multitude of cosmetics. For example, one day was devoted to cheeks with color and contouring, another to eye shadows, another to lip liner and lipstick, and so forth, until her entire face had been dissected and mapped. It was a great show, and well worth the price of admission. Madeleine was very patient and listened intently to every step. But like most Hollywood stars, they know what they want, and her idea for her character was not high fashion. She told me she had to be patient and kind, but on-screen, Madeleine's makeup was designed by Madeleine.

THE CARRADINES

The Carradine family is to the acting world what the Westmores are to makeup. In the early 1940s I grew up in North Hollywood, a suburb of Los Angeles. Everyone in the neighborhood had one relative or another working in the movie business. My house was located on a street filled with apricot trees. All the houses were nestled amid a former orchard, and ours backed up to another where a boy named David, two years older than me, would later make his mark in Tinseltown. He was the son of the legendary and prolific character actor John Carradine. When David passed away in 2009, it brought back memories of us as little boys who used to run around our back-yard fantasy world, me with my clothes on, and David wearing only one of his father's signature black capes. As David ran and jumped in circles, the cape would fly freely in the wind. Then the two little grasshoppers grew up.

I didn't see David again until 1972. My uncle Frank was his makeup artist on the popular television series, *Kung Fu*. Since he wouldn't shave his head, David had to wear a plastic bald cap every working day. With so many cap applications over the run of the series, Uncle Frank was able to write the book on how to make someone appear bald very quickly. Around this time, the Academy of Television Arts and Sciences was just starting to recognize the art of makeup in its Emmy Awards. I told my uncle that he should submit *Kung Fu* for an award, but his reply was "No" (actually, more like "Nah"). He didn't have time for such silliness, so I picked up the nomination ballot, filled it out, took it to him for a signature, and personally delivered it back to the Academy. Thanks to his artistry and David's head, he won. Every time I saw his Emmy displayed proudly in his den, it was a reminder to me: "If you don't try, you can't win!"

Occasionally I would visit the set to say hello to Uncle Frank and David. David's personality on the series was like a flower child floating along in time and space. To me, David *was* this character in the real world, offering kindness and love to all. On one visit I reminisced with David about his famous father, John, who I would occasionally see at Universal Studios in the late 1960s.

I came into contact with David again in 1978. He was hired to play four different characters in the film *Circle of Iron*, including one that was half-man, half-creature. The movie was to be filmed in Israel, and would later earn a cult following. Producer Sandy Howard hired me to design the creatures that would inhabit this surreal world. In my lab I designed and manufactured full exotic latex heads, faces, hands, and feet. When I was finished, I packed them all up and sent them to Israel, not knowing who was going to apply and paint them because this film was to be made on a very low budget. The production company had a reputation for producing inexpensive films, and they lived up to it. They did have an impressive cast of performers for this film, however, which brought to life a martial arts fantasy.

One of David's characters had to wear silver fangs. I had been trained by the best in the business on how to construct lightweight false dentures, and was prepared to make a pair, but the production company insisted on sending David to a professional dental lab where the fangs were cast in metal and chrome-plated. When I saw David before he left for location, he told me they were extremely heavy and uncomfortable, and that they kept falling out.

I had to take a cast of David's feet and face to create various slip-on animal feet and partial masks, for the character that morphed from man to creature. After I made my plaster casts, he washed the residue off his feet and face and strolled off barefoot down my driveway, into the setting sun. Just in case he might come back for them, I held on to David's shoes for several years.

In 1985 I was asked to create a disfigured latex face for Keith Carradine, David's brother, who was starring in a murder thriller called *Blackout*. Once again I reminisced with a Carradine about our historic families. Later when Marion, McKenzie, and I were in New York on a theater tour for McKenzie's graduation, we were lucky enough to get tickets to see Keith perform on Broadway in *The Will Rogers Follies*. When the musical ended, we rushed around to the stage door, which was open, with no doorman on duty. I found Keith backstage in his dressing room, where I introduced the family; we exchanged our mutual admiration for each other and our families. Keith has had a wonderful career. He even gets to be president on the popular television series, *Madam Secretary*.

I will always treasure these memories of the past, of one of acting's first families, and a pair of shoes.

REDD FOXX

The producer who requested me to complete *Bosom Buddies* also asked me to complete the last six episodes of *The Redd Foxx Show*. What you are about to read is not meant to be a put-down or to present a bigoted point of view; rather, it's an account of an experience I had on the other side of the fence.

I was born, grew up, and worked in a very liberal atmosphere, and being related to and having worked with many African Americans, I was not mentally prepared for the next six weeks. My first day on the filming stage I was told that Redd didn't wear any makeup, but after rehearsals he began to perspire, a lot. It was time to do my job. I approached Redd's forehead, dripping with sweat, with a tissue. When I was almost there his eyes glared at me and a hand shot out of nowhere and grabbed my wrist. I was pulled aside and instructed not to touch him. I had never been confronted like this, before or after. I have had great working relationships over the years, lasting from one day to several years, with Ray Charles, Johnny Mathis, O. J. Simpson,

Michael Jackson, Carl Weathers, Barbara McNair, Whoopi Goldberg, LeVar Burton, Michael Dorn, and Avery Brooks.

The news that I'd just won an Academy Award for *Mask* quickly circulated around the crew. Redd, also informed, was really proud of having an Oscar winner working on the set. Instead of me being congratulated, he would introduce a female assistant makeup artist as the coveted artist on the show. She was too embarrassed to deny his flamboyant introductions, so I just sat back, kept my mouth closed, and enjoyed the show.

Near the end of the six weeks, a friend of Redd's who had a nonspeaking role as a cashier approached me. "I want makeup," he demanded. Okay! He hadn't worn any for the past five weeks, but that was all right. My makeup partner was off the set and I was covering the cast on my own. I suggested he come over to my makeup table and I would be happy to accommodate him. His reply: "I want to get made up where the white people get made up." Needless to say, not too many white people got made up in the trailer, as this was a predominantly black show. The production manager gave me permission to leave the stage to satisfy his whim. Whether it was curiosity or a test, I don't know, but he never asked for makeup again during the remainder of filming.

These and similar experiences led to my thinking about quitting the project. When the actresses on the show became aware of my feelings, they were extremely kind and pleasant, as I had known several of them from previous work. I went through my bit of racial discrimination on this set; it's too bad it has to exist at all. I had nothing to do with the Confederacy. Redd was well known for his generosity and love; I just didn't get my share.

ANNETTE FUNICELLO

I was asked to apply makeup to Annette for a television commercial, and was told to report to her house with all my cosmetics and brushes. Before starting, all those new to working with Annette were asked to come aside and quietly informed that there were three subjects not up for idle discussion: Mouseketeers, peanut butter, and breasts. Over the years I have often tried to mentally compose a sentence using all three.

PRINCE CHARLES

While filming the movie *2010*, Prince Charles and his entourage visited the interior of our spaceship. The one thing that has stood out in my mind more than the prince was the small machine guns that his entourage had strapped to their bodies, beneath their suit jackets. My first instinct was, Don't get too close, and stay out of the line of fire.

KING OF JORDAN

Unannounced to any of us on *Star Trek*, one day the Prince of Jordan, Abdullah II, arrived on the set. He was a fighter pilot at the time, and was returning to Jordan. He was also a dedicated fan of the show. Each department—art, camera, makeup, etc.—had their opportunity to give him a royal tour. He enjoyed himself so much that he threw a party that night and invited all of us to attend. Due to my early morning schedule the next day, it was impossible for me, but some of the lucky ones continued the party and were invited to visit Jordan. The young prince with the wide inquiring eyes became the man who would be king.

A. C. LYLES

At Paramount Studios resided a man who was more famous in the entertainment industry than most celebrities. His name was A. C. Lyles, and he knew absolutely everyone. Many times he recounted to me the stories about a little black book that he shared with my uncle Frank. We are told that A. C. introduced actor Ronald Reagan to Nancy and was the best man at their wedding. Sometime before Desert Storm he popped into my makeup lab with Colin Powell, because the general wanted to see where it was all created. I was told that General Powell was a big fan of *Star Trek*, and in his travels he was supplied with films and tapes of our space odyssey. At President Reagan's funeral, A. C. was there in the front row, and again at Gene and Majel Roddenberry's individual services.

NO BUSINESS LIKE SHOW BUSINESS

A very well-known executive producer called me into his office one day with a simple request: Would I make a plaster cast of his erect penis so he could give it as a gift to his girlfriend? I don't remember if it was for her birthday or Christmas. With my back to the wall, I sounded excited and agreed so I could bide my time to think about this.

Once out the door, I thought to myself, *What did I just agree too? This can't be real.* Oh yes, it was! We hadn't talked about money; I guess that might have changed my mind. Viagra hadn't come on the scene as of yet, so I was able to back out of my agreement by telling him there was no way to keep it at attention as the cold pudding-like molding material was being applied. (Besides, there wasn't a category in any of the Hollywood awards shows to be recognized for such an upstanding job.)

HAPPY BIRTHDAY, MR. PRESIDENT

The House of Westmore, located in the middle of Hollywood on the Sunset Strip, was the most famous beauty salon in the world. After it opened its doors in 1938, women from every corner would make a once-in-a-lifetime pilgrimage there to be groomed and pampered by the best makeup artists and hairstylists in Tinseltown. What made this adventure so alluring was that a client could rub elbows with the rich and famous any time of the day.

My uncle Perc—the dean of Hollywood makeup, and known for his many Warner Bros. film credits—would actually try to meet and greet everyone at the front door. Ola, Uncle Perc's fifth wife, was the overseer of this Beautyland, and the caretaker of all the femmes fatales. On any given day a housewife from Iowa could sit under a hair dryer next to Bette Davis. Even my mother-in-law Olga made her pilgrimage upon arriving in Southern California. The exterior of the building is unique; it still stands today just off Highland Boulevard, recognizable by its high slanted roof. Across the front of the building, which is facing Sunset Boulevard, large script letters spelled out "Westmore's Salon of Beauty." The interior was spacious, with double-high ceilings and extravagantly draped windows. The large foyer designed in an art nouveau style was the typical architecture of the 1930s.

In the middle of the foyer was a stylish reception desk, manned by a bevy of beauties. One in particular (who shall remain nameless) had long flowing red hair. One day, as a new week started and the doors opened for business, "Red" was missing. Later in the day my aunt received a long-distance telephone call from her, saying how sorry she was for being late, but she'd spent the weekend in Palm Springs, California, the city of fun and sun, and she was still there. As Red was trying to sputter out an explanation, a very recognizable man's voice interrupted and asked if she could stay a little longer. As Aunt Ola recounted to me, all she could reply was, "Yes, Mr. President."

SIXTY MINUTES OF FAME

We always hear about a person's fifteen minutes of fame—some get a little more, some less. Over my career I have accumulated sixty minutes, most of them, spur of the moment. I was immortalized when thrust in front of the camera at the last minute. My costars were the likes of Elizabeth Taylor, Robert Wagner, Jason Robards, Jane Alexander, and Paul Newman.

On my first adventure I was working on a film at Universal called *Winning*, starring Newman and Wagner. The director decided he needed a bare Wagner leg from the knee down. Robert wasn't available, so the director shouted out for every male to pull their pants up. Robert had thin legs, and I was a perfect match. Many times in movies there are body doubles for the stars. In *Winning* I am the leg double.

Another Universal sci-fi feature was *Andromeda Strain*. As the story begins, the military discovers an isolated town where all the inhabitants are dead. The strange thing about each body is that their insides had turned to dust. To graphically demonstrate this phenomenon, in our lab we created a fake arm with hair and nails that when cut open across the inside of the wrist, a fine powder would pour out and billow into the air. The outer skin of the arm was constructed out of rubber, and inside were lengthy, thin glass tubes that were filled with a fine dust called "Fuller's Earth." This powder, which was used forever in the motion picture industry, is now on the no-no list. Inhaling the extra fine particles can injure your lungs.

To mold, rig, paint, and punch hair into each arm cost several thousand dollars. We were budgeted to construct three. On the day of filming, the sliced-wrist scene, I carried the three dummies down to the stage. The director Robert Wise had me instruct the actor playing the surgeon exactly where to cut with the scalpel and how to bend back the wrist at the right angle to allow the dust to pour out. Roll the camera. The director shouts "Action." On arm number one, our make-believe surgeon didn't slice it properly. On arm number two, the slice was okay, but he didn't bend the arm properly for the dust to fall out. The director then said, "Take the wardrobe and surgical mask off the actor and dress up Mike Westmore." This is when I became the attending physician with arm number three. Perfect slice, perfect bend and pour. Yes, that's me, the man behind the mask.

In 1983 I was in Kansas City filming *The Day After*, a TV special about the atomic missile crisis we all lived through in the 1950s and '60s. On the last day of filming everything was "Hurry up, hurry up." We had a plane to catch in the late afternoon (and I had a famous barbecue joint to stop at before boarding). We were all around the

Kansas City War Memorial. In the scene were Jason Robards and his on-screen daughter, Kyle Aletter. The two of them had a walk and talk around the Memorial. Jason and Kyle did all the close-ups of their conversation, and now it was time to film the wide master shot. The actors would look like ants, but everything else was in panorama, and it would establish the location.

There was no time to waste, as Jason had to redo his hair and wardrobe for another quick shot in another scene. Director Nick Myers looked around for a photo double. As a selected few stood next to Jason, they found that I was the same height and weight, and had a similar haircut. The difference: Jason was fifteen years older than me, with gray hair. (He and my brother Monty had attended Hollywood High School together in the early 1940s.) I watched Jason walk for a minute so I could replicate his body language and gait, and then I went to the makeup trailer where I had my brown hair colored white and slipped into Jason's clothes. I made my on-screen walk with Kyle twice. I thought I was great in take number one (Nick promised me it wasn't my fault that he had to do a second take).

My final fifteen minutes of fame came with Elizabeth Taylor and Jane Alexander, during their period TV movie, *Malice in Wonderland*. (As previously mentioned, this film depicted the lives of and competition between Hollywood's famous columnists, Hedda Hopper and Louella Parsons.)

In one of their notorious meetings at the studio, one star was being replaced by the other. The new star, Louella Parsons (Elizabeth Taylor), had inherited Hedda Hopper's (Jane Alexander) dressing room and makeup artist. In the scene the director wanted the makeup artist to be applying makeup, and he wanted it to look real. I had already applied Elizabeth's makeup earlier in the day. Since this was quickly planned a day in advance, the wardrobe was able to find the exact style of clothes that my father had worn back when he was the makeup supervisor for *Gone with the Wind*. This time they even gave me a line (more like a single word, which wound up on the cutting-room floor).

So between my body-double parts, I was able to appear on-screen four times. Fifteen minutes of fame times four equals sixty minutes of stardom.

NEAR DEATH

It is one thing to place your life in jeopardy while working on a motion picture, but quite another to experience it while lying in your bed at home. I don't remember the exact date, but it was a rainy night and we were living in Studio City, California. To this day I still vividly remember my near-death experience. At the time I wasn't feeling well, and started to contract a high fever. I slowly fell into a peaceful slumber, ignoring Marion's plea to call the doctor. She felt something was wrong and continuously stroked my head for reassurance, while repeating the Lord's Prayer.

Upon awakening I was not familiar with my surroundings. Somewhere in my nightly journey I started to feel a very warm, comfortable breeze encompass my body and found myself slowly approaching the distant entrance to a large cavern. The air around me was slowly churning in the form of a gray translucent mist, but nothing else was visible except the cave's black opening. As my feelings beckoned me onward I was assured I had nothing to fear.

Later, I recalled that I was not physically walking, I was levitating. As I entered the cavern I saw a distant light, and knew why there was nothing to fear: Standing along the sides of the walls were all my friends and family that had passed on previously. No one spoke, but their smiling faces welcomed me and urged me to continue my journey. Decades later, their faces are still as clear as if they were here today.

By now the light at the end of the tunnel had become very intense. As I approached its edge I could distinguish the outline of a figure and could feel my father's love, a father who used to hide candy in his pocket for me when coming home from work. He left on his eternal journey when I was only two years old. I tried to reach out to him but was pulled back at the same time. I said, "No, I have to go." At that moment I reversed out of the passage and inhaled the cool breath of life. I had a loving family that needed me, and this was stronger than my selfish desire to continue onward. I wasn't ready to leave Marion and the children.

Was it a dream, or reality? My story is not unique. It has been told and retold by many people over the centuries who have entered the world of "the near-death experience."

FARRAH: MEMORIES IN PASSING

Ring . . . ring . . . When I picked up the phone, on the other end an unknown voice said, "Farrah Fawcett has requested you to apply her makeup; are you available?"

Was I available! This was one of those dream calls every makeup artist yearns to receive. Of course I accepted, and on the day of filming, everything that was rumored about her was true. She was an incredibly sweet person who created her famous hairstyle by rolling her hair around rollers that were the size of beer cans, and she had the most perfectly straight, white teeth. When she smiled, that starburst you see in toothpaste commercials occurred naturally.

While working on another project in the late 1960s I casually met her for the first time when her then-boyfriend Lee Majors was guest-starring on the TV Western series, *Alias Smith and Jones*. One day Farrah came to visit and I mistook her for a hairstylist I knew; there was such a close resemblance. I approached her and said, "Hi, Susie," and found out very quickly that she was a very gracious person.

When she returned to guest-star in a later episode of *Charlie's Angels*, she called me again to take personal care of her face. At that time each "Angel" had her own personal makeup artist and hairstylist attending her. What I was told upon arrival was that the three makeup artists had made Friday-night reservations to ship out on an overnight deep-sea fishing trip, and they had to leave by seven p.m. Friday night in the movie business is famous for filming from midnight till dawn, just to squeeze out everyone's blood before the weekend. All three artists passed me their lady's individual powder puffs and sailed out the door. There was one more catch: One of the Angels with a late work call hadn't yet had her makeup applied. I was left with three high-maintenance women to touch up, and one to fully complete.

As I was applying makeup to number four, her eyes kept following me; she finally said in a soft voice, "Do you remember me?," and I replied with some intelligent response, like "Ohh . . . umm . . ." She had been married to an actor on a popular Western series where I was the department head. As his makeup artist, it was part of my job (in his mind, and for my job security) to forewarn him whenever she arrived for a visit. He had a propensity to entertain other ladies; she knew it, and she knew that I knew she knew it. We laughed about it. It's much more fun to laugh when you're sweating than to be recoiling in fear. The rest of the night I spent juggling powder puffs and lipstick.

I don't feel that Farrah ever reached her full potential in life. Her calling went far beyond the screen. She was a great artist and decorator, and we would often talk about color, forms, and textures. Her insight into the balance of the art world was brilliant in thought and design. Since I had been an art major, I could fully appreciate all her Texas talent.

One of her best TV films was *Burning Bed* in 1984. I had been called to her house to change her perfect teeth by constructing an imperfect slip-on plastic denture. To create the false teeth I had to take a plaster impression of her real teeth. I laid out my materials and tools in the small bathroom off the kitchen as she was preparing dinner.

In 2009 Farrah publicly aired her struggle with cancer. While viewing her on film, I could still see the power and love within. I kept her plaster tooth mold for many years. Her teeth were perfect, as distinguishable as the lady herself.

HITCHCOCK

Even though Hitchcock was English, like the male side of my family, there was no fraternal bonding. I don't think he liked the Westmores, especially Uncle Bud, and me by association. Bud was the makeup department head for Universal, and MCA/Revue was a studio located in Studio City, California. In 1958 the two joined forces, and MCA/Revue moved lock, stock, and barrel onto the Universal grounds. Hitch had two films to produce and direct, *The Birds* and *Marnie*, both starring Tippi Hedren. Hitch was so upset that Jack Barron didn't get Bud's job, he didn't want anything to do with Universal's makeup department. Jack ran both of Hitch's new shows.

As a gesture of goodwill, Uncle Bud had a beautiful, life-size bronzed bust of Hitch mounted on a pedestal like a Greek god. It was a gift of appeasement, or friendship, whatever worked. This thing was not light; it stood at least two feet tall and weighed more than fifty pounds. I think I drew the short straw, as I was selected to make the delivery. I had to carry it down the hill for a couple hundred yards to his office.

I entered his official, intimidating waiting room and told the receptionist that I had a gift from Bud Westmore for Mr. Hitchcock; I guess it was obvious, as cradled in my arms was a life-size head of her boss. I was announced and buzzed into the inner sanctum. There he sat in a big chair behind a big desk, with that unmistakable profile. His face was blank when he saw the bust in my arms. Without so much as an acknowledgment, he made a vague gesture; I placed the bust gingerly down on a table and stole out. (In retrospect, I guess I should have backed out of his room East Indian style.)

I hiked back up the hill to the two-story makeup department with the red doors. Uncle Bud anxiously and excitedly asked, "What did he say?" and I got to repeat Hitchcock's immortal words: "Put it over there."

SANJEEV KUMAR

Hollywood does exist in India. Although the word *Bollywood* has become linked with most Indian films, that is only one particular area of India's massive film industry. In

1981 I was contacted by an East Indian film company to create some special makeup effects for a very big film, both in size and popularity. It starred one of India's most famous actors, Sanjeev Kumar. This was one of India's first attempts to step out of their world of beautiful people. Sanjeev was to wear numerous transitional latex prosthetics as his face was transformed in the Indian version of *Dr. Jekyll and Mr. Hyde*.

Each Indian star has his or her own personal makeup artist, and the name of Sanjeev's artist was Sarosh Modi. They both arrived in Hollywood and stayed for the next month. Sarosh would show up at my lab every morning and sit and watch me prepare the masks. I couldn't convince him to go to Disneyland, not even for one day. After a month of sculpting, molding, and painting, we were ready to test each phase of the makeup. After our application and approval test, I had to manufacture enough faces for Sarosh to take back to India with him, as the mail and Customs couldn't be counted on to deliver. What I remember most vividly about Mr. Modi was his reaction to a question I asked; before inviting him over to the house for dinner, I inquired if he ate meat, or if was he a vegetarian. He replied, "I am an eater of meat, not an eater of grass"—so we had steaks.

KAMAL HAASAN

My next encounter with the world of Indian filmmaking occurred around 1987, when I was contacted by a woman named Varni Haasan. She wanted to learn the art of cinema makeup so she could travel with and be useful to her famous actor husband. Varni learned very quickly. What other students take months or years to learn, she became proficient in within a matter of days. To make traveling in California easier, she stayed with friends in Woodland Hills. She would catch a city bus and travel to Studio City, where I would drive down the hill and pick her up for the day's lesson. At the end of the day I would take her back to the bus station. This became our normal routine; she even changed her native sari for Western fashion. What she didn't change or remove was a very large diamond that was pierced into the side of her nose. She thought nothing of it, although her fellow passengers would look at her inquisitively each day. I convinced her to remove it as long as she was using public transportation.

At the end of our classes her husband Kamal arrived and we talked about some of his projects. We have been friends ever since. From that moment Kamal accepted the challenge to incorporate special makeup into his career like no other Indian actor. He was and is a total visionary, adept not only at acting, but also screenwriting, songwriting,

THE MANY FACES OF KAMAL HAASAN

Courtesy of Kamal Haasan

As Kalifullah Mukhtaar . . .

As Avatar Singh . . .

As Krishnaveni . . .

As Avvai Shanmughi in the Indian re-make of *Mrs. Doubtfire* . . .

As Christian Fletcher...

As Balrum Naidu...

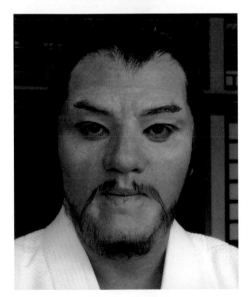

As Shinghen Narahasi...

As George Bush...

And as Kamal Haasan himself.

producing, directing, singing, working as a lyricist and choreographer, doing stunt work (he says he has broken every bone in his body), wardrobe, lighting, makeup, and hair-styling. When he sets his mind to anything, he learns with proficiency. It is said that he is the leading method actor of Indian cinema, and is known for his versatility.

When I first met Kamal Haasan, at my house, he inquired about making a few simple scars for his upcoming film. Since I wasn't traveling to India, I made a small plaster scar mold and taught him how to fill it with plastic from a squeeze tube. After the gooey plastic dried, Kamal could peel it out of the mold and apply it to his face.

On another film he played the part of a man who is the sole survivor of a terrible bus accident. The man is left with a horribly scarred face. This time I made a larger mold with epoxy, which is more durable than plaster. Kamal is such a thorough individual that this time he brought a camera and filmed every step that he would need to follow in order to create and apply the numerous scars.

Kamal loves to watch the movies of filmmakers from around the world. He was so impressed with the American film *Mrs. Doubtfire* that he wanted to do an Indian version. To accomplish this, I needed to create a latex face that would fill and round out his masculine features. It was amazing to see the transformation once Kamal was in costume and makeup. He became the embodiment of his Indian Mrs. Doubtfire, in both appearance and movement. Not knowing exactly how many faces he might need, we decided to have enough so that a new one would be ready to use each day of filming. The final count was fifty, but I only had one mold, and it took eight hours to create one face. The plaster mold with the latex inside had to be heated at a low temperature so as not to destroy it. Needless to say, it took a while to finish all fifty of them.

One of the most popular dialects in Indian films is Hindi. When the Indian *Mrs. Doubtfire* was released, it became a box-office hit. It was so popular that Kamal decided to film it in another Indian dialect, known as Tamil, the language of his birth. This created a new challenge, because the new version couldn't simply be voiced over or dubbed. The Tamil version had to be completely reshot with different costumes and sets, but the same makeup. My face mold was on its last legs from the first go-round, but I resurrected it and nursed out fifty more faces.

Nothing like this transformation had ever been seen on the Indian screen. When it came time for the Indian equivalent of the Oscars, the film won an award for makeup.

I continued to supply Kamal over the years with anything he could conceive of. On another occasion he played Gandhi's assassin. For this project I had to duplicate the resemblances of both real-life characters.

The latest film for which I collaborated with Kamal took two and a half years to prepare and film, and I would consider it any makeup artist's dream. Kamal was featured wearing ten different, individual makeup applications. The special pieces needed for each character ranged from full latex faces to partial faces, with items as small as a nose tip, upper lip, or earlobes. In conjunction with the latex appliances I also used wigs, eyebrows, mustaches, beards, false teeth, and colored contact lenses.

When it was all prepared Kamal arrived in the United States so we could test all our makeup ideas on film. Our test consisted of a blue-eyed European, President Bush, a Sikh, an old woman with wrinkled arms and hands (my favorite), a giant with a long face, people from different East Indian castes, and another favorite, an Asian. Kamal wanted to test the ability of the Asian character to fly, so after applying his latex face, eyelids, long black wig, eyebrows, and Fu Manchu mustache, he was hoisted off the floor with nylon ropes that were slung over a ceiling support. Like the flyers in Cirque du Soleil, the character named "Shingen" did a few successful circles around the room.

The name of this film is *Dasavatharam*. Don't try to pronounce it. It is known as one of the first modern sci-fi films made in India. To date, it is one of the most expensive films ever made, and included the largest makeup budget ever seen in the East Indian film industry. Unlike American films, *Dasavatharam* filmed eighteen hours a day for a total of six hundred days. It is easy to see why Kamal over his long career is the most decorated actor in terms of awards in the history of Indian cinema. If he was performing in the American film industry, he'd have a shelf full of Oscars. He actually was honored with a Living Legend Award, bestowed by the Federation of Indian Chambers of Commerce and Industry (FICCI). The press has noted that he has an obsession with needless perfection. I have found his obsession to be an excited, driven desire to make everything visually perfect, not so much for himself, but for the art of the cinema. Because of this obsession, *Dasavatharam* became the highest-grossing film in the history of Tamil cinema.

In 2016 the French government awarded him the Chevalier de l'Ordre des Arts et des Lettres (The Knight of the Order of Arts and Letters). The order is part of France's premier award, the Legion of Honor.

Kamal's philosophy: "When you do what you believe in, you don't get tired. I have no holidays because I don't have any working days."

WHAT'S NEXT?

Where did my journey take me after *Star Trek*? I spent the next year and a half creating the many different cultural disguises that actor Kamal Hassan had to portray in his

East Indian movies, and I continued to record more of my career adventures, the people I have touched and how they influenced me. In recent years I received a Lifetime Achievement Award, presented by the Hollywood Beauty Awards. I was quite honored, as that trophy will be known in perpetuity as the Michael Westmore Award. I was selected by the Motion Picture Academy to be the first makeup artist to have my entire career documented for the Motion Picture Academy's historical archives.

I have always enjoyed lecturing and teaching at conventions worldwide. In the last few years a golden moment arrived when I was asked to participate in a makeup-competition television show on Syfy called *Face Off*. My task is to mentor the competing makeup artists who bring their talents from all over the United States.

In 2016 *Star Trek* will celebrate its fiftieth anniversary. I will proudly attend the conventions and share stories from my time in space. To close out the year I will be creating a special exhibit, which will be displayed at the University of California, Santa Barbara, museum. It is called *Lifeforms, the Makeup Art of Michael Westmore*.

As to what the rest of my journey has in store for me, only time will tell. Let's have lunch, and I will tell you more tales of my life behind the camera.

Awards, Honors, and Nominations

I have had the privilege of being honored and recognized in my career with over one hundred nominations and awards in the motion picture and television industry and the theater, along with worldwide educational exhibits, written accolades, and featured guest appearances.

Academy of Motion Picture Arts and Sciences

Academy of Motion Picture Arts and Sciences Member (1982–)
Motion Picture Academy Award, *Mask* (1986)
Four Academy Award Nominations (1984, 1986, 1987, 1997)
British Academy Award Nomination (1985)
Three Saturn Award Nominations (1996, 1997, 2002)

Academy of Television Arts and Sciences

9 Emmy Awards (1976–1996)
42 Emmy Nominations (1973–2005)

Awards of Honor

Motion Picture Hall of Fame (1981)
The Hollywood Walk of Fame, Star #2370 (2008)
Marquis "Who's Who in America"
Marquis "Who's Who in Entertainment"

Academy of Science Fiction, Fantasy, and Horror Films, "Golden Scroll Award" (1981)
Two Resolution/Recognition Awards from the City of Los Angeles (1981, 2008)
Shooting Star Award (1999)
Lambda Chi Alpha Order of Achievement Award (2001)
Hollywood Makeup Artist and Hairstylist Guild Awards, Nomination (1999)
Hollywood Makeup Artist and Hairstylist Guild Awards, Award (2000)
Canadian Sci-Fi and Fantasy Award, "The Spacy" (2007)
Kryolan's International Golden Mask Award (2013)
Hollywood Beauty Awards (2015)
Critics' Choice Award, *Face Off* (2015)
Critics' Choice Award Nomination, *Face Off* (2016)
Motion Picture Academy Oral History Archives (2016)
Distinguished Alumni Award for Performing Arts, University of California–Santa Barbara (1978)

Theater

Mark Taper Forum, Los Angeles, *The Sorrows of Frederick*, (1967), *The Devils* (1967)
Pasadena Playhouse, *Mask: The Musical* (2008)

Exhibits

Honoring the Makeup Artistry of Michael Westmore, twenty cities (1987–1993)
Permanent exhibit at the American Museum of the Moving Image, New York
Permanent *Star Trek* exhibit at the Oregon Museum of Science and Industry
The *Star Trek* Experience, Las Vegas
International exhibits, Canada, Italy, Scotland, and Germany
Art, Design & Architecture Museum, University of California–Santa Barbara

Instructional

Awarded a Lifetime Community College Teaching Credential
Outstanding Alumnus and Instructor, Los Angeles Valley College
Instructor at University of California, Los Angeles (UCLA)
Alumni of the Year, University of California, Santa Barbara (UCSB)
Author of *The Art of Theatrical Makeup for Stage and Screen*
Coauthor of *Star Trek: Aliens & Artifacts*

Photo Credits: Studios, Photographers, and Artists

Eleanor and Franklin, ABC TV movie, makeup test
Capricorn One, Warner Bros., Bruce McBroom
Arcana, David Bowie

1980s

Raging Bull, United Artists
True Confessions, United Artists
First Blood, Carolco/Orion Pictures, Joseph Lederer
2010, MGM Studios
Why Me?, TV movie, Lorimar Productions
Iceman, Universal Studios
Mask, Universal Studios
Elizabeth Taylor, Family
Clan of the Cave Bear, Warner Bros.
Masters of the Universe, Cannon Films
Blood of Heroes, New Line Cinema
Johnny Handsome, Tri-Star Pictures
Oscar Presentation, Academy of Motion Picture Arts and Sciences

Star Trek

CBS Consumer Products, Paramount Studios, John Van Citters, Marian Cordry, Holly Amos
Star Trek: The Next Generation Tribute, Gary Hasson, Carole Kabrin
Kamal Haasan Montage, Kamal Haasan

Additional

Frank Taylor, Bison Archives (Mark Wanamaker), Paul Harris Lab
Cover photo by Scott McClaine, Imaging Arts, courtesy of Art, Design & Architecture Museum, University of California–Santa Barbara

Index

Italic page numbers indicate photos and illustrations.

About the Author

Michael Westmore recently completed visual and oral recordings for the archives at the Academy of Motion Pictures Arts and Sciences, said to be one of the longest archival sessions the Academy has recorded. He is currently appearing on the Syfy TV show *Face Off*.

Jake Page is the author of over forty books of fiction and nonfiction, including natural history and Native American themes. He was the founding editor of Doubleday's Natural History Press, as well as editorial director of *Natural History* magazine and science editor of *Smithsonian* magazine. He has written more than forty books on the natural sciences, zoological topics, and Native American affairs, as well as mystery fiction. He died in 2015.